Searching for
SanViejo
"St. Old Guy"

Notes to My Younger Self

LARRY MOFFITT

SanViejo™
PUBLISHING

Bowie, Maryland

Cover illustration: Hannah Hunter

Interior illustrations and cover and interior design:
Marina Kirsch Design

LMoffitt@sanviejo.com

www.sanviejo.com

SanViejo™
PUBLISHING
Bowie, Maryland

For Honey Nim

Live in both worlds.

Contents

INTRODUCTION

There is a Japanese song, *Seinen no Ki Yo* ("Tree of Youth") in which the lyric, "... sincerity and love comprehend the universe," pretty much sums up life for me. It's not a hundred percent of what drives me, but it's a big chunk. I have done my best to instill as much of those two things into this book as I can. Interspersed with appropriate doses of wisdom-infused absurdity and humor to clear the palate.

In my current role as an obscure, early-twenty-first-century essayist, I offer you this book of personal observations that have been instructive to me, and which I hope will be useful for you. My checkered life has taken me to sixty-something countries, including North Korea (twice). I've been blessed to see and do more than anyone has a right to ask for out of life. Some of the stories from those travels, and lessons from them, are also in this book.

I began compiling these writings in 2007, after encountering my own mortality. The alarm clock at the end of the universe told me to get my life's priorities straight, to shift the paradigm ("PARA-diggum" in Larryspeak). I looked around at all the dead people I knew, and pondered what they were able to take with them to the next life. Their stamp collection? Their electric-blue Ferrari 488 GTB? The keys to Graceland? Nope, nope and nope. Not even the stick of beef jerky they were eating when they went bingity-bangity down the stairs.

As far as I can tell, you only take your character, and perhaps maybe a toothbrush, with you. Your only possession is what you are. Most of my dead friends were not saints. I'm certainly not, and you're not either. Probably. So whatever state your character is in, that's what goes with you.

"SanViejo" originated from when I and my family lived in Buenos Aires at the end of the 1990s and I was director of editorial operations for the nineteen *Tiempos del Mundo* newspapers in the major capitals of the Americas.

I did something kind and briefly labor-intensive for some Catholics (the regional vicar of Opus Dei). My son, David, then 13, asked if they had paid me for it. I said no, I was just doing them a favor and added frivolously, "but maybe they'll make me a saint."

David mused for a second. "Hmmm … Saint Old Guy." *SanViejo* in Spanish. It sounds better in Spanish, more distinguished somehow. I liked the ring of it and have since infused the name with meaning it didn't start out with, and adopted the moniker and what it connotes, as shorthand for the last big quest of my life's journey.

SanViejo is a saintly old guy, man or woman, who finishes their life having acquired an honorable character. No matter what kind of a liar, bully, thief or trailer-park Hitler a person may have been while growing up, if, by the time they take their final breath, they have found redemption among their enemies and reconciled with the people they have hurt, made restitution with society and have acquired an honorable character—then we might conclude that such a person finished well as a human being.

At some point between the very second I finish typing this sentence and half a century hence, I hope to also finish well. I'm still a bit gnarly around the edges, and finding the SanViejo within me, is my personal goal for myself.

It takes a lifetime to build one's character and the kind of life that makes others happy that you exist. I wish someone had written for me, when I was in my 20s, a book like the one you're reading now. Something with a bit of wisdom and thrilling true life adventures, occasionally funny or profound. There's random poetry in these pages; sorry, just deal with it. God has been involved in my growth process, and so God is in here as well. I don't mind if that irritates you, I just try not to irritate God.

If a genie in a bottle gives me three wishes about my life, I would tell her (if he was a man he would be a gene) these three things: (1) I never want to be put in to a position to have to take another person's life. (2) I never want to crush another person's spirit or block that person's ability to find their happiness. Conflict exists; I just don't want to crap all over people needlessly. And (3) I want to live an existence that has a good purpose. At the same time, I reserve for myself the right to occasionally be playful and frivolous, and do crazyass things I will regret later. Repentance is good for the soul, and if I never do anything I need to repent for, that's not going to benefit my soul, is it? Irish logic. You will be happy to know I remain gloriously, spectacularly—flawed.

I count as treasures the people in my life who, aware of their own flaws, try in some way every day to connect with something higher than themselves. They meditate, pray or practice mindfulness or seek out words of inspiration from others. Collectively, they adhere to every faith tradition, or no tradition in particular, while respecting all. You are welcome to join this community; there's room for everybody. There really is. We all help each other keep the delusions of grandeur at bay, and we know the medicinal healing value of caring and laughter. And tears.

This book is a compilation of short essays and things I have thought about in my still-ongoing quest to find SanViejo. I seek the true me even as the sun gets lower and the shadows grow longer.

Some things herein, I have published elsewhere. One thing you will notice about the topics covered is that the important things sit right alongside the absurd. In that sense, this book mimics your life. There is humor in these pages. We all have different ways of coping with existence. Some people collect antique coffee mills, some take over countries and enslave the people. I find humor in things.

Here's what I've done to be helpful to the reader. The chapters are short enough so you can keep it on the bedside table and finish one before you fall asleep. My own practice is to read in bed until the book falls on my face three times. I hope you enjoy it, and that it makes you ponder your own switchback journey to the true you, that it makes you want to write your book (if only to correct the errors of this one), and that it causes you to think. And even laugh deeply now and then.

The reason I wrote this book is because writing is what I do, and because after my first book of true life adventures was self-published in the mid-00s, I still kept living and stuff still kept happening.

Larry Moffitt
September 18, 2017
LMoffitt@sanviejo.com

High tea with lowlifes, pinkies extended

There are six different ways to kill a man with a lemon wedge. I know all of them, and have personally used three. However, I am forbidden by the Government of the United States from revealing them. And anyway, that's not what this story is about.

The plush Atrium Lounge of the Makati Shangri-La, in the heart of the top of the social food chain in Manila, is enormous. On Sunday afternoons, a string orchestra made entirely of gorgeous young women plays classical and popular music while people sip tea and nibble hors d'oeuvres in the quietude of elegance. The wall behind the orchestra is solid glass rising three stories, overlooking a perfectly manicured garden beyond.

I was the only one sitting near the indoor fountain. It had been a tough week and the sound of falling water soothed me. A tea candle floated on a tiny raft amid purple orchids in the centerpiece, its flame nudged into a gentle hula by ions produced from the oxygenation of the fountain.

A couple of no-nonsense Godfather extras suddenly stood in front of me, interrupting my reverie. One of them, with a folded over ear, asked if I wouldn't mind relocating to another part of the room so they could have that area for a "private conference."

They were muscled, trying to smile, but it wasn't really working for them. They looked only barely this side of nasty, wearing the *barong* shirts of Philippines business casual attire. Their shoes were scuffed and dirty. One of them was big, a human truck. The other, who did the talking, was a dark, thin stiletto. Behind them by the bar, a group of nicely dressed gentlemen stood talking, studiously not noticing the meeting arrangements being negotiated for them. That's why henchmen were invented, to do the heavy lifting in community relations.

"If you don't mind," the smaller of the two, the asp, said impatiently.

I eyed the lemon wedges on the plate beside the teacup, then thought, *nah*.

"I don't mind at all," I smiled. And I really didn't. I stood as a waitress and a very relieved maître d' rushed in to scoop up my tea and hors d'oeuvres and whisk me over to a table with a good view on the other side of the room. I felt good because now the Atrium Lounge owed me one.

"Would you like to try the crispy Thai chicken?" the maître d' asked. "It's our specialty." Then he added, "on the house."

Would I like the first violinist to soothe my fevered brow with a cold compress?

The scruffy guards were dark pillars of soot, chatting on the edge of the commandeered area a discreet distance from the meeting. They created an unspoken no-fly zone for that part of the room. The cascading water made it impossible for a hidden microphone to pick up what was said, and I wondered if that had anything to do with why they had chosen to sit there. The three gents were soon joined by two equally well-turned-out elders with distinguished touches of gray at the temples. They shook hands and all sat down to plot high crimes and misdemeanors.

I tried to allow for the possibility of having misjudged them. But I was pretty sure I hadn't. Occam's razor: the simplest answer is usually the correct one. Something about polite, confident men of elegance and poise being protected by dark beasts they themselves had raised told me they were not meeting about how to bring clean water to the slums.

I watched the gentlemen. The first three were subordinate to the two elders. They quickly offered their business cards, a submissive gesture that was not reciprocated. The body language and attempt at lame humor from one of the three, said this was their first time to meet. I imagined the two elders as they would appear twenty-five years from now, alone and bereft of loved ones, unless they were lucky. Even for those who rule the earth, and can buy all the love they need, the time comes for all of us when we will be wholly dependent on the kindness and care of others as we sit, diapered and *non compos mentis,* staring up at the skylight in the day room of a geriatric home. And although that time will arrive in the blink of an eye, for now the two lords had full shocks of expensively cut hair, polished dress shoes and powerful appetites that would be catered to by the world they had built. They were the bottomless Mariana Trench of need.

Consider this: All that separates my golf game from the great Jack Nicklaus is distance and accuracy. Just two things, but it's a matter of scale. What separates a wealthy robber baron, from a wealthy person who gives it all back? Heart basically. And nobody can really know the heart of another. I thought, *what if that meeting over by the fountain really is about bringing clean water to the slums, or field trips to the zoo for crippled orphans?* But no, everything about it was all wrong for that to be the case. The simplest answer was telegraphed by the borderline fear in the deference of the wait staff, the maître d's quiet urgency to mollify me, the air of menace surrounding the goons. Occam's damned razor.

Jeremiah, the prophet, not the bullfrog, said, "For from the least of them even to the greatest of them, everyone is greedy for gain. And from the prophet even to the priest everyone deals falsely." No wonder they threw him in prison. He probably said it to some high priest. But his point is well taken. Two members of the "least of them" sitting in front of me, greedy for gain, looked like lifers. But really, I wondered, *what kind of epiphany would it take for them to whip out their checkbooks and fire off a few thousand to Mother Superior's orphanage?*

Figure another ten or fifteen years before immortality ceases to be an illusion for them, like it already has for me and most of my friends. They're slick gangsters, savvy guys at the top of their game. You'd think they would try to investigate what comes next after the big roulette wheel they're on begins to slow, and ultimately stops. Do they really think it spins forever? At some point a person thinks, *Hey, I have enough money and clout; I don't need any more.* Don't they? Don't your priorities shift at some point? How do gangsters relax anyway? Do they take time to stop and kill the roses?

The question is, if I had possession of the magical and corrupting Ring of Power, would I throw it into the Fires of Mordor to save the world when the time came? Pretty much all of existing literature says no, and history seems to agree with that. However, I would like to challenge the automatic assumption of greed. I am neither Gandhi nor Spartacus nor Joan of Arc. I generally sit in the average Joe section, somewhere in the middle. But even so, I would still toss the damn ring into the flaming pit without a second thought. I kid you not. You just watch. I think many others would as well.

"If I were the king of the world, tell you what I'd do. I'd throw away the cars and the bars and the wars. Make sweet love to you." Book of Jeremiah. The bullfrog Jeremiah.

At some point in my musings I made eye contact with the two nose tackles. We smiled, nodded. Each of us had gotten what we wanted. Over in my part of the Atrium, the Thai chicken lived up to its billing. They brought more tea and, sipping with pinkie extended, I listened to the All Pretty Girl Orchestra. I never saw the check.

Mapping the Goodness Genome

Can we sequence the DNA of goodness? Does the elusive goodness genome even exist?

The falling "Newton's apple" that triggered this for me was the onset of autumn.

Autumn is the season when everything does a lingering waltz toward dormancy and death. Standing on the doorstep of winter's sleep is strangely invigorating. Even as we prep for our long nap, blazing displays of orange and red leaves set against skies of the deepest robin's egg blue thrill our souls to the rafters. Seasonally it's bedtime, and yet we are jazzed, ready for action, as though we had suddenly decided to drink coffee at 10 p.m. That's the paradox of autumn.

If spring is a lime green Corvette with the top down, autumn is a bright yellow one of those, with orange stripes accenting the contours.

Energy, happiness and goodness are cousins, each playing "can you top this" with the others. I'm not going to twirl around like Julie Andrews in a Bavarian mountain meadow, but the energy I get from walking under red and orange leaves stimulates me to consider how goodness operates, and how it is transmitted between one person and another. Whatever else they are, peace, love and harmony are airborne viral infections of the goodness genome.

The search for the goodness genome itself is a matter of sifting through clues. Sometimes the negative spaces, where goodness isn't, can help reveal where it is. In the way that shadows show us what light is doing, what do the times when there is little or no goodness to be found tell us about its adaptive powers? One of the darker parts of U.S. history was when the forefathers of some of us were committing genocide on the American Indians, and enslaving black human beings.

It's natural to wonder what God was thinking. I'm pretty sure all the better religions espouse that God loves *most* people. Or maybe *many* people. Anyway, it's a lot, so let's all try to stay calm. Let's suppose for a minute that we're all in this together.

If we assume God cares for everyone, it is not a huge stretch to imagine that ninety-nine percent of human history must have been unspeakable torture for God to observe. There has been so little goodness out there, even on the good days, it would be easy to conclude that we're on our own. Or that God has attention deficit disorder, or is impotent or non-existent.

Is there even such a thing as a naturally existing goodness genome? Good question. Incredibly, and in the face of all the crap going on, intuition still says yes, there is. It may just be that God is insanely patient with everyone. If God were to smite humankind for the atrocities we commit, there would soon be nobody left, and we would all be stuck in the slime pits of hell. Then who would be left to comfort, and atone for, history's shattered victims?

M.L.King said the moral arc of the universe is long, but it bends toward justice. I take that as an article of faith, for the sake of life's victims.

It sickens my heart to think that Declaration-drafter Thomas Jefferson was a slave owner. It required a bloody, fratricidal war to atone for slavery, and some say the matter still isn't settled. We came close to being permanently divided into two countries—north and south. Had that happened, I seriously doubt America would have been cohesive enough to defeat the Nazis 80 years later. I doubt we would have been able to oversee the collapse of global communism, a scourge that owns all the records for mass murder.

But that was then, and the goodness genome mutates to accommodate the unique challenges of this age.

For most of history, goodness faced invading armies. Today the enemy is our own culture.

In the context of cultural changes, we are frogs, who were put into a kettle of cold water in the 60s and placed over a low fire. Today we are immersed in a hypersexualized rolling boil. Community standards are in tatters. Christianity is on the ropes, utterly unable to control its collective, ecclesiastical penis.

If only immorality were an enemy race we could dehumanize on recruiting posters. But it isn't. As Pogo said in the cartoons, "We have met the enemy and he is us."

At exactly the instant I am thinking of all this, I walk out of Barnes & Noble book store (where I saw the Pogo cartoon) and find myself directly in front of the large display window of Victoria's Secret, the lingerie store of dreams. Right on cue, the culture shows up and I realize this essay is now writing itself.

The underwear model in the high-resolution photo, way bigger than life-size, is wearing a smile along with key lime green panties and a pushup bra worthy of Mauna Loa.

Her belly button is the size of Dead-Eye Dick's eye patch, and her other parts are to the same scale. And that's basically nothing compared to other things going on in public everywhere these days.

Goodness has to contain a chromosome for self-governance to offset the absence of external societal standards. A lack of standards puts people in the position of having to define goodness for themselves, unless they have a faith community or tradition to look to for guidance. These not always being available, goodness has to be up to the task. It has to mutate to protect a child surrounded 24/7 by unrelenting internet porn, desensitizing graphic violence and public school classroom demos on how to put a condom on a cucumber. Goodness has to be self-maintaining, at least until the popular culture stops trying to outdo the fall of Rome.

Part of the evolution of goodness may be manifesting in thinning the barriers between this world and the next, allowing for a person who exercises introspection, to get a clearer sense of right and wrong, and where they stand in the big gray area between good and evil.

The way it was in the old days, when you died you would meet Mr. Death.

"Hello, Death Nim."

"Here you go, son," and he would hand you a big fortune cookie. You opened it and inside it would tell you whether to pack your bags for heaven or hell. And that would be it.

Today, with some self-analysis, I believe it is possible to be aware in advance, what will be your fate in the so-called "afterlife." I chalk it up to growing harmonization between the physical and the spiritual, and the evolution of goodness, caused partly by the continuing development of humanity's spiritual consciousness. This is something people of all different faiths, politics and sexual orientations are sensing—at least those willing to speak to me—and so I feel emboldened to suggest it as a positive mutation in the genome.

Many religious traditions believe that an anthropomorphic, sentient being God is firmly in the driver's seat. I recognize an engaged God, but I also think goodness can function, grow and mutate very well in the hands of people and their consciences. I believe God gives us more responsibility than we think. Or want.

I personally find this scary because much of the responsibility is on the individual to clean up his or her act. It always has been, of course, but now it feels more like working without a net. Deep down in the dust bunnies of our soul, we know right from wrong. When I arrive at the Pearly Gates the excuse that I wasn't warned won't hold up.

My conclusion, therefore ...

Goodness exists. The genome for it courses though our corpuscles. It's a force as dependable as the toast falling jellyside down.

We were given a conscience in order to govern ourselves. That doesn't leave us a lot of wiggle room because conscience eliminates every last speck of plausible deniability we can allow ourselves. We can disconnect our conscience and live utterly without remorse. I don't know how well that holds up in the long run, but there are some very gnarly people who seem to be able to do just that. For the rest of us, however, the conscience knows all and doesn't stay silent. An individual either does right or does wrong, and the truth of it is clear to the individual even if people around him are fooled. Our mandate is, not that we *look* good, but in fact that we *be* good. The conscience is actually quite harsh. Hence occasional crushing guilt.

If capital-C Conscience were to govern all of society, if The Whole Truth were known to everyone all the time, like "Jack the Ripper is me" written across the famous serial killer's forehead—that would be useful to know. But constant public announcing of The Whole Truth means that, "Well, yes, that dress does make your butt look fat," is also written across someone's forehead. And that's not always a good thing because sometimes silence really is golden. Having The Whole Truth out there all the time might be a case of the goodness genome running amuck, producing results that are not necessarily good. Could any family reunion, office Christmas party or wedding survive the tyranny of truth?

It's hard to talk about conscience without mentioning forgiveness. Forgiveness is the wiggle room that keeps the conscience humane. Forgiveness is dealt with extensively elsewhere in this book so I will just say the forgiveness component of our humanity, this club in our spiritual golf bag, is what keeps the conscience from being a wildcat in a suitcase inside each one of us. Forgiveness is a necessary marker in the goodness genome.

What about the political sphere? Where does the goodness genome come into play in politics? Answer is it doesn't. Or almost never does. The utter nastiness of politics is why the most qualified and best of the best often decide not to seek public office. Suppose God, or we and God together, could help the goodness genome acquire another couple billion nucleotides of DNA and become a dominant ... thingy. Here is how it would impact politics: There would be little or no campaigning. A representative group of qualified men and women would gather in a room every four or six years and would draw straws. The one with the longest straw would be the Prez. The vice president would be selected by playing rock, paper, scissors. Imagine such a process presided over by people above reproach, who are guided by their fully involved conscience in unity with God himself ... herself ... ourselves.

SPACE-TIME CONTINUUM BLUES

Snuck up from behind in the lunchroom,
my three-ring binder sails over the meatloaf surprise,
arcing through the air slo-mo, in grace and beauty
until you stomp it flat and shove me back on my butt.
It is sooooooo freakin' funny!
You laugh; your friends laugh; all the students laugh;
the cute girls laugh; the ugly girls laugh; the teachers laugh;
the mayor laughs; the goddamn president laughs.

But what if instead …
I had deftly intercepted your arm?
What if I had calmly turned your wrist over,
applied just enough pressure
to drive you to your knees and hold you there
while you scream bloody murder, as your
carpel tunnel nerves send hook and ladder trucks
up your arm, down your spine, through your balls
and into the living roots of your teeth?

If I had done that, all order would be sucked from the world,
gravity would flow in reverse; meaning, existence and reason
would march back to some previous age in a bizarre
parallel universe we never knew existed,
where your friends would stand in line to kiss my ass
and the homecoming queen, heart aflutter,
would beg to have my child.

A VIOLIN IN THE WIND

Shoveling the sidewalk and driveway today. It was snowing like a busted open pillow and I went out to shovel, thinking I might keep up with it. I finished one pass and turned around to see the pavement was quickly being covered again. "Hey!" I shouted skyward, "I just finished this and you're covering it up again."

The only sound was "the sweep of easy wind and downy flake," as Robert Frost wrote. The language of that is so subtle and sublime, like we're looking at the cover of a romanticized Christmas card with a kindly old man sitting in a one-horse open sleigh. All around me the snow came down in buttons. This snowfall is heading for the record books and I knew my puny efforts to keep up with it would hardly matter. More than half an inch had already covered the pavement I cleared twenty minutes before. Not a problem because I wasn't out there to *accomplish* anything. I was out there to be Robert Frost. "My little horse must think it queer to stop without a farmhouse near. He gives his harness bells a shake to ask if there is some mistake."

It's good to spend time meditating. This falling, layering curtain of white must do what it must do. And so must I, and I wonder if it is possible for us to do it together. "These woods are lovely, dark and deep." It is so quiet inside the curtain. I stop scraping the driveway so I can stand inside its white velvet folds and listen to the silence. At once, a hundred other kindred silences appear and stand beside me. I am in an empty church. I am sitting in a *zendo* wearing loose-fitting clothing. I am kneeling in a garden. I am locked inside a deep pine forest. I stand over a high canyon on a decrepit railroad trestle, unused for a hundred years, looking into the abyss. Inspiration transmits on all channels, already familiar with turning my soul's reception to my own unique frequency.

Prayer is different from meditation, except for when it's exactly the same. Either way, prayer-slash-meditation can motivate you to build an ark or go there and do that, or transform yourself into this. The best contemplation alters your points of reference, which changes your perspective, shifts your paradigms, puts more colors on your palette, enlarges your catcher's mitt, so then you can feel confident to take full ownership of your initiative to build that ark or a maybe just a better lemonade stand.

Maybe you're like me and others who pray while driving or washing the dishes or otherwise rocketing through the twenty-first century. We think we're attaining a higher level of success when we're efficient like that, like a machine that pulls water out of the air on a humid day and uses it to cool the engine as it moves down the road. When did it happen, our unreasonable love of forward motion? I realize, out there at the end my driveway the sublime virtue of standing perfectly still.

George Orwell said that, at age 50, every man has the face he deserves. By then you have become a vessel made up of your laugh lines and your sorrows. The aggregated total of your deadly lies, as well as your secret integrities and good deeds unknown to others, are compiled there as well. All your charities, brutalities, brash moves and nuances, gross motor and fine motor. Your money and how you came by it. The loves you kept and the ones that got away; or that you squandered. Your past becomes a road map imprinted on your countenance. In addition, these things become the frequency at which your spirit vibrates. Heartbreaks and joys especially accumulate around the eyes, creating erosion lines and the beginnings of meandering rivulets and deep arroyos. Only the eyes themselves let the world know whether it was heartbreak's resignation, or joy, that eventually carried the day.

A violin held just right in the wind, will hum. Likewise, an introspective person will reverberate so that they hear the sound of their soul tuning itself to their own perfect frequency. It is unmistakable to their heart. It hums at a pitch only they can hear. The one next to you perceives the divine still small voice on a different frequency, based on the unique resonance of her molecules. Not being you does not make her less, nor ignorant. It just means she's a C and you're a D-sharp minor. Symphonies need both. With patient practice you can learn to glide home on your best natural wavelength, as personalized for you as your own fingerprints, as individual as every snowflake in that vast transcendence of white at the end of my driveway.

Receiving inspiration seems to be unrelated to external happiness or comfort. Some of the most gifted and accomplished artists and the most authentic saints endured lives of constant physical pain and unspeakable heartbreak. Paradoxically, it doesn't seem to be about being righteous either because some who appear to me to have done everything right are miserably poor, and there are others in big houses who have children with straight teeth and scholarships, but whose hearts are blacker than the inside of a goat. Saints understand this, which is why they are saintly, and why they have much to teach us. Teresa of Avila, the great sixteenth-century Catholic reformer and mystic, has been an inspiration to millions. Working through great physical and spiritual torment, and persecution from her own church, she leveraged her ill health and excruciating migraines to turn her spiritual violin into the wind at just the right angle. Go read her story and never again complain about anything.

At the end of the driveway snow is visibly rising around my feet. Looking back toward the house it looks deeper than it did when I began. I laugh. Noah built an ark. I read about it. Took him less than one page to do it. I could be out here all night and not clean one cubit of pavement. Lead my people out of Pharaoh's bondage? I can do that too I'm sure, but right now I need to make a path back to the house. I will aspire to greatness later, I'll catch up with Moses next week, but right now this is not about rising to sainthood or even about clearing snow. It's only about being here in the whiteout, limiting the vision and making all sounds indistinct. I cannot travel, I cannot see or hear. Therefore, I must exist fully in this moment and no other.

I imagine what it must be like to be a violin in the wind. I wonder how many other people are standing at the ends of their driveways thinking similar thoughts, and I see myself as one chair in a vast orchestra of a hundred thousand violins. All up and down the eastern seacoast of the United States, we are standing out in this snowstorm of biblical proportions, all of us laughing at the amazing wonder of it all.

Apropos of absolutely nothing, I think of these guys in New Paltz, New York, I read about. Three college students discovered $40,000 in green cash money tucked under the cushions of a second-hand Salvation Army sofa they had purchased. After doing battle with the little angel on this shoulder and the little devil on that shoulder, they decided to try to track down the owner. And they did. She was an elderly widow desperate to find it. It was her life's savings, "banked" in the sofa which was given to the thrift store by well-intentioned relatives. What are the odds that these modern young men would each resonate on their perfect frequency at the same moment and then conspire together to search for the owner of that money? "For I have promises to keep. And miles to go before I sleep." They must be standing in their driveway in New Paltz right this very minute, where it is snowing even harder than it is here.

I want to resonate like that, on that perfect frequency. I want so much to be a violin in the wind. I want to be in that community of people who try to do the right thing when the opportunity presents itself. Those are the people that all get together now and then to cook a big community lunch and give foot rubs to passersby. Every person who is one in heart with the Creator God, is one in heart with every other person in the world who is one in heart with God. Heaven is meant to be here and now. And we walk in its midst.

What Percy Shelley taught me about being remembered

Percy Shelley's famous "drowned rat" statue at Oxford

On July 8, 1822, slightly less than a month shy of his 30th birthday, Percy Bysshe Shelley drowned in a sudden storm while sailing off the northwest coast of Italy in his schooner. Shelley, who could be morose even on a good day, may even have wanted it that way. His body washed up on the shore with much of the skin eaten away, his clothing nearly gone and a boot missing.

That's all that was left of the Percy Shelley who wrote *Ozymandias*, Shelley, the image of brooding romanticism, philosopher-poet and husband of the author of *Frankenstein*. What was left of Shelley is what's left of all of us: guts, tissue and soul. Shelley had a rampaging soul. The long, lyrical phrasings of his poems can leave you searching for a place to breathe. A privileged and mystic iconoclast, he never let the silver spoon in his mouth get in the way of expressing his rage against the machine. His writing style conveys what I imagine as a personality of great drama and intensity. Not someone whose drink order you would want to get wrong at the Eagle and Child.

There tends to be lamentation, grief and a wet, rotting leaves kind of language in much of Shelly's poetry that can leave you in a deep contemplative discontent.

> *The dead are sleeping in their sepulchres*
> *And, mouldering as they sleep, a thrilling sound,*
> *Half sense half thought, among the darkness stirs,*
> *Breathed from their wormy beds all living things around,*

Incredible beauty in those words, but after reading Shelley, I need a hug. This is not to say that Shelley couldn't write a love poem as romantic as anyone. The same Percy Shelley who wrote "'Poetry is a sword of lightning, ever unsheathed, which consumes the scabbard that would contain it," also wrote, "'Poetry is the record of the best and happiest moments of the happiest and best minds'—both comments in the same essay, *A Defence of Poetry*.

The sculptor Edward Onslow Ford created an unusual memorial statue of Shelley. It wasn't a rendering of the poet in a coffee house with goose quill in hand or sitting at the hearth being urbane with Lord Byron and Keats. Instead, Ford sculpted a likeness of Shelley's soggy, lifeless, naked body, a marble version of the way he looked lying on the beach where they cremated him.

Shelley was kicked out of Oxford 200 years ago for being an outspoken atheist. I think of the offending essay, *The Necessity of Atheism,* as the poet in his punk-rock youth just keeping it real. Centuries later, after Oxford itself became atheist, they built a special nook for Shelley's drowned rat statue with inset mood lights capturing snippets of his poetry on the surrounding walls. It's there today, sitting on an ornate pedestal borne up by carvings of the requisite bare-bosomed lass and a couple of winged creatures from someone's nightmare.

The statue is highly acclaimed as a work of art, but it seems unfair to have one's best-known memorial be a sculpture of one's waterlogged carcass. Where's the dignity? What was Edward O. Ford thinking?

I wonder what the poet himself thinks as he strolls the halls of Oxford's University College on a moonless night.

John Keats, who lived at the same time, started writing poetry at 19 and died from tuberculosis at 25.

For a poet, dying young can be a good strategy. If it were not for Keats' verse, I doubt there would be one person who would remember him today. Keats' literary work was semi-ignored while he lived.

John Keats at medical school

His untimely death, however, gave his work a quality of rarity (plus it is honestly very good work), and by the end of the 1800s, he was revered everywhere. There is a dignified bronze statue of him at Guy's Hospital in London, where he studied medicine. He is depicted smaller than life-size, sitting on a bench, his hands resting on a book in his lap.

His statue sits apart from everything in an inner courtyard in the historical buildings of Guy's college, surrounded by a lush lawn bordered with flowers. He sits under an arch taken from the original London Bridge and transformed into a quiet alcove. Everything about the statue and setting exudes dignity and reverence.

So why is Percy Shelley's memorial the way it is? Maybe, through no fault of Shelley's, he was simply chosen by an instructive Fate to be an object lesson for us all in keeping it real. Or hey, maybe it's just a statue. When I gazed over at the carving of Shelly's dead, atheist cadaver at Oxford's University College, it was not with scorn. As I lurch tenuously through my own life, I am in no way fit to judge him. However, a day later, when I saw John Keats' statue in Guy's Hospital near London's Tower Bridge, I was strongly impressed with the contrast in the types of remembrance available to any sculptor who wants to take a shot at "doing you" after you're dead and defenseless.

Isadora Duncan, the great American dancer had a spectacular demise in 1927, worthy of her flamboyance.

While standing in the passenger seat of a convertible, she ostentatiously threw the long flowing scarf, for which she was famous, around her neck and trailing behind her as she shouted a devil-may-care *"Je vais à l'amour!"* ("I'm off to love.") to her friends. Some say her final words were *"Je vais à la gloire!"* ("I'm off to glory"), but that could have been post-mortem whitewashing. The scarf hung outside the roadster, where it was picked up by the back tire and wrapped as the car sped away. Ms. Duncan was yanked backward out of the car and onto the pavement, her neck snapped.

Numerous statues of her have been created showing her in dance moves that rightly depict her as the free spirited, inspiration and barrier-breaking revolutionary she was in life. She is often rendered topless or nearly so. This is good, because everyone knows if you're a woman, you have to be naked to get into a museum. A New York Times writer observed that only five percent of the art in the major museums has a woman as the subject. However, of those women, eighty-five percent of them are naked. But that's a future essay.

There are lessons galore in death's circumstances. Nelson Rockefeller died of a heart attack, tongues wag, while atop the lovely Megan. "Rockefeller Comes and Goes," one headline read. The joke that emerged to top all others is that Rockefeller died from low blood pressure—70 over 23. His wife had him cremated, like, instantly, bypassing the autopsy required by law (eliminating any errant fluids). But history knows how it went down, and we await the statue with some trepidation.

If I were ever invited to an orgy, I would worry: What if I choke on a chicken bone at the buffet while I'm there? What would my statue at the University of Texas at Austin look like? I fear it would depict me naked and clutching at my throat amid disreputable surroundings, instead of the way I look most of the time, including weekends, standing atop a mountain, gazing sagely into the distance. With chiseled abs.

I try to think, what are the deal-breakers of my reputation. Consider Judas, who could have been an Eagle Scout with Oak Leaf Cluster for all we know, but whose one misstep (selling out Jesus), seems to be the only thing people talk about these days regarding him.

Likewise, a lifelong reprobate can come through in the last minute. John Newton repents for his part in the slave trade, turns pastor, and writes the hymn, "Amazing Grace." I get teary-eyed when someone sings Battle Hymn of the Republic, so you can imagine what I must look like after listening to one of these stories about a scoundrel repenting, calling out in gratitude for "the hour I first believed."

Nobody gets out of here in one piece and without regrets. And truthfully, not without stains and blemishes either. Shelley wrote, "Life, like a dome of many-coloured glass, stains the white radiance of Eternity." We exit imperfectly and with a few dents and scratches, in other words.

In truth, my final minutes are not as worrisome for me as my final two or three decades. But that also is another essay. There is this brief life allotted to everyone (your mileage may vary), and then there is the eternity that comes after. Many proclaim with certainty, what that eternity is all about. But nobody can prove it. My two cents is that the odds favor the importance of creating happiness while you're alive, making meaning, family, beauty, joy and love in one's life, as opposed to sowing destruction, and living by taking, taking, taking.

Your memorial statue could be around a long time, not to mention your melancholy soul, lingering in the hallways of your *alma mater*. You can go ahead and take a minute to ponder eternity if you want. We still have a little time here. What is eternity anyway?

"Eternity is really long," Woody Allen said, "especially near the end."

Tipping Point at
TIKAL

She said "Hi."

Her red bandana headband was saturated from the sweat pouring off her face and forehead, and my hair, under a soft straw panama, was also soaked. We both stank to high heaven. "Hi," followed by conversation, happens easily on the road, easier even than in line at the supermarket. It's the backpacks. They proclaim we are both strangers here and neither of us has any turf to defend or local image that needs propping up. As *mochileros*, backpackers, we have nothing to offer but ourselves, no story to tell but our own.

We sat on opposite ends of a ten-foot-long granite stone chiseled to the shape and angled precision of a stick of butter by someone two thousand years ago using ... what? A piece of flint? Banana leaves? This stone, which must have weighed two tons, may have been the entire life's work of the carver. The edges were worn rounded now and the surface was a pitted moonscape, as you would expect from its having sat out in the rain all this time, the last half-century of which was laced with acid.

The stone was alongside a courtyard near a pyramid-like temple rising 200 feet above the rainforest floor. Between the big bang and sometime in the 1800s this tower was the tallest man-made structure in the Americas. We had just climbed up and down it, a rite of passage for visitors to Tikal, a Mayan ruin in the jungle of northern Guatemala, abandoned and entombed by Mother Nature for a thousand years except for a few acres that have been restored to near-original grandeur. Before "Hi," we hadn't met or spoken. We had climbed the steep narrow steps with a half dozen others, gripping the chain handrail that ran up the middle. We stood in an anonymous group at the top, transfixed by a view that sent our imaginations out across a never-ending carpet of treetops.

At the moment, both of us were keeping an eye on an inch-long ant, black as obsidian, crawling over and around the irregularities of the rock's surface. My interest was based on not wanting it to sneak up on my hand and take

a chunk out of it. Beverly's interest stemmed from being an entomology grad student from the University of Florida. "Pre-working on my pre-dissertation," she said. A master's degree freshly under her belt, she was in the process of deciding if she wanted to jump back on the treadmill for the long journey to a doctoral.

If you're a bugologist, the high-canopy rainforest of Guatemala will probably have what you're looking for. Not that Florida doesn't have enough insects of its own to follow around, but you know what they say: the bugs are always greener on the other side of the fence. And if you need some space to just get your head together, well, there's plenty of that here too.

But right now, Beverly was baking in a palm's half shade like me, chugging bottled water. She was early 20s, perky and earnest, wearing the uniform of the day: T-shirt, jeans and the required minimum of at least one item of clothing purchased at Banana Republic—hiking boots in her case. She carried a day pack with water and a couple of those health bars made from factory-seconds dog biscuits. Her passport and money would be in there too. Nobody leaves that stuff at their campsite. She met the world through eyes of an indistinct brownish blue that seemed to be trying to observe everything in case there would be a quiz later. As we talked, she did my eyes and then checked out my hat, upper body, shoes, belt, hands, then a surreptitious check of the perimeter around us, and back again, all the while making the most casual conversation. A survival trait of women who travel alone; I've seen it a lot. I wonder if they even know they're doing it.

Her face was more angular than round, with a strong jaw and chin being her best features. Too many nights sitting in the grad school library and scarfing down student union chili dogs had not helped her hips. But they weren't too bad at this point and she was young enough to effect whatever lifestyle disciplines she cared to in order to stay fit. She struck me as nice-looking, and cleaned up, would be even more so. And of course she was blithely immortal as she spoke of her studies and the future, as though her life would always be as it is now. No one in their 20s ever says, "Thank God I have my health."

"Cockroaches," she replied when I asked about the nature of her research. She was doing some kind of comparison between two variations, one in Florida and one in Guatemala, of the same basic brand of roach.

"Really? What kinds?" Like I would have a clue. Getting her to open up about roaches was easier than getting pupae to pupate. She was looking at similarities (or was it differences?) between the genus *latinword latinword*, which are all over the place in Florida, and its cousin, *latinword latinword*, which you can find under every other leaf in this part of Central America. Her dissertation title would easily fill three lines in print and seemed to imply some kind of theory about twins being separated at birth and evolving into separate cockroach armies. It had "parallel evolution" and morpho-something in the name, that's all I can tell you.

Did you know there are thousands of species of cockroaches? Of course you didn't, but Beverly does. Did you know that the flying cockroaches infesting South Florida originally came over from Vietnam in fruit shipments and in fact the merchant marine is the cockroaches' global interstate highway system? They get on with bell peppers in California and get off in Japan. On with mutton in Australia and off in South Africa. We spray and fumigate and stomp the little buggers but cockroaches are tenacious clingers to life. Hearing her describe her crunchy little friends made me feel like things were crawling on me. It must be interesting having an avocation that gives people the creeps. I wanted to ask her what's a nice girl like you doing in a field of study like this, but didn't yet know her well enough.

"So what is this?" I pointed, figuring here's where I learn the Latin word for ant, *eatibus anythingibus* or some such.

"It's an ant."

"I see." An entomologist outside her specialty is as Joe Sixpack as the rest of us.

"Look." She pulled a small magnifying glass from her pack and held it over the ant for me to see through. I bent down close. On the other side of the glass it tripled in length and had pincers the size of hedge clippers. As calmly as if she were marking her place in a book, she placed her finger down in front of the ant and wiggled it to see if it would latch onto her fingernail. It did so with a vengeance, lunging into the attack.

"Atta girl," she said, and dragged it forward an inch or so. The monster ant wrestled fearlessly with the fingernail. I was impressed that she had the wherewithal to get so personal with one of nature's most voracious eaters and that she would risk it shooting over the nail and biting into her finger. Okay, fine, so she was different from Joe Sixpack.

She asked what I did and I mentally weighed two options. I could say I was a writer, which impresses the heck out of people for some reason, especially young women, but really wasn't true since I spent probably 90 percent of my waking life on administrative work in an office, completely unrelated to actual creative prose. On the other hand, while saying I was a paper-pusher would have zero charisma, it would nonetheless carry the armor of truth and a virtue that is undeniably its own reward.

"I'm a writer."

We decided to walk over to the Jaguar Inn for some lunch, the only eatery in the park functioning at that time. That's when we met Ray, walking along the same road for the same reason. Middle-aged and affable, Ray would fit somewhere inside everyone's notion of average. Of medium height, he wasn't fat, but his chest had sunk into his paunch. He had short hair, thinning on top in the back, and an almost perfectly round head. He had found a trekker's hiking stick and poled himself along with it.

Like us, Ray had a tent in the park at the campground where most overnighters stayed. There weren't any showers anywhere, but there was a pump with a handle that, after a few quick pulls, would yield water. A sign on the pump warned that the water was limited for drinking only and strictly forbade using it to wash clothes or bathe. The sign might just as well have had another sign appended to the bottom telling you to ignore the first sign, for all the good it did.

In late April, we were still a few weeks away from the start of the serious rainy season that would run well into October. The heat and humidity, and mosquitoes were not nearly the force they would shortly become. With a modest amount of repellent, it was possible to sleep unmolested at night in the string hammock I had haggled for in a market in Oaxaca, Mexico. Still, it was midday in the jungle and the heat was on.

The Jaguar Inn, a few bungalows and a cafe located in the park just a half mile away from the ruins, was the area's sole provider of "indoors." Lunch at the Jaguar was the same as breakfast and dinner—black beans and rice, and eggs. And cold beer. The service was slow and the waitress still mixed up people's orders on the three-item menu. On the other hand, it had a ceiling fan and was a place to sit where the sun and mosquitoes weren't. As soon as the cold beer arrived all three of us snatched up the bottles and touched the icy wetness to our necks and faces. The chill stung exquisitely, like a love bite.

In the silence that settled in around us, Bev asked Ray about himself. The friendship was an hour old and she had already transformed from a Beverly to a Bev, and now the whole tapestry of our existences seemed to be fair game for discussion. That's how fast it can work with strangers who know they will never see one another again after a day or two. Inquiries that would be impertinent in any other context are acceptable in this one.

That's why we were surprised when her request, "So, Ray, tell us about your life," threw him into a deep brown study. In the unnatural silence we sensed an uncauterized wound had been touched by the most routine of questions. She hadn't asked him about his work, which would have been easy for him to handle. A person can hide behind his job all day, and besides we had already covered that one. He told us on the walk over that he was a contractor who built things on U.S. Army bases. He traveled all the time doing this. He also played the piano and after hours jammed with pick-up bands of soldiers, other pretty-good musicians who got together when they could.

The waitress brought the food. Beans and rice with a fried egg on top for all of us, along with a basket of fresh hard rolls and a second round of beer. We ate a little to fill the spaces in a conversation stranded high center. We could see Ray's composure was walking on eggshells. Finally he spoke. "I'm sorry."

"Want to tell us about it?" she asked reflexively, with a slight grimace of her mouth that begged a pardon if asking was making another mistake.

And that's when Ray told us about the inconceivable dual reality he had been living for twenty years. One life was spent as a straight-arrow husband in an empty marriage, the father of two children. A self-made businessman and amateur musician. Regular churchgoer. The works. In life number two Ray was addicted to all manner of homosexual activity, mostly with enlisted men, in rec halls on the bases. There had been officers too, even a major. He described furtive gropings in bathrooms and public buildings. He held nothing back. As he unrolled his map of two decades, we were riveted. He operated on one set of standards at home and a completely different set on the road. As much as anything else, we were struck by the utter aloneness of his existence.

Lately, and increasingly, the separate colors of his two lives had started to run together outside the lines. A lover from somewhere on the road had somehow gotten his phone number and called his home a few times. He counted it a miracle that he gotten to the mailbox first on the two occasions when letters came from a one-night stand whose requests were particularly graphic. "How did he find out where I live?" Ray asked the middle distance in front of him.

"Army bases have computers," Bev offered. "You're a contractor, so you're in the database. I was madly in love with my biology professor a couple years ago. That's how I tracked him down. It was easy ..." The last couple words flattened out as she trailed off, expelled a betraying sigh that wound down to a tiny puff. In nothing more than a parenthetical fragment, I thought we may have seen a door behind which lay a world she had sealed off for good.

"He drives past my house," Ray said. Public exposure loomed, and with it community revulsion, heartbreak, devastation. Divorce? In addition his business had been in a long rough patch and was in serious jeopardy of going down. The crows were gathering and Ray was feeling maybe it wasn't worth it. None of it worth anything.

Ray had come to Tikal to decide whether or not to kill himself.

When somebody tells you something like this, you're supposed to reach out, touch them meaningfully and urge, "No, wait, don't ... *all human beings are infinitely precious*, etc.," and Bev did just that. In almost those exact words. She leaned in close, across the table and stroked his arm as though trying to nurture him back to life. I felt sorry for him, but I've been around. Life, in many cases, is unrelieved pain. Part of it is the hand you're dealt and nothing more, and I wondered at the time how long or happily everyone is supposed to live.

I have changed a lot since then. I believe everyone has a right to, if not happiness, the unfettered pursuit of it without barriers being put in place by others. I hope that my compassion has deepened, as well.

It would have been useless to remind Ray that, on the whole, double lives are good things to avoid, because there are enough deceptions and gray truth to keep track of in just one life. So I went for the more practical, "Were you thinking of taking a dive off the temple?" That was the start of Bev kicking me under the table.

"Oh my God, no," Ray replied. "I'm much too chicken." Not wanting to inconvenience others, Ray would do something less dramatic with drugs or gas when he got home. He had started to accumulate a lot of life insurance and would try to make it look like an accident. "But I did think about it when I was up there," he said.

I tried again. "So you got all this stress and anguish. And the idea of killing yourself is to escape from that into oblivion?"

ka-KICK!

"Something ... anything ... I just don't want my family to ..."

"But what if peaceful nothingness isn't what happens when you die?"

He was wary and irritated at where he thought I was going with this. I got an inkling we weren't the first people he had had this conversation with. "Oh, yeah, the burning fires of hell," he said. "Well, I don't buy into any of that."

"I don't either," I said, "but of course we never know. And that's the point. Nothingness is only one of a zillion possibilities. What if you kill yourself and your suffering still exists in your heart, and you're still trapped in it somehow? I mean isn't that why ghosts hang around and haunt things and rattle chains, and are always pissed off?"

Ray was speechless. I had moved my leg and Bev's kick caught the post under the table.

Bev, ever the good cop, jumped in. "This isn't something you've definitely made your mind up about is it?"

"No."

She added, "...because it sounds like you're thinking out loud about ... I feel like you're trying to desensitize yourself ... like you're working up your courage to ... do something." Direct enough, I guess, considering what she had been doing to my shins for saying what I thought was much the same thing. Neither of us had any way to know how far along he was in his plans, how definite, or if he was a serial crier for help or what. But I thought Bev was right. In front of us, two strangers he would never see again, he seemed to be seriously test-driving the idea.

"Well ... maybe I am," he answered.

Bev and I didn't have a plan for where to take this, but we were connecting. Bev had ventured into euphemisms early on, borderline homosexual, bisexual and such, but I felt almost certain that wasn't true. I was sure Ray was gay as a box of birds and that whatever had been going on with him and his wife the past twenty years, he had been faking it all the way. That was my two cents and Ray didn't contest it when I brought it up. Bev sat beside me, and Ray across from us, alternated looking at me, then her, then me—eyeball to eyeball with each of us. Every time my turn came around, I was consciously aware I was looking deeply into the eyes of a man who bats for the other team.

"Ray, you need to get real," I finally said. "You've obviously built a life you don't like and your business is going into the toilet, but you're talking about killing yourself, pulling the plug for all time. Forever. I think you need to quit playing games and think this thing all the way through because *death is pretty fucking irreversible*." That last part may have been delivered just a smidgen too loud. Every head in the place whipped in the direction of our table.

We stayed in the restaurant for three hours, holding down our corner as the rest of Tikal's gringo tourists, "banana republicans" we had christened them after their sartorial sameness, drifted in, ate their beer and beans and left. I told them of my own decision-in-progress, about whether to keep on working in an office or risk all doing the writing I really wanted to do. If it didn't also involve my wife and kids, no problem, but not being able to provide for them, that was the scary part. On the other hand, the fantasy of being a famous writer was superb: Getting up in the morning, taking my coffee cup and laptop up the ladder to the tree house in the woods out back. Banging out deathless prose to feed a world of hungry hearts. Coming down only to put on a tux and go to White House dinners.

"Nice hallucination, huh?" I concluded.

"The best." Ray winked.

Ray eventually began to lighten up a bit. Nothing like a few cockroach stories from Bev to put everyone in a festive mood. Did you know some kinds will eat your eyebrows while you're sleeping? Life stories of broken loves were swapped and it was determined that nobody gets out of this world with their heart in one piece. In the end, a conspiracy was hatched between us: Sunset on top of Temple IV. Maybe the Mundo Perdido temple, because it would be less of a tourist magnet come sunrise, if we decided to do an all-nighter.

The only problem were the guards posted after the ruins were closed to the public. "Leave them to me," I assured my companions. The universal language that unites all mankind isn't love. It isn't even money or the barrel of a gun. It's cigarettes. Marlboro cigarettes. American Marlboro cigarettes have gotten me through more closed doors and gates and into the good graces of tinpot dictator bureaucrats with rubber stamps in more places than I can remember. I don't smoke them, but it seems like everyone else does.

When we arrived though, the guards were nowhere around. They shooed the tourists out of the park before dusk, hung around to guard for awhile, and then left themselves. Maybe they were off smoking that day's Marlboros. Or maybe they didn't care to be jaguar bait. Either way, they were gone and I was unable to demonstrate my bribing prowess.

The path into the restored part of Tikal was ours for the taking as the sun hovered through the treetops at a steep angle but still decently above the horizon. We scampered along the trail as quickly as we could move, aware that down here, below the high canopy, nightfall arrives a good half hour earlier than it does above the trees.

Provisioned with beef jerky, two bottles each of piss-warm beer, three-quarters of a bag of sat-on Oreo cookie dust and four useless packs of cigarettes, we scampered up the high temple, giggling like kids sneaking into the exit at the cineplex.

We arrived atop the temple in time to watch the sun fall into the seamless covering of treetops spread out below us. We listened to howler monkeys, which sound like jaguars, and jaguars (which also sound like jaguars), down below and around on all sides of us—staking out their territory for the night. We were way out in the middle of deadly earnest, non-Disneyland jungle. And now it was dark. In retrospect, smart people would not have been where we were. I wondered if these temples were where they left people at night so they could be eaten by jungle cats.

"What do you suppose killed this civilization?" Bev asked. "War?"

Ray knew. "They ran out of sacrificial virgins. They had nothing left to appease the gods with, and so naturally the gods destroyed them."

More thinking aloud than speaking, I added, "We're pretty much out of virgins back home, as far as I can tell."

"Not a good sign," Ray said.

While waiting to be eaten, we held a free-flowing, warm beer fueled, all-night dissection of the souls and destinies of all three of us. Ray wondered if I had any personal objection to gayness. I felt no need to pony up that trendy and shallow response, "I have many friends who are gay." I simply told him I only know the people I know as individuals, and that I have perceived deep in the dust bunnies of my soul, a kind of frenetic lostness in many of them. "Ray," I said, "I think you're loster than Moses, and what I want for you is to be at peace, and happy in whatever skin you're wearing, whatever that looks like." Ray shrugged, said, "Me too," handed me a busted Oreo. I took it. "Thanks."

I recited a couple of poems and was rewarded with their laughter and approval. They really liked "Attila the Hun," the poem I could remember, and concurred that my life would be better spent pushing words around on paper than pushing papers through the colon of the machines of officialdom. We worked on our jaguar growls and Ray and I taught Bev "Me and Bobbie McGee."

Bev found another giant ant, or rather it found her. She dispatched it with a swat and then started to demonstrate the fingernail bit with one of its friends. If it clamped her nail and didn't bite the finger, we decided, Bev would take it as a sign from God that she should pursue her dissertation. We had been urging her all afternoon to go for the Doc, and the ant backed us up. The little bugger clamped on her fingernail and held on to beat the band. Ray hailed her "Dances with ants."

We even discovered a use for the Marlboros: mosquito repellent. We lit six at a time and set them all around us. We would have been driven mad by "blood-sucking Arthropoda" (a bugologist in the jungle can be endlessly informative), but the breeze above the trees kept most of them at bay, just as the stars and our felt companionship anchored us there until night melded into daybreak. The sunrise would have been outstanding if it hadn't been for the fog. In the dark of predawn, as the dew was forming all over us like rain appearing out of thin air, the night's coolness and the still warm earth married to produce a pea-soup shroud that rose from the jungle floor. Before it surrounded us and blocked out the stars, the fog climbed the temple stairs until it covered the treetops at our feet, washing us in reflected moonlight. We pretended to be the last three survivors of a castled city built on a cloud.

Somewhere in the night, I said, "Ray, you need to figure out what you are, and then have a talk with your wife. Maybe the first real talk of your whole marriage. Chances are she already suspects you're gobbling army men since you've had sex with her like what, twice?"

Bev, agreed, "I'm sure she must know, or suspect, but maybe doesn't want to know." There on the top of the temple of ancient Tikal, we made Ray raise his right hand and swear before the orchid-bedecked primeval gods of a vanished people that he wouldn't do anything dumb like the Mayans may have done. No human sacrifices. And that he would tell his wife what he should have told her twenty years and two children ago. At dawn, we descended back into the present century.

The tall wet grass soaked our boot tops as we headed along the path from the ruins, past surprised guards who had come on duty shortly after sunrise. We walked back to the campsite to say goodbye and roll up our gear. We all hugged, and meant it. Gradually, we departed on separate buses to our individual fates, however enriching or pathetically tragic they would turn out to be. The fearsome threesome, unlikely to have met and even more unlikely to meet again. Dances with ants. Dances with words. Dances with soldiers.

ATTILA THE HUN

Attila the killa
Attila the Hun
Attila the Hun and his horde.

Attila would walk on the bed in his shoes,
get close to your face, and sneeze.
He greased his chin with a mutton shank
then slept with his wives
and their fleas.

Attila the Hun was such fun.

You must be this tall to smash Hitler's balls

How can the aggrieved innocent torment Hitler in hell without being stuck there themselves?

Despite the title, the topic of this piece is central to human happiness. A couple of "givens" obvious to some of you, but which I have to insist upon when speaking to my glitterati café society friends, is that when you die you don't just go *poof* into fairy dust. There are those who believe life is an accidental joke, a brief and meaningless journey from birth to oblivion. I don't. I think you will continue to exist in some form. Your consciousness, your spirit, lives on in some manner, with your thoughts and feelings and personality intact.

No matter what you believe.

In addition, I assume people in the spirit world are still able to learn things and grow from them, the same as they did when they owned a physical body on earth. This implies that, with some effort, a person would be able to right some wrongs and put one's difficult life behind them and start anew.

As well, they might commit additional wrongs, making their situation even worse. Some may choose to hang onto their grudges and haul their earthly emotional baggage and regrets with them for perhaps a very long, long time. There might be a hell and a heaven and places in between. I haven't been there, so you could say all this is speculation. But it seems to me that, based on what we have managed to figure out about good and evil, and about our own human nature, the following is an entirely logical—and certainly not an impossible—scenario.

If heaven exists, I do not expect to see people lounging around in their bathrobes reading the Sunday Times at 10 a.m. (nor lazily strumming those harps). I think people will have assignments and real work to do in the spirit world, and that the higher realms must have a lot of energy. I envision they hit the floor early, grab a cuppa joe, then roll up their ectoplasmic sleeves and get to it. Life is eternal; you do stuff there just as you do stuff here. Just the packaging and the physics, are different.

One of the most interesting dead people I know is Adolf Hitler, the poster child for evil, a man so wicked that today it's against the law in Germany and Austria to have Hitler as a family name. They retired his jersey, so to speak.

I read an article written by a man, Dr. Sang-hun Lee, who had died and was apparently communicating via an earthly medium with some recognized ability. He had been a scholar in his earthly life and had a reputation for academic integrity. In his messages from beyond, he said he had been assigned to visit all kinds of people and talk with them about their lives, what they did right and wrong, etc., and then report back to us, the "living."

I acknowledge that some people (though surely not you, gentle reader) think the existence of a spirit world is bunk, and therefore think any kind of communication between there and here is bogus. Then there are those, the same people who think, "If it's on the internet it must be true," who believe every utterance from the spirit world is gospel. I tend to take a practical approach. I think a no-good, lying, cheating bastard here is a no-good, lying, cheating bastard after he dies. In fact, most people are a mixture of good and bad, with most of us being somewhere in between. People are guided by their habits, intentions and motives, and that forms their character. Their character goes with them intact, to the spirit world. Dying doesn't suddenly make you a good person, or all-knowing. But neither is everyone over there full of beans.

All this is just to say that interaction with the spirit world is an inexact science, and although I have experienced a very few of what I consider to be genuine communications from spirits, even from God, in response to prayer I believe, I am sympathetic with anyone who thinks the whole idea of spiritual communication is a crock. I know some people who communicate regularly with the spirit world and are crazy as a clown car. Until we have cell phones to chat between here and there, we're stuck with relying on intuition.

Back to Dr. Lee. Our intrepid and still-dead reporter, described an arduous search for Hitler before finally finding him hanging out in a desolate, gray and featureless place. Literally hanging out. He found the former *Führer* suspended a few feet off the ground, against the side of a tree. Tied by his arms and feet, he hung spread-eagle and naked.

Dr. Lee reported seeing an enormous throng of people stretching down the street and off into the distance. A nearly limitless parade of enraged souls filed past Hitler, and as they did, they screamed at him or scratched him, struck him with a club or, if they were tall enough, reached up and smashed his testicles with a chunk of jagged brick. If I were Hitler, this treatment, especially the testicle thing, would get old really fast.

Reading that, it seemed an unimaginable hell for everyone involved. I envisioned a pile of bricks and rocks stacked alongside the path near the tree. Each person picks out a nice chunk, hefts it, approaches the tree and gives Hitler a solid whack to the privates. They toss it back on the pile and walk all the way back down the hill, around the corner and over the horizon to get in line again. Their anger, self-fueling as the sun, has never been quenched or even abated by a single degree since Hitler took his life in the *Führerbunker* in April 1945.

With the caveat that any discussion of what goes on in spirit world is tinged with a certain "woo-woo factor" and requires flexibility in one's conventional knowledge, I have no trouble picturing this horrific scene of resentment that cannot be resolved, simply because it seems possible that there are crimes that cannot be forgiven. An unending circle of evildoer and victims are locked together forever in a macabre dance that eventually acquires its own self-contained feeling of being "normal."

Now for the part that's really, really hard to think about. Dr. Lee spoke through his earth-side medium about meeting a young Jewish woman there. She was innocent, a virgin we assume, who was part of the mob crowding around Hitler. She had been killed under horrific conditions, possibly in a concentration camp gas chamber. I wondered what a relatively blameless woman would be doing in this cold, gray hell with Hitler for the past 70 years. There is no reason for her to be there unless she was unable to move on, unless she was "bound" to Hitler by her inconsolable sorrow or hatred, or whatever strong emotion kept her there.

All we were told about the woman is that she had been there since the war and was utterly miserable and bitter. Her circumstance begs an enormous *why?* that has important implications regarding the nature of the spirit world. This young woman should have been, if not in ÜberHeaven, any number of higher and brighter places than where she was currently. A Jew in Nazi Germany, her only crime was the bad luck of having been born in the wrong era and place.

It seems Hitler, by his extreme evil, not only consigned his own soul to hell, but keeps millions of others stuck there in that awful griminess, unable to get past the blockage of their own pain and resentment at having been murdered by the Nazis.

Sometime after Dr. Lee's article came out, I read something else that mentioned Hitler somehow being "liberated," in that he was allowed to finally get down from the tree. Not to be confused with forgiveness, this was "liberation" or perhaps a kind of grace so that this whole grim scenario would not have to be stuck in stasis for eternity. But apparently he was taken down off the tree. Many who happened to read about this reacted with derisive contempt, including myself. Another big *why?* emerges. Where is the justice in liberating Hitler? Why should Hitler be given a Get Out of Hell Free card? The thing is, I don't think that was the case.

I had always assumed the "unquenchable fires of damnation" were eternal. And also, nobody ever said anything about the victims spending time in hell with their perpetrators. And certainly not for eternity.

BUT … if we believe, as I do, that ultimately God's own happiness is contingent on having a way to eventually eliminate hell itself, then there needs to be some process by which this can happen. Even if it takes eons, there has to be a process for healing. After smashing Hitler's balls there has to be a choice other than getting back in that line again. If Hitler was allowed some respite from his well-deserved torture, it may actually have been for the purpose of healing the innocent souls trapped there with him.

If Hitler could be taken down off the tree and be allowed to be out working on his penance, then maybe the people in that long, bitter queue could get on with their own destinies as well. Maybe all those victims could finally step into the light, so to speak, and go on to brighter, warmer, happier places.

In other words, a favorable justice can liberate *everyone*.

And what of Hitler's penance? Between 60 and 70 million people were killed in World War II, and Hitler may be partly accountable for all of them. So when I use the word "liberation" for him I keep having to put it inside quotation marks because the word is being used in a decidedly relative, tenuous sense. I wonder if his existence, and his penance, may have finally transitioned into a different kind of suffering, an anguished atonement of begging forgiveness, one-on-one, for a long time to come.

Perhaps it means he is allowed to at last begin the long and painful course of his own restoration. If Hitler, now a wanderer in the spiritual realms, is required to have his ticket punched by everyone for whom he is responsible for their physical, emotional or spiritual destruction, I can't imagine how long this would take. His road to forgiveness could require a few millennia to complete. We don't know how sick in the head Hitler might be. We don't know his state of mind or to what degree he even realizes the extent of the evil he begat.

Dr. Lee's report did help me understand that God really is all about healing and patience and love. If I were as merciful and far-sighted as God, I think I would have altered Hitler's circumstances, too. *For the sake of the Jews.* My sympathy would be with that young woman, somebody's daughter, who was never able to become a loving wife and mother—whose life was cruelly squandered by the most brutal arrogance. For her to be able to finally get on with pursuing her true course, to be set free to experience the joy that is a human being's birthright, instead of circling endlessly around Hitler's tree, consumed by loathing in that grease-water swamp—for her to be unshackled from her resentment—would be worth any price.

Imagine that freedom multiplied times 70 million.

I would think it worth even peeling Hitler off that tree and sending him out on his long march of expiation, over endless mountains through unnumbered towns and villages in the spirit lands, looking people in the eye, begging the forgiveness of millions. One person at a time. Yearning, maybe even praying, for all this to someday be over.

A beautiful Christmas story

Walking through a storybook snowfall in early December, I visited an art dealer to sell my beautiful hand-finished mahogany and glass display case so I could buy Taeko an exquisite mother-of-pearl safety guard for her chainsaw and the down payment on a monster truck.

Christmas morning she opened her gift, picked up the beautiful chainsaw safety guard, inlaid with pearl's mother, and began to smile while weeping softly at the same time.

"What's the matter, Honey?" I asked.

"Nothing, Darling, nothing at all," she replied.

Then she told me she had sold her chainsaw and her heirloom brass knuckles a week ago to buy the femur of John the Baptist from the Sultan Suleiman's reliquary in Istanbul, to put in my mahogany display case.

We fell into one another's arms in tears.

SPRING'S DEEP, WET KISS

Science tells us that around December 21 the sun is directly above São Paolo, Brazil; Puerto Leda, Paraguay; Kruger Park, South Africa and Alice Springs, Australia. Meanwhile in the northern hemisphere, it gets dark a few hours after sunrise. People fight their way through frozen slush on salted pavement, surviving on party food in an ambiance of air kisses, robotic shopping and road rage. The fortunate hunker down with families and a few close friends to ride it out. Not to worry, science says, the Sun will return in all its glory and we are not doomed to endless cold and darkness. For at that moment, science assures us, the wobbly Earth begins to tilt back to the upright (relative to the Sun), and the long, warm days will return to us.

This of course is rubbish.

The truth is my pagan ancestors saved us from dying alone in the frozen darkness, abandoned by the Sun. Every year they brought back the sun with their dances and sacrifices in the forest. By heroic effort, on nights of icy rain in thigh-deep snow, peasant farmers worldwide stopped the sun from vanishing altogether using time-honored rituals and liquor to keep warm. If they hadn't stepped up to the plate, the sun would have disappeared altogether, leaving us in everlasting darkness. There would be no spring planting, no crops, and all life on earth would have come to a dead stop forever. And so every year unschooled people cut a deal with The Great Turtle, doing whatever it took, offering whatever they thought was needed. And every year The Great Turtle was pleased, and the sun began to return. Don't let anyone ever tell you animal sacrifices don't work. You're welcome.

Today people are in a hurry and so we tend to go with science's explanation, which is … the tilting Earth's axis, starting in late December, makes the Sun appear to move northward, creating longer days up here. The Sun is directly above the equator around March 20. That's *equinox*, the moment day equals night and spring arrives in the northern hemisphere.

The onset of spring is gradual, beginning with a string of days of perfect temperature, interspersed with chilly rain, followed by warm rain, and still melting snow. Then, one day, a comforting sun hits our little patch of ground and stays, carrying some invisible magic. We realize we hadn't been breathing for a while; the pulse quickens. We sigh and exhale, climbing down off the ledge and into the light, the warmth and the grass. The shoes come off. Whoa, baby!

Many say the Creator is fully half masculine and fully half feminine. This idea is supported by observing that all creation appears to have been divided into masculine and feminine expressions. Boys and girls, boy animals, girl animals, boy plants, girl plants. It seems to have happened across the board, all the way down to protons and electrons (maybe not exactly boys and girls, but polar opposites).

The result is that in order to see what God really looks like, and for things to resemble what the whole of God is like, looking at just a man or just a woman alone won't do it. You have to put them back together in order to fully understand what God is made of. When it comes to putting man and woman back together, I don't think I need to convince anyone that the most intense form of "together" for males and females, is mating. And everything from people to hamsters to magnetic north and south are trying to do that. Goldfish and katydids do it without drama. But people, omigod, fill the air with sweet, stupid love songs, with insipid Valentine's Day poems and any excuse to rhyme moon with June.

This happens in the spring like no other time. You can pinpoint the start of the madness to the first warm, sunny days after the snow goes away. It's as though jumper cables have been attached to every living thing and someone cranks up the juice all the way and everybody gets a little crazy. The angel of somber responsibility sits on one shoulder and the angel of spring on the other, whispering in your ear twenty reasons to skip school or work. All of them good. Not just good. *Fabulous.*

Life that we thought had died from months of freezing cold was only hibernating, biding its time. *Where did all these wasps come from? You guys were supposed to be dead.* Spring is in its bacchanalia, a glorious Fat Tuesday for which there is no tomorrow, and in which nothing is held in reserve. Mother Nature is the extravagant life of the party. She is a drunken sailor three sheets to the wind who will do anything and everything to ensure that the male and female of every hop-toad and slime creature find each other and share spit. Everything is over-the-top excessive. Where a few thousand minnows will do, nature needs millions just so their own parents can eat most of them. Some species of mayfly have an adult lifespan of only 30 minutes. A queen ant can live for 30 years. There don't seem to be any rules.

The rush is headlong and pre-wired, without conscious thought. As a young adolescent boy in Oklahoma, I saw a Hereford bull destroy a sturdy oak and wire fence, hitting it again and again with a half-ton of momentum, until he broke through, bleeding and grinning, to mate with the heifers on the other side. It inspired me beyond belief.

However, it's the male praying mantis who wins the award for giving all for love. After he mounts the female to copulate, she turns around and severs his head with her buzz saw jaws. Now headless, he continues to mate for the next several hours, until he falls over or she eats the rest of him, fortifying herself for the gestation. There are a couple of ways to look at this, aside from understanding that men don't require brains for sex. You can choose to see it as a testimony to the cruelty of nature or you can see it as a sacred, supreme sacrifice for the future of the species. I choose to see it as practical. If your lover can also be your protein source, that's a lot more convenient than stopping what you're doing to order in some chicken wings.

Burgeoning springtime begins below our feet. Most of the planet is dirt instead of one big rock because the bacteria, protozoa, fishing worms and tree roots have been burrowing through it and eating it for eons. The earth is also a giant compost heap, like the one near your garden, with plant matter, egg shells and decaying bugs. We call the process "rotting," but fungi, amoebae, mites and arthropods call it "the good life."

A single spade of dirt from my little victory garden has some 200 species of insects and other life forms, most of them too small to see. Fungus spores, cicadas, several varieties of beetles, wasp larvae, caterpillars and others are there too, each hosting an impressive variety of parasitic insects, some of whom host their own parasites.

There are 200 million insects for every person on earth. Of beetles alone there are up to eight million different species, with new ones being discovered all the time. One out of every four animals on earth is a beetle. And you thought there was only John, Paul, George and Ringo.

Ants are in that same spade of dirt, spilling over the edges, each one trying to save suddenly exposed eggs. Amazon ants from Brazil, now found also in the American southwest, are one of a few species of "slave-raiding" ants who steal the pupae of other ants, raise them and put them to work as unpaid help to care for the young. Wisely I think, because the long, piercing, dagger jaws of the Brazilian ants make them unsuited for infant care. Think about it. Would you want Edward Scissorhands changing your kid's diaper?

Ants of course are eaters. Last week the café car on my Amtrak train, fully stocked for the run from Richmond to Boston, ran out of sandwiches and sodas within the first hundred miles. The server shrugged, "A hundred teenagers got on at Lynchburg." Amazon ants could learn from them.

"April is the cruelest month, breeding lilacs out of the dead land ..." wrote T.S. Eliot. April rudely awakens comfortably dormant acreage and shoves it through messy changes. As any fetus will tell you, in birth, hunger is also born. The little guy has to scream bloody murder to get fed. Only a day before, everything was provided without asking, so beautifully tranquil and undisturbed. So yes, April is cruel, and its motto is: "Get a life!" While sitting at your local cantina some Saturday night, watching two drunk cowboys in a knife fight over who said something to whose girl, ponder why the magnetism between male and female was created to be so intense, and why it is only this bonding, and nothing else, that creates new life from one end of time to the other. The reason love and mating are the most powerful engines, second only to hunger, is because *they have to be*. You can forget to pay the rent because you will still exist after getting evicted, but you can't forget to eat and you can't forget to have sex because that's how life continues.

By the way, the longest day of the year for us northerners will happen around June 20. The axis of the earth keeps tilting until the Sun sits directly over the northern shore of Cuba. There the wobbly Earth will reverse its tilt, sending the Sun back down to warm the bikini beaches of South America. The insanity this creates in Brazil is their problem. We're told, "God is love," but it's more than that. God is the very author of the mating frenzy. All this is his fault. The surviving cowboy in the

Saturday night knife fight won't get away with pleading that The Great Turtle made him do it, but the Creator's fingerprints are in the DNA. God is a love-junkie just like us who are made in his image. I believe he wants to be right there in the middle of everything we do, especially when we're creating new life. If we are bug-eyed and joyfully unhinged when spring fever hits, we are simply chips off the ol' block.

Therefore, I don't have to ask who wrote the book of love. I know exactly who put the *bomp* in the *bomp bah bomp bah bomp* and the *ram* in the *rama lama ding dong*, that made my baby fall in love with me.

HUMOR HURTS

Why do you think they call it a "punch line"?

True story. High winds contributed to a huge multi-vehicle pile-up on a major thoroughfare near our house during a big outdoor event with parades and pageantry. It was like this: An 18-wheeler jackknifes in gale-force winds, strewing its cargo of bananas, cream pies and pre-inflated whoopie cushions all over the road and into a crowd of bystanders.

Order instantly turns to chaos as dozens of people begin slipping on banana peels and falling butt-first onto the pre-inflated whoopie cushions. Pie fights break out randomly. The screams of pie victims are all but drowned out by the fart sound "raspberries" of the whoopie cushions. Fruit pie is everywhere. The carnage is horrific.

A quick-thinking bystander searches the faces in the throng around her, shouts imploringly, "Please ... please ... somebody ... anyone ... is there a humorist here?"

I had been watching the whole thing, expecting I might be needed. I calmly stepped out of the crowd. "Yes, ma'am, I'm licensed to commit humor."

The woman's shoulders slumped with relief. "Oh, thank God!" she said, her voice shaking. "Are you ... are you funny?"

I smiled reassuringly. "Check this out. What do they call a boomerang that won't come back? A stick." *BADA-BING!*

Two muffins are in the oven. One says to the other "Boy it's hot in here" The other one replies, "Omigod, it's a talking muffin!" *BADA-BING!*

"A dyslexic man walks into a bra ..."

"Wonderful, you'll do fine," interrupts an overly buxom matron wearing a corseted 1890s dress and a grotesquely wide-brimmed, ostrich-plumed hat, as a golf cart filled with clowns sporting lapel squirt flowers rounds the corner.

The cart skids on the bananas, knocking the Boston-educated matriarch face-first into a cream pie held by a fussy British waiter wearing a monocle, top hat and formal wear. Both of them go sprawling at great force into a group of ballerinas carrying large bags of feathers. The ballerinas, in turn, are sent flying into a group of workers from the Acme Hot Wet Fertilizer Company who carry bags of fetid, steaming manure, fresh from the cow.

Ballerinas and hot wet fertilizer workers collide like bowling pins. Bags fly into the air, split open and are whipped by the swirling winds into an enormous dark toxic cloud of hot, stinking, slimy cow shit mixed with feathers. The viscous mass, stretching now from curb to curb and low to the ground, is quickly borne on the wind, hurtling southward down the street at tremendous speed …

… as northward up the street comes the Annual Ku Klux Klan Pride Parade. Four hundred men and women, desperately white, dressed in freshly laundered, pristine bed sheets. Emblazoned on a banner at the head of the marchers is this year's theme which reads, ironically, as it turned out, "If You're Brown Get Outta Town!"

This really happened.

THE EVOLUTION OF GOD

When evolution is outlawed, only outlaws will evolve.

I don't approve of the way the argument over evolution has evolved. Darwin thoroughly yanked the chain of collective Christianity regarding natural selection.

He published *The Origin of Species* and suddenly, by the trends in Christianity at that time, it somehow became a mandatory assumption that an evolutionist is also an atheist.

Darwin was an unreconstructed racist, claiming superiority of white over black. Less well-known, but mainstream for that era, was that he was a thoroughgoing sexist, writing in his autobiography, "The average mental power in man must be above that of women." Not so strangely, these two notions didn't bother the Christian establishment one bit in 1859. That's the part of Darwinism they *liked*.

Robber barons like J.D. Rockefeller and Andrew Carnegie, along with Karl Marx and Hitler liked those parts as well, in addition to natural selection.

Bummer.

Today, all religious people accept that a faster wolf will catch more bunnies, will eat, thrive and breed—and will give birth to a new crop of fast, or faster, bunny hunters. We assume that Leonardo Da Vinci's kid could probably draw well. The original natural selection burr under the saddle of Christianity is a non-issue these days among a great many of them, if you will forgive this undoubtedly inaccurate broad brush.

There is still the problem of evolutionary qualitative leaps when seemingly entire new species are apparently created out of whole cloth. Are such occurrences a case of random spontaneous creation or was it collateral fallout from the creative frenzy of God and the helper angels busting their chops to get everything done in a six-day work week? They had to create complex ecosystems within ecosystems, while agonizing over the details of building, say, more survivable spiders. ("Ooh, look how she eats her mate. Let's call this one a black widow.")

Can randomness result in order? What about the idea that billions of chimps flailing away at typewriters would eventually write "Hamlet?"

Or hey, even a clean limerick. This urban myth always assumes the monkeys would type in English.

That a gazillion chimps could do this is one of those "cocktail party truths" some guys think they can use to impress geeky girls with thick glasses. (Today's strange parenthetical remark: I used to think girls with thick glasses were smarter, which made them better suited for survival and reproduction, and thus more desirable. But as it turns out they're mostly just regular girls who don't see well. I stumbled through post-adolescence as a walking study in failed social theories. Darwin would have had fun with me.)

But I digress. The "infinite monkey theorem" (cool name, huh?) has been shot in the head pretty thoroughly by real scientists. The odds of chimps typing even one grammatically correct sentence, not counting two-worders like "Jesus wept," are some fraction of a googolplex (a number so big the universe doesn't have enough room for all the zeroes).

Statistically, it approaches never. They wouldn't even come up with "Häagen-Dazs," a nonsensical marketing word invented to sell ice cream by sounding Danish. So how do new species suddenly appear? How would I know? They just do, or appear to. But I have some thought as to *why*, although I can't prove it. It comes down to my understanding that God, as in The Creator, is both a parent (of humanity) and a passionately creative artist. From there, I extrapolate based on people I know who are also parents and creative. The creative urge in people is hardwired to the same creative urge that drives The Creator.

I wouldn't exactly call the creation process random, because randomness is not the backbone of artistic endeavor. However, intuition is heavily involved and that can seem random. Or in fact sometimes is. Therefore, the artist can be surprised by the results, which is why creativity is thrilling. For my example, I return to bugs mentioned in another essay. At last count there were 10 quintillion insects alive on Earth (1 with 19 zeros behind it). They represent around a million-and-a-half species, and that's only somewhere between 20 and 80 percent of the bugs we think we know about. That's science's way of saying we don't have a clue how many.

I've never thought of God as a control freak, and the insect situation informs my intuition that happy accidents might be somewhat routine in the big workshop upstairs. That's not to say there isn't a working divine blueprint guiding things. I'm only saying that if I'm doing an oil painting of a landscape at sunset, and I decide on a whim to put in a purple cloud that seems to resemble two lovers kissing, why can't the ultimate Creator do likewise? It could be that the only blueprint for evolution is the heart of an engaged Creator artist.

Until Moses appeared, man related to God with burnt offerings. Simple, but kind of hard to know where one stood, grace-wise. At one point, God gets a bellyful of our shenanigans and floods the whole place. After it's over, God has regrets and promises not to do that again. This indicates rethinking and growth.

When Moses came along, God put it in writing and we had ten clear laws. The Commandments helped, but it was a hard world and there didn't seem to be a lot of mercy to go around. In the eons since then, God is learning and growing as a parent. At the same time we are learning and growing as children. Everyone is evolving.

Then we come to Jesus. It took Jesus to finally call God "Father." Jesus also popularized the idea of *forgiveness*. This was completely new, and it was huge. Mohammed, Buddha, Confucius, Bahá'u'lláh, Zoroaster, Sun Myung Moon, and others added pieces to the picture puzzle. We no longer burn people at the stake for insisting that God is *both* male and female. Or that men and women are co-equal, or that science and religion share a lot of DNA. Some are okay with all this; others hate it. But the conversation is happening.

This is evolution of the heart, and I think it is a much more important level of development than even bugs and apes. I also think the environmental world of critters emulates somewhat the evolution going on within God's creative soul. Sometimes progress happens in increments and sometimes in big, inexplicable leaps. But it's all natural.

Consider your own children. As they grew, didn't you also grow as well? As the parent of a young adult, you are emotionally more evolved than you were when they were in diapers. Their world is more intricate than it was before, and your love became more multifaceted to accommodate that.

I don't think God was born finished. What parent is?

Therefore, I believe God walks a continual road of self-discovery and continues to create, learn and grow as we do. This implies that God is not only deeply attached to us, but that in fact God's happiness desperately requires unrestrained love from human beings to a degree much more deeply felt and intense than we ever imagined. We're a lot more important to God than perhaps we thought.

I get my understanding of this from how my heart reaches out to my own children. From stepping back and examining my own yearning for the happiness of my sons and daughters, I conclude that we really might have an inkling of how bottomless, how ardent and relentless is God's longing for us.

A STREET FILLED WITH SPIRITS OF THE LONG-TERM DEAD

It's morning rush in the spirit-filled streets of Seoul, at the corner of overpriced hotel and shoe repair guy. The cup is held close in both hands, fingers of hot, steamed aroma gently massage my face. I pause to solemnize the moment before taking the first sip. No other taste of coffee the rest of that day will be its equal. My early-hour grogginess and that very first slurp run toward each other in slow motion across a meadow, jump into each other's arms and tumble as one into the waving wheat.

People who want to live to be a hundred and ten never eat chocolate-filled croissants, but I heard on the bedside radio that today is National Self-Sabotage Day. I'm always good for a holiday. People have written whole chapters in cookbooks about the natural harmony of coffee and chocolate. You would instantly trust the intentions of a country that had a steaming cup of hot coffee and a chocolate-filled croissant on its national flag. That would be a nation that knows peace.

At a back table of the coffee shop by the window, my attention is drawn to something unusual outside and I briefly touch the glass. I am watching spirits plod along. Spirits usually know they have died when they naturally cross over. These folks I am watching may not have gotten the memo. They appear to be earthbound spirits, marooned between here and there, and for about twenty seconds I see them. There are hundreds of them walking along, still going to work, as they must have done for decades during their lives. They look less distinct to me than the living. They are dull and slightly faded. The living, also walking by the window, and the dead pass among and through each other without noticing. As a group, the spirits look less hopeful or expectant than the living commuters. The spirits look as though they have exhausted their to-do lists. There is nothing new to accomplish, no new appointments or meetings, no calls left to return. Not a one of them looks content. A few are obviously anxious. Perhaps they know something is amiss, but what?

None of them conform to my image of Marley's ghost. They don't rattle chains or make scary faces, maybe because they don't know this is expected of them. Just above them, about ten feet off the ground, I see a second layer of spirit pedestrians. They look very much like the ones on the ground, faces creased with worry lines. The two groups don't appear to notice each other and they don't look much different to me. When someone tells you, "I'm sick and tired of being sick and tired," the person is describing the deep funk malaise my ethereal pedestrian friends look like they're mired in. Spotting this second layer, I thought, *Oh yeah, for sure those are spirits*. But aside from that one minor incongruity of appearing to float in the air, everyone looks more or less normal. I wonder what they're thinking. I imagine it's something like, *Why does it seem like I've been walking along this street forever? Why do I have so much time on my hands? How come nobody responds when I speak? I'm out of smokes.*

It's my assumption that we, the currently living, more or less know we carry our own spirits around inside us. It's the essence of spirit we're seeing when we look into a person's eyes. As we move through life we seek out kindred spirits and glance into their eyes even while talking about ordinary things. It's our nature to want to find those who are like us, and once found, we make them into friends. We bond with them, we grow together, we marry them. Looking into someone's eyes is not a surefire way to separate the warm and fuzzy from partners in crime. We can all be fooled by a false heart, or by our own expectations and hopes for what we want that person to be. I read somewhere that spiritually sensitive people who regularly visit the spirit world find it easy to distinguish heavenly spirits from hellish ones there. But I have also been told by such a person some years ago that Lucifer himself is quite beautiful, gentle in manner and smooth if he wants to be perceived that way. Haven't had the pleasure myself, regarding Lucifer, but I can tell you none of the folks trudging past the coffee shop window looked particularly charming. They just looked defeated, worn-out and weary to the bone.

It may turn out that the differences between existing in the physical world and existing in the spiritual world are ridiculously minor. Transitioning from the former to the latter, via so-called "death" may be nothing more than a metaphysical grand-plié, a vast sweeping vertical gesture of your entire being that moves you up and out in one fluid motion. But then there's also shooting through that highly-touted tunnel with the light at the end, spoken of in many near-death experiences. Either way, what's left behind is your body; what goes with you into the spirit world is your character, how you love in the form of altruistic caring, as well as your ability to manage your self-serving hungers. This info is courtesy of religious writings, various spiritual people and my own intuition.

So it seems life goes on, in a manner of speaking. To the extent love determined our actions in life, or didn't, we are so compelled after we go incorporeal.

My grandmother told me, "Your character is all the things you do when no one's looking." In other words random acts of kindness as well as eating the entire pint of rocky ripple. For some there are even stronger, darker desires, hatreds and compulsions to self-serve that can mire a person down in one place in the spirit world.

For example, an earthbound spirit, formerly a thief, is stuck in the hardware store shoplifting the same crescent wrench over and over again. A man and woman, who lived high on the social ladder, are dressed for a night on the town in 1928. They remain forever standing in front of the Waldorf, wearing the implacable faces of the gentry class, still waiting for the limo that no longer exists. Their Rolls-Royce Phantom has long since been crushed into a tiny cube, melted and made into a battleship that is now itself scrap.

Spirits stand a hundred-deep around the doors of every strip joint titty bar in the city. You don't know it, but you walk right through them to get in, and a dozen or so grab ahold and ride in with you to savor whatever you savor and feel penetrating pulsations courtesy of you.

A fantastical digression here: There was a time, pre-history, when I began every Tuesday lining up dates for Friday and Saturday night. I could not imagine a weekend evening spent alone, solely taking stock of myself. I went to great lengths to avoid introspection, fearing solitude the way a jackrabbit jumps away from a hawk's shadow. Life was "dates." I date; therefore I am; therefore, I am desirable and worthy. A date amounted to taking Suzy Earthmother to go hear Greezy Wheels at Armadillo World Headquarters in Austin. We had social media back then, but we called it conversation. Had I not had an awakening and relocated to my inner Walden Pond at some point in my life, the dating treadmill could have been the hunger that defined me for all time.

Or maybe I would have pursued wealth as my drug of choice. It is ironic that material wealth does not quench one's hungers but rather increases them. Regarding both empty-calorie love and money, the more you have of it, the more you need. Had it been my lot to be filthy rich instead of an obscure, early-twenty-first-century essayist, I'm afraid I would not have been a noble exception to the rule. I am not special. I likely would have been a robber baron like the rest of them. I could have had golf balls handmade from platinum and smacked them around into the forests and water hazards, and over the far horizons of my imagination.

Such images, whether they ever inspired me at all, certainly now do not hold even the slightest appeal. I don't want to rule a financial empire; I only want to rule myself. And I do want to be utterly engaged, my arms and mind stretched from my childhood tree house to the moon.

We human beings want to be in the fray, intensely involved. It's encoded into our software. Unfortunately the quality of intensity that swirls through the general population is pursued through a brew of sex, booze and dope, money and domination of the innocent helpless. For the dead grays in the aftermath, intensity is exactly what is missing in the spirit-filled streets. Without their physical bodies, stuck at street-level, self-absorbed, do they miss savory? Do they long for the touch of hot and salty skin? They're out of smokes. Thus continuing their pursuit of intensity over and over.

Coffee is ordered hot or iced. Nobody ever tells the barista, "Make mine tepid." But these earthbound spirits are trapped in tepid. Their voices are like whispers drowned out by the wind, their colors muted in the low-contrast ambient light. The body language of the street's culture is hunched shoulders and mumbling. No one makes eye-contact. They would tell you with a straight face that being dead isn't all it's cracked up to be.

Where do these walking wounded go from here? What's the endgame for them? I'm unsure, but it is an article of faith with me that people desire to improve their lot, whether in this world or the next, and will seek to do so if they can.

Can we, the living, get through to them and help? I want to think so and therefore will give an enthusiastic yes. We traditionally communicate with the other side via some kind of focused thought such as prayer and meditation. Whatever name you want to give this focused thought, it must be driven by sincere intent. I think a genuinely sincere earnestness must be conveyed from this side and will be somehow perceived in the spiritual realms. Perhaps that's how we can help "the long-term dead" as I think of them. Know this: there really and truly is life after so-called "death," I guarantee, or your money back. But there can also be death after death, and that's somewhat the situation of these ethereal listless coffee shop passersby. Mr. and Ms. Nowhere Man.

Sincerity is the *one key factor* in moving energy in the spirit world. Spiritual healers call this "intention." Prayer, as an example, is not mumbled words; it's passion. I think what one utters in prayer is not nearly as important as the force of one's sincere intent. Spiritual intensity has two edges and can be good or evil, either giving life or taking life.

For example, altruistic intensity is grounded in healing others and seeing to their well-being, oneself included. Base intensity is grounded in fleshly desire, addiction, fear and the sacrifice of others for the fulfillment of oneself. Investing the force of your will into the latter is a really, really bad thing to do.

In my limited experience with sincerity, there is something special about tears that is way more important than laughter. You and a group of friends can spend an evening laughing your asses off. It becomes a good memory for all of you. But if you cry with another person, holding each other, mixing tears and snot, you will remember it meaningfully and deeply for the rest of your life. It is exceedingly rare for earthbound spirits to shed tears for another person. I would even say never, because if they had this level of outward caring, they would not be stuck on the ground, or even hovering a mere ten feet above it. In the spirit world, cries of repentance or intercession, emptied out from the gut, come from the highest realms, and most especially from God. When heaven cries, the effect transcends both worlds. I think of tears as spirit-soluble, liquid gold in that they overlap and go beyond the physical and the incorporeal, dissolving the self-centered crust enveloping this world and that one.

Wait, what?! God cries? Well ... you tell me. Think about it. If you were the parent of a lot of children whom you loved more than life itself, and most of them were exploiting, murdering, raping and torturing one another in the cruelest ways imaginable—exactly how merry would your life be?

Tears shed totally for another person, one's own troubles put aside, are rather rare coming from anyone. Sincere tears shed for complete strangers and future unborn generations, are virtually non-existent. Only saints and messiahs do that kind of crying, and unfortunately, history shows they are often killed despite, or because of, their compassion.

Looking out through the steamy window, I'm neither repenting for the earthbound spirits, nor shedding tears, nor even praying. I'm actually kind of stunned, aware this is a very unusual thing going on, and not wanting to breathe, lest I shatter the moment. I just get real quiet and watch patiently, and ask nobody in particular, *How many layers up you have to go to reach heaven?* No response, of course. Silence. The only answer was a lone piece of paper trash, a solid, physical-world hamburger wrapper blowing down the street. With that, I knew the vision had subsided. I looked up and saw only empty air and low clouds. The people on the sidewalk were your average Kim and Choi walking to work.

I spent the rest of the day trying to sort out this brief tableau. The takeaway for me was that I realized anew the reality of a post-earthly existence. I understood that I need to pray more often, more profoundly and about a wider spectrum of things. I knew that if I were to unpack that nameless hoard of people shuffling along, were to spread them out and look at them closely, one by one—each one would have a story as deep, wide, passionate and interesting as my own.

I wanted to go back into the vision, step in front of each one and stop them. I wanted to say or be something that would be meaningful to them —that would make them look up at me, and then look around. And then together we would call for assistance from whatever angels or whoever is in charge of helping people advance in the spirit world.

But there was no going back. I could pray for them on their behalf, which I did, and will. But I want the personal relationships, as well. I want us to matter in each other's lives. But they have left this life and their situation may be best handled over there.

Most productive I figure would be to apply my energies to the people living right now, especially the young adults around me. This is their moment to carve out great destinies for themselves, to catch a spark, seize it and pursue their dreams. These younger versions of me should not wait until their sixth or seventh decade to find out their destiny is eternal, and not just for the period of their lifetime on earth.

At the end of that day, just before dinnertime in the early evening, I was still out on the busy streets of Seoul. I had one of those ongoing prayer conversations as I walked around, bending God's ear.

"Hello, God," I said. "Thank you so much for this morning. I think I'm starting to figure it out. Those gray folks actually helped. I'll write it all down, but you know … nobody's going to believe this."

As often happens, I felt God's presence and reply coming through the still, small voice within: "Larry, as you sometimes say in our little talks, 'screw that.' There are a lot more people out there like you than you think. And I mean a *lot*. Go find them for me."

THE NEW BARTER PARADIGGUM

They say the barter economy is lurking,
cash money will peter out and it will be
chickens and eggs for a visit to the doctor,
three days of yard work
for an oil painting of bluebonnets.

We will never write a memo, or hire a lawyer
to speak for us in tedious, freeze-dried prose,
messages we would rather have arrive
a day late on wrinkled school-ruled paper,
with brown smudged eraser marks
and a blotch of melted sucker in the margin.

We will trod across town to return twelve cents
accidentally pocketed because while we talked,
a woman walked by singing to her daughter
and even after they went around the corner,
her song still poured out of the roses.

You will never grow tired of noble ideas,
and will sit up stupefied, shocked, a little scared,
while trying not to smile at amazing possibilities
when someone unexpected comes to you to barter
a love poem for your hand in marriage.

Watching Nagasaki blow

To my mother-in-law, the atomic bomb
looked much closer than it was

"11:01 AM"

© Andrew
Marston, used
with his kind
permish

Setsuko Sonoda was a girl of 13 on August 9, 1945. She lived on the same land she does today, now at age 82. The family farm is outside Yatsushiro on Japan's southernmost island of Kyushu, just across the bay from Nagasaki.

She was out in the garden at 11:01 a.m. that morning when she heard a thunderous reverberation. She knew it was a bomb because she had heard plenty of them. Every factory and railroad station in the country had been taken out by that time.

She looked up from weeding the chard. The bone-rattling roar brought everyone out of their homes. Over the rooftops of her neighborhood, she saw a mushroom-shaped cloud climbing. It went higher and higher and higher. They were a few miles inland from the bay, and because the cloud was so huge, it had to be far away, at least a couple of towns over. And yet there was something that didn't add up; the perspective was off.

This was way too big to be that close, and the rumbling was too distant. Could this be happening all the way over across the bay? Even as far as Nagasaki, seventy miles away?

The cloud from the Fat Man's mere fourteen pounds of plutonium continued climbing and spreading for long minutes. A solid wall of black dirt, running from horizon to horizon, began to rise up as well, creating the contradiction of a beast brighter than the sun consuming the daylight.

Whenever someone mentions how many died from the two atomic bombs, someone will always ask-slash-remind, "How many died at Pearl Harbor?" I understand, and this story is not about assigning blame. Brief digression: War happens. In war everybody kills everybody until one side stops fighting. Nothing even remotely compares to how much war sucks. The prize for winning is freedom, and that the bodies of most of your dead young men will be identified. The prize for losing is that you get to rebuild your entire infrastructure, and will never be certain where or how your son or your uncle died. We will have peace when we love our children more than we hate our enemies. But don't hold your breath. End of sermon. Thank you very much.

Now fast-forward thirty-four years from that morning in the garden to October of 1979.

Setsuko Sonoda is in her garden again. I am there too, marrying her daughter in a Shinto wedding. Meet Taeko Sonoda of Yatsushiro, daughter of Setsuko and Sueo Sonoda. We are at her parents' home, surrounded by all the relatives and most of the neighbors in the small farming village.

My father and mother are there as well. Dad had been a Navy pilot long ago who had just finished flight training and was preparing to invade Japan when the war ended. The village is far removed from tourist destinations, so although everyone has seen American television shows and movies, some of the more elderly had not seen an American in the flesh since the early post-war years. When Taeko and I strolled along the road next to a rural school, little children rushed over to walk along with us as far as the end of the playground, looking me over and peppering her with questions. They asked her if I came from television.

Like all weddings should be, this was joyous. There was lots of singing, and the Sonoda women did their locally famous chopstick dance. The men approached me one by one to toast our marriage with sake. We each drank, and turned our cups upside down to demonstrate we had drained it. Problem was, there were sixty of them, and only one of me, but my mother-in-law secretly kept my own sake flask filled with warm water, which saved me from having to be carried from the room. They marveled at my capacity, but I and the women knew what was going on.

At some point, her father spoke, saying nice things about me.

Then my father spoke, saying nice things about Taeko. It's not an easy or particularly pleasant task for a young Japanese woman to translate effusive praise about herself, but she was the only one there who could handle both languages, and she got through it with a minimum of blushing and seizing up.

Then it was my turn. With Taeko beside me, we sang a Japanese song call "Homeland." Every Japanese has a lifetime familiarity with the song, but it seemed particularly moving for them to hear it coming out of a western mouth in their own language. Taeko sings beautiful harmonies, which made it even more special.

After the song, which I filled with a way cool harmonica bridge in the middle, I said a few words about things Taeko and I had noticed about our two cultures. These are things we had talked about during our engagement, and also that Reverend Moon had expounded on numerous times. He had spent a lot of time on both sides of the Pacific and was a keen observer of people.

I told them the East and West fit naturally well together. You could even say they need each other, as two halves of a sphere. The Japanese have a culture of family and filial piety. Americans excel in pragmatic realities. The Japanese tradition (Confucian and Buddhist) is vertical, with a strong connection to the past. The American character is horizontal (Christian), looking to the future. Each completes gaps in the other. We make each other better and should never have fought. The greatest tragedy for all of us is that we never knew each other very well. I told them I didn't come to Japan to steal your daughter, but came to join your family and to ask you to be part of mine.

Neither Taeko nor I had expected our remarks to have anywhere near the impact they did. The sweetest girl in their tiny town had gone off to the U.S. and come back with a pink and white American. There was also the historical backdrop. To people of a certain age, regarding certain events, forty years ago was last week. The presence of my parents served to remind them of the last time they had seen Americans, as enemies across a battlefield and later, as occupying troops. And now everyone was older, and no longer menacing. So much water had passed beneath that bridge and they saw each other differently now. When we finished, everyone in the room had tears. Even the men were dabbing at their eyes.

Our speech concluded the "formal" part of the reception. As people mingled, Taeko was drafted for translation duties when several of the old men approached my father. As they touched their glasses to his, the Japanese farmers expressed their deep regret that there had been hostilities between the men of their generation. My father, his eyes moist, echoed that regret on his part.

I don't want to make more of it than there was, but it was as quietly profound a moment as I have ever witnessed. If there is such a thing as trains of spirit that can merge onto one set of rails from parallel tracks, unfasten and refasten their couplets together and then move out as one long, unified, ancestral train, I think that's what happened.

If life searches for ways to make things come together to be healed, then what better place to do that than in a village on the other side of Nagasaki Bay? I didn't know at the time that Taeko was my destiny and would be the love of my life. But I suspected it could be so. And hoped it would.

FORGIVENESS SAVES YOUR BACON

A man steals $10,000 from the loose change basket on his father's dresser. He flees his home and spends most of it on blackjack, vodka shooters and fast women.

The rest he squanders.

Too ashamed to go home, he becomes a drifter. After sinking to the depths of degradation, and weary of his job tuning the piano in a whorehouse, he returns to his family home, and to his father, with a remorseful heart. He hands his father everything he has left, which is two $5 poker chips.

The father tearfully embraces the son, and orders that the fatted calf be killed for a feast. This is your basic repentance and forgiveness. Forgiveness is something that was invented, simply because it had to be. I don't think forgiveness was part of God's "Plan A" because I don't think the Creation Planning Committee even had a clue that such a thing would ever be necessary.

God (over lunch on Day Five of creation): *"Alrighty now, Earth is pretty much finished, the air, dirt, water, plants and animals anyway. They're all good. Now we'll make beings. We'll call them people and they'll come in two sizes—men and women. They'll have sex and, everyone will be great friends."*

Head Angel: *"Cool."*

Men and women. What could possibly go wrong? You don't design a building thinking how difficult it will be to implode when the time comes. You design it thinking it will be your eternal legacy. I feel certain nobody was thinking the man-woman thing would get as out of control as it has.

But here we all are, eight-hundred gazillion years later, hating and forgiving (or not forgiving) each other all over the place. Parents forgiving sons and daughters, and vice versa. Forgive President Nixon? Forgive Chairman Mao? Forgive Andrew Jackson for betraying the Cherokee? Forgive O.J. Simpson? Forgive your no-good, lying, cheating, wife-beating slut of a husband? (The majority of sluts are men, by the way. Seriously.)

It gets harder. Consider forgiveness for entire races and nations. At the creation of human beings probably nobody was thinking about the thing called *war*. How do you forgive Genghis Khan or the Nazis? Put pillage, rape and genocide in your pipe and smoke it. Does the horror ever stop? No. Not In your lifetime anyway.

Not everybody even *wants* forgiveness. Nations and people who are very good at pointing out sins committed against them, are equally adept at denying their own historic atrocities, their enslavement of others and all the massacres they committed. They go to offer an apology and end up rubbing salt in the wounds with insufficient atonement and tepid constructs of flaccid phrasings like, "mistakes were made ..." in speeches delivered two hundred years too late, and that fall way short of the full grovel that needs to include expressions like "deeply, deeply sorry" or "our people are without excuse."

Furthermore, the atonement speech should be uttered from behind a wall of tears and mucus streaming down the face of the offenders' ranking representative. That's how you do it. Anything less than that, or its equivalent, is putting lipstick on a pig.

Offenders would do well to also pay for a concrete and bronze monument that honors the victims, that further acknowledges the perpetrators' blame, and carries the victims' names on it if they'll fit. In addition, they should pony up a few scholarships, endow a university chair or library, and have a moment of silence at a football game on significant anniversaries. Is that enough? Maybe, maybe not. It's case by case.

In relatively modern times, the gold standard for national apologies was established by German Chancellor Willy Brandt on December 7, 1970. The chancellor had gone to Poland to lay a wreath at the site of the infamous Warsaw Ghetto. During their 12 years of Nazi occupation, the Germans murdered an estimated three million Polish Jews and three million Polish Catholics.

It was a stop on his schedule, planned as a nice gesture. Perhaps a cross between an act of apology and a photo opp. It would have been okay for that starched-shirt era, but eminently forgettable.

Brandt apologized on his knees. © Bundesregierung/Engelbert Reineke

However, after placing the wreath, Chancellor Brandt departed from the script, casting aside protocol to do something very different and shocking. He spontaneously dropped to his knees and stayed kneeling silently for about a minute. Writing about it in his autobiography, he said, "Carrying the burden of the millions who were murdered, I did what people do when words fail them."

It was an act of political courage that a legion of attorneys would have rushed to advise him not to do. But what Brandt did mattered, and it forever changed the relationship between Germany and Poland. Or at least it was a very solid beginning by many people's reckoning.

However…

It depends on who you talk to. Illustrating why national atonement is such an inexact science is, for example, the experience of Julian Kulski.

Mr. Kulski joined the Polish resistance in 1939 at age 10 (recruited by his Boy Scout leader). He killed his first German soldier at age 12, and a great many more after that. You would be hard-pressed to imagine any form of modern warfare cruelty and horror he has not witnessed or personally experienced. He was 16, and a hardened veteran, when the war ended. Jumping onto the back of an American truck was the only thing that kept him from being swept up in the net of the advancing Russian Army.

His response to Chancellor Brandt, told to me personally, was, "I am not impressed. Asking forgiveness is easy to do." He has a point. Cain and Abel can forgive one another with a handshake and a hug when they're just two people. But lasting, eternal, forgiveness between Cain and Abel at the national level involves millions of people and covers every degree of pain and wrongdoing. Some acts are so horrific that the resulting hatred never diminishes within a person's lifetime, and stories of that are passed onto their descendants, "lest we ever forget."

Still, what the German Chancellor did, deserves mention and no small amount of credit. Few who were there or who read about it afterward could forget Willy Brandt's silent, and most eloquent, apology.

There are a lot of apologies that could use a dose of Willy Brandt's silent eloquence. A few that come to mind involve the slavery of blacks in the U.S., the genocide of American Indians, South African apartheid, and the Mountain Meadows massacre in 1857 by leaders of the Church of Jesus Christ of the Latter Day Saints.

Korea and Japan finally came to some agreement in 2015 on atonement for the crime of some 200,000 Korean women being forced into sexual slavery as "comfort women" by Japanese soldiers during World War II. But again, that doesn't mean it's over for every Korean family.

Atoning for big atrocities is a long, drawn-out process. It can take decades, even centuries, and some amount of repetition. The apologizing party is not qualified to say when they have repented enough. Only the victims' families have the right to tell the offenders when they can get off their knees and receive an embrace. When the family stories change and descendants on both sides moisten their stone cold faces with their own tears, and reach out, only then can closure happen and life continue. And maybe that will do it. But again … *maybe*.

Hearts are complicated. Forgiveness takes a long, long time and there is no short way around it. There are probably very few people today still passionately enraged about Persia's King Xerxes sacking and burning Athens in 480 BC. But I'll bet the number is not zero.

Sometimes, for a lot of reasons, you won't get the act of contrition your people deserve. I hate this, but at some point you and your grandchildren have to move on, apology or not, if only for your own sake. It isn't easy for the wronged party to hear this, but your life and the lives of your children become easier when you are finally able to accept an apology that was never offered. While Jesus was hanging on the cross, nobody from the government came forward to ask his forgiveness, but he granted it anyway as almost his last words. Sometimes that's your only option.

There are tons of workarounds for this grace thing. A friend's assistant borrowed his laptop and accidentally corrupted umpteen files, including a third of an unfinished novel. After inventing curses that would have made a pirate blush, my friend went shopping and bought her a *gift*. He told me it was the only alternative he could think of to ripping her head off. If there existed a Nobel Prize for Not Murdering, he would have been a contender.

And, by the way, I am fairly certain I am also the problem. Right this minute, someone, somewhere, is probably struggling to find a way to forgive me, and I have no idea this is going on. The problem is me walking around thinking I have nothing that needs forgiving.

I received a touching letter once from a woman I knew only casually, socially, but on cordial terms. The letter inquired if she had ever offended me in some way and, if so, she expressed her most heartfelt apology and asked me to please forgive her. I tried to replay all our interactions and came up with only friendly encounters. I was certain she had never done anything to cause me the slightest distress. This got me wondering if I had ever done anything to slight or offend her. Again I drew a blank. I wrote her back (an actual paper letter with ink on it and a postage stamp), expressing my gratitude for her friendship and assuring her I held nothing in my heart but the fondest of feelings toward her. Six months later she died from cancer.

At the time of her letter I had no idea she was gravely ill. It occurred to me long after her passing that what she was probably doing was going over every person she knew and was carefully evaluating her relationships to see if there was the slightest possibility she had left the air cluttered with hurt between her and them. She knew how ill she was, and what the probable outcome would be, and she was taking no chances in her determination to leave this world with the slate wiped as clean as she could get it.

Lee Atwater did something similar. He was a top advisor to Ronald Reagan and George H.W. Bush during their presidential campaigns in the mid-and-late 80s. He was their pit bulldog on the campaign trail and left carnage in his wake. He had loyal friends and fierce enemies. In early March 1990 he collapsed at a political fundraiser. Doctors found a particularly aggressive brain cancer. He lived one more year, confined to a wheelchair. During that final period, Atwater converted to Catholicism and called on all his enemies, and they were legion, to beg their forgiveness. He was truly sincere in his repentance and I believe he received absolution from every person he requested it of, including some whose political careers he destroyed—Michael Dukakis for one. Atwater made a point of publicly asking Dukakis' forgiveness for the "naked cruelty" of that campaign. To his great credit, and the astonishment of many, Dukakis gave it—which says as much about Michael Dukakis as it does about Lee Atwater.

In February 1991, a month before his death, Atwater wrote in an article for Life Magazine:

> My illness helped me to see that what was missing in society is what was missing in me: a little heart, a lot of brotherhood. The '80s were about acquiring—acquiring wealth, power, prestige. I know. I acquired more wealth, power, and prestige than most. But you can acquire all you want and still feel empty. What power wouldn't I trade for a little more time with my family? What price wouldn't I pay for an evening with friends? It took a deadly illness to put me eye to eye with that truth, but it is a truth that the country, caught up in its ruthless ambitions and moral decay, can learn on my dime. I don't know who will lead us through the '90s, but they must be made to speak to this spiritual vacuum at the heart of American society, this tumor of the soul.

The anguish we carry around with us, whether its origin is our conscience for the harm we have done to others, or whether it stems from our unresolved anger at the injustices done to us—attaches itself to our spirit and drags us down until we are able to release it. Atwater had to repent to save his own soul; Dukakis had to accept that repentance in order to save his.

In the end, we are judged, not by a bearded, frowning God reading from a big book of our sins, but by our own conscience. Truth always gets into the game to bat cleanup, even if it takes its own sweet time doing it. Reckoning ultimately happens, and, we hope, forgiveness. Only then can calming waters settle over the sunken wreckage we have created, and outrageous pain be stilled by a comforting touch. Or by the image of the German Chancellor on his knees.

COCKFIGHT

Cockfighting is more about us than the chickens.   Larry Moffitt/2009

Cockfighting in the Philippines is second only to basketball as the most popular sport. You see it on television most nights, and every town has a small circular arena with a dozen rows of circled bleachers seating a couple hundred men overlooking the dirt floor cockpit surrounded by a low, clear plexiglass wall.

I had no idea what to expect, so one of the Ortega cousins, who ran the arena, filled me in on the particulars. "In the Philippines we use a blade this long," indicating a 3-inch length with his thumb and forefinger. "It varies country to country. Mexico uses a one-inch blade, sometimes just a short spike."

Answering the question I was about to ask, he added, "I don't know why; it's just the way it is. Mexico's fights last longer. We have a ten-minute limit, but it's rare for one to go longer than a minute or two. Most are over in the first 20 seconds."

Looking at the blades, I could see why. They're lightweight polished steel, curved slightly. The inside of the curve is more than sharp enough to shave with. Blades are attached to one leg of the cock with the sharpened edge facing up because the killing stroke is downward, the way a chicken scratches.

Cockfights are swift, carried out with a stunning viciousness. The cocks are brought face-to-face by the owners for the same stare-down that human boxers engage in before combat. Set on the ground, they charge toward each other and leap into the air chest to chest. There is no way the human eye can follow the whirlwind of feathers, legs and beaks. All you see is that when the chickens fall back to the ground, one of them is noticeably weakened. Usually both are injured. One or more blades are coated thick with blood. That's just the first hit.

The cocks lunge at each other with instinctual fury again and again. But quickly, after only a few clashes, one or both of them are too injured to respond, other than lying inches apart trying to peck out each other's faces. The referee holds them close together in the air and drops them. They attack with beaks or, if one of them is still capable, he will jump up and slash away with the knife at his helpless opponent. Sometimes both of them are mortally wounded, but still go through the motions as their instinct drives them to do. Often the winner is simply the last one to bleed to death.

The fighting knife slices away feathers and chunks of living flesh, exposing guts as easily as Dad carving Sunday dinner. A thigh, a wing, a breast, a drumstick. The savory parts are slashed and laid bare in the arena as blood-saturated tissue, and you see what chicken really looks like, rather than the battered and fried bits of food that no longer remotely resemble what they actually are.

A friend—a member of a prominent family in the Philippines—had driven me five hours out of Manila to a small provincial capital. And, again, I was there because I had asked to be. This is what I do. I was put on earth to find out stuff and report back, first to myself, then to you. The downside is the danger of becoming what we watch, acquiesce to, laugh along with or cry over. Emotion has gravity like Jupiter. Some activities change the observer forever. Prolonged exposure to cockfighting could have a negative desensitizing effect on a person, I think.

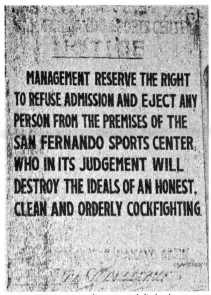

We run a clean cockfight here.
Moffitt/2009

I sat in the sweat-stained bleachers with an average Jose Sixpack in jeans and t-shirt inscribed "Sorry, girls, I only date models." The people there are not hard or unfeeling. They are not cruel. They are generous and welcoming to strangers. They are a close-knit family who have little, but who would give it all to a brother in need. There is blood and death and a palpable camaraderie. It is complex and runs deeper than an outsider's ability to comprehend.

My host said if you want to make it in politics in this town, you have to be accepted here in the cockfight pit. I could see the truth of that.

Something interesting happened. I was kneeling on the cockpit floor, looking at the result of a particularly awful fight. Both chickens were bleeding out, the winner and the loser stared blankly up at the ceiling. My gut was churning from watching chickens turning each other into monkey meat.

Before I had entered the arena building, I prayed what I like to think of as my standard pre-cockfight prayer. It's the prayer for guidance I utter whenever I am in a situation beyond my understanding: "Please show me what to feel and think about all this. What should I learn here?"

It begins with strutting and posturing (the gamecocks) and trash talk (the folks in the stands). The trash talk is good natured since everyone grew up there together and they do this every weekend, and the wagers are not for huge amounts of money in these local arena fights. But then less than a minute later, severed arteries are expelling life so rapidly the victims, in chicken terms, can hear the rush of blood in their own ears. Limbs shake uncontrollably and the bowels let loose. Gasping air, the eyes search, lost. Spilled blood cakes the dirt of the arena. Cold envelops the combatants as the mind loses all interest in what was the only important thing in the world just seconds before. And finally one of them is a lifeless piece of carrion, now lifedead and souldead amid the cheers, lying in blood-soaked feathers. The guys whose chicken lost, wadded up bills and tossed them across the arena to winners.

I have witnessed and written about something that obviously calls for a moral conclusion on my part. So here it is. Cockfighting is shitty. You can argue that this is their culture, not mine, and who am I to sit in judgment, etc. No. Simply no. This is not about it being another person's culture. It's a blood sport and I'm okay with that in principle as long as the combatants choose to be there. Such is the case with two boxers who pound each other into hamburger.

But these are chickens. This is about chickens, and in the larger and blatantly obvious sense, about mercy versus cruelty. I'm a carnivore and I understand that chickens are for killing quickly and cleanly, so that you and your family can eat and grow strong from the protein provided.

The effect of this experience on me was to set in motion a reverberation that was slow in building, but which has been continuous over the years since. I've always thought that part of my job as a human being who writes is to find out everything I can about everything that happens, and report back to you. That includes the bad stuff. I still think that. But it does take a toll, and that afternoon has affected me a lot more than I thought it would. It doesn't haunt me, but I do think about it.

Cockfighting parallels human existence in all the most disturbing ways. It's a knife fight by proxies. It's the Roman Coliseum with chicken gladiators. The problem with cockfighting is that cockfighting is *us*. It's you and me. Nobody gets a pass, not even Gandhi and Mother Teresa. By our position at the top of the food chain, we were given responsibility by the universe to be stewards of creation. We're the adult supervision, and therefore we don't waste things. We don't drop trash on the ground and we use cloth bags instead of plastic. We also don't cruelly waste animals for our own entertainment.

Unfortunately, it's a macrocosm issue. God sets humankind up in business to be equal partners. We're literally the boss' kids. "All that I have is yours" is the message relayed to us through prophets. The shingle hanging in front of the shop reads "God & Sons and Daughters."

But what kind of business did we humans start with our seed money? We opened up a liquor store with a cockfight out back, next door to a girlie show and a roadside stand that sells candy and landmines to children.

Cockfighting is not the worst thing people do. It's not the rape of Nanking, but it adds to our karmic overhead. The last thing human beings need is another metaphor underscoring the littleness of our existence.

HOW I GOT THIS WAY

My grad school application essay

Question: In a brief, third-person narrative of 800 words or less, describe yourself, including pivotal events that have made you the person you are today. (You may write on the back.)

My essay:

Larry Moffitt is an ancient soul, having traversed the space-time continuum through countless lifetimes since the dawn of creation. Born a Devonian Age trilobite, Larry, together with his pals, spawned up a storm and owned the seas until the power balance was shifted in favor of fish with jaws and teeth strong enough to crush their hard outer shells. Seeing the end was near species-wise, he transmigrated to an avian form, having seen unimaginably beautiful birds soar above the waters, seemingly without effort or care. Unfortunately he did not choose his breed well and lived a thousand score lives as a flightless dodo on the island of Mauritius.

Looking for a way out of what was essentially a dead-end existence, Larry transmigrated into a human being. He drew the first rough draft of the plans for Stonehenge, and in a later female incarnation, while in the throes of a particularly vicious bout of pre-menstrual rage, invented the crossbow. He lived eight brief consecutive lives (some male, some female) during the Black Death in France and Italy, becoming more than a minor expert on the illness. His dying words, gasped out at the end of his final plague-era incarnation, were, "… don't quote me, but I'm pretty sure it's the fleas on the rats."

Weary, in need of rest, Larry returned to the stifling comfort of dodohood for a couple hundred years. And you know, there's a lot to be said for the unhurried simplicity of the dodo life. Of course everything has its downside, too. After being clubbed to death by a Portuguese sailor in 1520, he opted to become a Galapagos Islands tortoise, where three years later to the very day, he was again clubbed to death by the exact same sailor. He decided to give Homo Sapiens another try, having learned there are three important factors when choosing your place on the food chain: location, location, location.

In 1799, as a young officer in Napoleon's Egypt Campaign (male incarnation), Larry was smoking near the cannons and accidentally ignited one, shooting the nose off the Sphinx. For that little stunt he was exiled to permanent guard duty in the western Nile delta village of Rashid (known to Europeans as Rosetta). While (drunk) on guard duty one night, he unearthed and took a leak on the Rosetta Stone, the famous carved tablet that was the key that led to the decipherment of Egyptian hieroglyphs. Of course he had no idea what it was, but it looked important. In a well-intentioned effort to save valuable time for Napoleon's learned historians, the young officer decided to have a go at translating the hieroglyphs on the upper section of the stone:

> *He picked me up at seven and he looked so fine*
> *da-DO ron ron ron, da-DO ron ron.*
> *Someday soon I'm gonna make him mine*
> *da-DO ron ron ron, da-DO ron ron.*

The translation, although spot-on accurate, was trashed by jealous rival academicians, and the officer was executed by firing squad for suspected deviant proclivities.

Fast-forward a few centuries to New Orleans where, as blues singer Blind Lemon Pie, Larry, again as a male, taught Chuck Berry the "duck walk," a subliminal skill retained from his vast dodo experience. In a female incarnation she was the original coiner of the famous phrase, "Be sure to wear clean underwear. You never know if you'll be clubbed by a Portuguese sailor and have to go to the hospital." Again, more past life bleed-through.

Larry was offered a shot at being born as John Wayne. Declined. Also offered were Marilyn Monroe, Hitler, Angelina Jolie and a rainforest tarantula. Declined, declined, declined, but he did give serious consideration to the tarantula.

Larry settled instead for an obscure middle-class incarnation, as the son of a guy who finds oil and gas for big corporations, and a mother who makes great Tex-Mex. That one lasted for decades, but there were bumps along the way. Having seen his idea for the hula hoop stolen and his lyrics to a song, "Let It Be," ripped off by a well-known British musical group, his milk of human kindness began to lose serious butterfat content by the mid-1970s.

He invented the DOS prompt (>) which made the computer age possible. Again zero credit for it. Earlier, his letter of warning to John Kennedy about going to Dallas was rewarded with suspicion and recrimination for years.

Today, with the help of friends (mostly bad poets and navel-gazers) he has managed to put most of that behind him. As a quietly enraged aficionado of extreme religions, he lives a fairly serene life in suburban Maryland where he is currently entertaining offers from several small nations to become their philosopher king, while eking out a modest existence changing lead into gold.

In 1972, Larry Moffitt was accepted into a graduate program in communication at the University of Texas at Austin, on a fellowship grant from the National Institute of Mental Health. The goal of the program was to train professional communicators for the mental health field. Getting into grad school in those days did not actually require a written essay, fortunately for Larry, because if one had been required, this would have been it.

FOR MAIDENS WITH MILEAGE

It's okay to wonder ...
did I buy the right life with my small pennies?
did I choose the right Indian to be a squaw to?

Listing your dowry assets, one by one, on your fingers:
your charm, your poise, patience, luck
your lucidity, sense of irony, affinity for the absurd
your breasts and legs
your devotion, wakefulness, your alive eyes
your biological clock
your ability to time the passing carousel,
knowing when to jump on
and off.

Stiletto heels and pantyhose, debutante
bait for married executives, done that.
As well the macrobiotic hippiechick
faded blue tattoos and the
half-remembered taste and touch
of indiscriminate skins.
At times, from decade to decade,
you've picked up your mail in both places.
Maybe I shoulda been an anarchist,
you wonder in your dreams, asking the sky
does anyone ever get extra,
or have I already dined on
the only bones with the only meat?

You could build a road to purgatory and back
With the oatmeal cookies you've baked
because it makes America strong, as you
take them to the neighbors on paper plates.
When you die they will make you into
a copper-green statue in the park
and pigeons will shit on your head.

But is that enough?

It's sorting-out time as you ponder the
late afternoon light and the day's dying breezes.
Leaning out your tower window,
you take in a view unreachable, sighing,
while even then, suffering the attention of
some dime-a-dozen handsome prince
trying to climb up your hair.

THE OLD PORCH LIGHT TRICK

It's a dark, dark night and I debate whether to flip on the porch light. Finally, I conclude that even if the electricity used equals the cost of a small coffee house *mocha latta frappiatto sotto voce* …

… it's worth it.

If it helps light the path of a lonely stranger passing through my neighborhood (in which very few people ever actually walk, now that I think of it, and never at night unless they're criminals) …

But what the heck. I go ahead and flick the switch.

In only 47 billion years from now, the current speed of space's expansion, the light from my front porch bulb will finally reach the outer edge of the known universe. There, nestled between the ether and the nothing, sits a small planet called Murray. Male and female non-carbon life forms, multi-tiered in their complexity, yet prosaic in their simple yearnings, will be walking along holding tentacles, when suddenly from out of nowhere, the light from my front porch bulb will arrive right in front of them.

"Whoa, what was that!? Omigod, did you see that!?"

"Sure did. Scared the FelgaGarb outta me."

I'm laughing to myself already, anticipating the looks on the faces of those two.

Non-carbon life forms, man, don't you just love messing with their heads? Seriously, it's almost too easy.

Searching for SanViejo

A meandering river through granite and soapstone

There're two kinds of knowing: regular knowing and *Omigod knowing!* In this last kind of knowing, I finally figured out my body is mortal, while my spirit is infinite.

Life fired a series of warning shots across my bow, reminding me to get serious about my pursuit of the true essence of SanViejo lying dormant within, as described in this book's Introduction, and those timely warnings have a lot to do with why I began pondering my mortality so seriously and started compiling the essays and other driftwood that ended up becoming this book. As I also wrote in the intro, the final task for me as I head down the "back nine" of life is to become SanViejo, which is shorthand for manifesting the best person I can become in the one lifetime I am allotted.

It's a worthy goal. I don't want to look back and be appalled at how much time and energy I spent being a selfish jerk or missed huge opportunities to be useful. Who does? Of course there's always reincarnation, I suppose, if you need infinite chances to get it right. I don't for a second believe in past lives and reincarnation, but I understand it operates whether you believe in it or not. :-)

The first of those warning shots came at me on the morning of December 31, 2007 when I awoke with a sharp pain running up and down my right arm. If it had been my left arm, I would have thought *hmm … heart attack, maybe this is it!*—but this was happening on the right side, and so I'm thinking torn shoulder, rotator cuff, or that something had chewed my arm off in the night.

I reported all this to Honey Nim, one pillow over. "I be profen," she said.

"I be sushi," I replied. *Etiam in passionem, ego belle* (even in suffering, I jest). She got up and fetched a couple of useless pain pills and a glass of water.

The MRI showed it to be a pinched spinal nerve and it hurt like a blind, screaming mother. The pain manifested as a continual shoulder ache accessorized with hot, electric needles shooting down my right arm. Sitting, standing, lying down, eating, taking a shower. Lying on my back downgraded the pain from excruciating to mere agony. It hurt to exist.

Eight hundred milligrams of Ibuprofen didn't cut it. I asked my doctor to call in the big guns—Vicodin, Percocet, morphine, heroin. "I'll only give you a few Vicodin, but that's it" he said. "It's easy to get addicted."

"Really? You say that like it's a bad thing."

One's spine is made up of individual bones (vertebrae), separated by little cream-filled gummy bears that keep the vertebrae from grinding together and make room for nerves to wind through the little tunnels in the bones. With age, or an injury, these gummy bears can start to lose their filling and go flat. When that happens, the bones rub together and pinch the nerves between them.

Friends gave me the names and phone numbers of orthopedic surgeons. "He will fuse your spine and you'll feel a lot better," one said. *Fuse my spine!? The only spine I will ever own?*

Panic was in order. There was no way I could go to work, and a million-scary-thought tsunami inundated me. Is this permanent? Even reality has escapes, but pain is invisible luggage that never gets lost. Every scenario looked bleak. I felt cornered.

My little arrangement

Before going further, it's time to reveal some personal background, so here comes a necessary digression in the narrative. I cut a deal with God back in the 70s. In my early twenties, I was window-shopping a lot of interesting religions, and had requested divine assistance in sorting them out. "Can you just quietly clue me in?" I asked. "Maybe just inform my intuition." I figured a person ought to settle on a religion at some point to have access to the big picture, and even offered to create one myself since all the good ones seemed to be pretty much the same.

As long as I was working my wish list, I took the liberty of adding a couple of preferences. I let it be known that I didn't particularly want prophetic visions and dreams. No burning bushes or angels coming through the walls please. I knew a few people who had this degree of spiritual openness, and most of them were crazy as hell.

I thought let's keep it subtle and just go with the "still small voice within." Perhaps if I paid close attention my intuition would come to recognize the signature voiceprint of God when I encountered it in conversations with trusted friends. Or in literature, movies, music. Or nature: "sermons in stones, books in running brooks," as Bill the Bard wrote. God is everywhere, right? Over time I figured I would learn how to distill any guidance I need from the background noise and chatter.

This approach seemed right and I offered it up in prayer one day with my higher power. I immediately felt an image of a guardian angel chewing on an unlit cigar as he flipped through the rule book before looking up and shrugging, "Yeah, we can do that." With one or two noteworthy blinding light exceptions (fodder for some other essay), a low-key, calm and undramatic, sensible approach to the conduct of spiritual seeking has been my M.O.

I have found that when I am in "Okay, world, educate me" mode, opportunities appear in front of me.

For example, some years ago I was in Ocean City, New Jersey, on business and found myself with an extra day and nothing to do. I awoke early, walked down to the water and presented the universe with my list of demands. I announced that I want to use this free day to have an adventure, I want to do something bold, epic, heroic and different.

The small restaurant nearby was crowded but an elderly woman who looked to be about a quarter-zillion years old sat alone at a table. She seemed bright and sturdy. I asked if I could join her and she smiled and said, "Of course."

We hit it off well, talking about her late husband and about my wife and children. We discussed history, hurricanes and even slavery (her great-grandmother had been one in Carolina. Not North or South, just plain Carolina). After an hour or so she invited me to come to her house for dinner that evening. Being epic and heroic, I boldly told her I would catch some fish and bring them to her and we could cook them. I was starting to hatch a plan.

After we parted, I walked over to the local newspaper, *The Sentinel*. I walked in, introduced myself to the editor and said I would like to write a feature about day fishing on one of the local charters, written from the perspective of a non-fisherperson tourist. He didn't look terribly thrilled but finally he said, "Okay, twenty bucks, if we like it."

With that, I had the confidence to walk down to the pier, go up to any charter boat and audaciously say, "Hi, I'm Larry Moffitt, with *The Sentinel*." It was media magic. The captain was happy to take me out for free in exchange for his boat being featured in a story.

Turns out I didn't catch a thing. It was a humbling experience. Seems that ocean fishing involves some skill. It also makes your legs wobbly and stomach queasy. When we got back to the dock, I went to the paper, found an empty desk and wrote the article. I touted the adventuresome fishing, praised the captain and the bountiful fish (some people were catching). The editor liked it and handed me $40, double our agreement. I took the money, went to a local fish market and bought lots of fresh fish and scallops for dinner. She welcomed me into her tiny cottage. We had a nice meal, good conversation, and the next morning I hopped on a bus for home.

It's a trendy cliché, this notion that if you put your intent or request "out there" that you will often get results. It's a cliché because it actually occurs fairly dependably. When I was in college (undergraduate degree in Radio, Television, Film; MA in Communication) I did a lot of hitchhiking around the country, including through Mexico, Central and South America, I would wake up some mornings, literally close my eyes, put my finger on the map and then go there for no other reason than to see what I would see and meet who I would meet. I did this a lot.

Among other places, I ended up with beekeepers in Aiken, South Carolina, and hung around a mom and pop store in Tapachula on Mexico's Pacific coastal underbelly. I was in Crested Butte, Colorado long before it was discovered, "developed" (and ruined, in my opinion) by skiers and boutiques. A rodeo clown picked me up in his truck outside of Quapaw, Oklahoma and took me to work with him. In a borrowed cowboy hat, I watched from the pens in the staging area, sitting next to some bodacious cowgirls who were drinking Jack and Coke, and knew how to pack a pair of size-7 jeans. Today those gals are probably retired, with mother-of-the-bride bodies and grandchildren.

There are so many other memories, and tons more I have forgotten. I have lost a few summers, or years, maybe most of a decade down the memory black hole. But I do remember being on a relentless spiritual search during all that time, asking "is there actually such a thing as eternal?" when I would meet a guru or someone I figured ought to know. They all thought so, of course, but I wanted the details, whatever those might be.

I tended to run into purveyors of fringe religions and would spend a day or two hearing them out until I came to the end of their cosmology and decided it wasn't for me. A few of them were quite insane, like a priest in full priest garb who celebrated Mass by himself every day in a small cabin on a mountainside in Colorado. He swung a huge incense burner on a chain that filled the room with acrid smoke as he shouted in Latin, blessing the hell out of everything. I had come upon his cabin while thumbing rides. I had to climb an impossibly steep driveway made of mud to get up there, knock on his door and ask for water. He answered the door wearing the full Vatican. He heard my entire convoluted confession and gave me absolution. He may even have been a real priest.

I spent a weekend with the Children of God near Thurber, Texas. They were an okay cult at the time, before they went very sexually weird and the women began trolling on the streets to find guys they could bring to Jesus over a cup of coffee followed by an orgasm and herpes. Anyway, when I met them they ran a monogamous and chaste farming commune. One guy, Mount of Olives (they adopted biblical names) told me he had taken LSD five-hundred times before he met Christ. I was not surprised, thinking if I dropped that much acid I would be taking long walks on the beach with Christ with sparklers in his hair. I wrote a friendly feature story on them ("Band of Outsiders") and sold it to *The Daily Texan* in Austin for gas money.

One day, I was finally able to distill into words what my search was all about. I wanted to know why love, which seemed like such a good thing, could only exist as fleeting, powdery light that arrived when you didn't want it and evaporated as soon as you wanted it more than you ever wanted anything in your life. In my twenty-somethings I was very intense, interested in *everything*, standing outside in a summer rainstorm, screaming at the sky, "I wanna cut through the bullshit!! I just wanna *know*!!"

I really did that. Where, you might be asking, was my adult supervision? Good question.

It scares me a bit, now that I am older and more set in my ways, to recall what a dangerously, horrifyingly unstructured existence it was to meander through the late 1960s and early 70s, along highways and through mountain passes, across states and countries, through dictatorships and revolutions—like a river eroding random bends through granite and soapstone. This is especially true when I see this exploratory nature in my children and think how much more perilous the world is now than it was back then. A daughter who works for an airline and can fly for free suddenly takes off to wander through five countries in Europe with her tiny carry-on backpack and a list of people on whose couches she can sleep a couple of nights. All five of our adult children have, in varying degrees, this gene that compels them to explore geography and inner space. In my own case, all I can conclude is that God must have been protecting me in my wanderings. I was too naïve and stupid to live. But I did. And in the process I became confident in the power of visualization. I learned to trust my intuition, and learned something about how to read the signs.

Still, I worry about my wandering children because I'm the dad. But then I'll remember arriving at dawn in a tiny village coming off the Bolivian *altoplano*, but still at 10,000-feet altitude, where breathing is a conscious act. It was July, the dead of winter in the southern hemisphere. A group of farming men and women were gathered around a vendor selling glasses of a hot and sweet starchy beverage that was yellow with swirls of deep purple it. So delicious and warming. I pulled the wrinkled, disintegrating copy of National Geographic out of my backpack and looked again at the picture of Lake Titicaca. That's where I was headed. In Copacabana, above the lake, I met a family who was walking the Stations of the Cross up the side of a hill, with inscribed markers at each stop. They shared their tangerines with me and took me to Mass that night. I was safe within that family of a father, mother and several children of all ages. When we came out of the huge cathedral, the moon was more full and clear and twice as near as ever. It seemed like, no matter what, God kept showing up wearing the bodies of strangers or looking up from behind a shop counter as I walked in. I have to trust that God still longs to be there for other pilgrims in every land, including my children.

Something important I learned while scouring the universe, searching like Dorothy in Oz for the Kansas that was inside me all along: if you can do this kind of wandering with your life's mate beside you, your enjoyment and ability to absorb all there is to see, feel and learn—will be increased a hundredfold. Encountering distant lands and cultures can temper the welded joints of your relationship so that the two of you will endure longer than Istanbul's fifth century walls built by Constantine, that still wind through the city today. If you want to wait, build a relationship first and then travel in your forties, you will still be young, you'll be a lot smarter than in your 20s, and the world will still be out there.

And a few rules: You are always required to use your own discernment. A revelation from God is different from the random voices in your head, but if you don't listen carefully and work the pause and replay buttons, you can mess yourself up. Therefore, never unplug your rational mind. Take full responsibility for your actions, and no excuses. When you ask the world to educate you, and you say it aloud, or shout heavenward prayers of determination with two exclamation points at the end, you'd better be ready for answers you don't expect.

I'm free to complain all I want to my friends or to God or the fairies on the bathroom wall. But nobody wants to hear me bitching and moaning about my bad luck or lack of planning. So just suck it, and go to Plan B. I may get a do-over now and then, like if someone I hurt agrees to forgive and reset everything back to zero. I am grateful when that happens. I think we're allowed a great deal of say-so in how we relate to the world, physically and spiritually. This includes the freedom to ignore God and the advice of your ancestors altogether. Unbelief is also a choice we're allowed to make.

Now that you have some background, this digression ends, and I return to where I am now in the search for SanViejo.

What my pinched nerves were telling me

I was *forced* to seek divine advice about the pain in my shoulder because nothing else was working. But when I prayed about my desperate situation, it was my own awareness that responded because, in fact, I already knew the answer. It went like this:

Larry, in case you forgot, you aren't going to live forever. Your life is finite. Therefore use the years and days you have left (or maybe minutes, who knows?) to improve your character and get yourself ready for the day you will finish your time here and go to the spirit world. Use this time to actually become SanViejo, not just your email address. Talking about it won't help, and you can't finesse it or bullshit it. You will either do it or not, so just do it.

That was pretty much it.

I think existence offers us—in the form of trials and hardships and those who are rude or who cut us off in traffic—the potential to dig out the saint buried within. And when we find our inner SanViejo, that's the original blueprint of ourselves. That's the row of corn we need to hoe, the tree to water, the garden to spend the rest of our lives investing in, preparing for the harvest.

If I could fit the specifics on a bumper sticker, they would be (1) perfect my heart by loving other people and (2) create a family whose members love each other and love the community and the world and (3) take care of the earth, the air, the water and the friendly bacteria and little doe-eyed creatures. I'm in charge of all this, and so are you.

I saw the pinched nerve as a wake-up call about my own mortality. It was a pebble in my shoe, a bell reminder about all of humankind. Eventually I found a doctor who used a blend of eastern and western medical approaches, acupuncture and manipulation of my arm and back. He eased the pinch and stopped the pain. *Okay, lesson over,* I thought. *Now onto other stuff.*

I was wrong.

Lesson Two: totaling the rented SUV

Exactly one month after the nerve pinch, at approximately seven-something on the evening of January 31, 2008, I was sitting in the driver's seat of my rented sport utility vehicle watching another sport utility vehicle the size of Moby Dick, heading straight for my door. The oncoming headlights were eye-level with me. I had inadvertently taken an illegal left turn and got creamed and rolled like a pill bug.

My head banged the window, knocking me cuckoo. I unfastened my seat belt and plummeted downward onto the passenger side door. I became aware of voices around the car asking if I was okay. I asked how the people in the other car were. What if I had killed someone? I was told they were shaken up but otherwise uninjured. Their seat belts and airbags had done their jobs.

When the fire department cut the back of the car open with the jaws of life, I mentioned to the medic who came in that I thought the car was totaled. He replied. "You're alive, and believe me, this car is of no importance." I thought that was an essential perspective from a guy who pulls dead people out of cars for a living. His words have stayed with me. Good friends of mine have been killed in auto accidents. I was smacked pretty hard, but it wasn't my time to go. Yet it easily could have been. There is nothing quite as helpful for getting your priorities in order as being smacked upside the head with a demonstration of how fragile your life is.

Lying in a crumpled rental, waiting for the paramedics, informed me at the visceral level, that life is short and that therefore, Larry should get off his pink-and-white ass and stop wasting time. *Good lesson. Thank you again. We're finished, right?*

Nope.

Lesson Three: blessed are the pacemakers

I should have known life's cosmic lessons come in threes. After all, it took three ghosts to teach Ebenezer Scrooge what he needed to learn. Goldilocks had three bowls of porridge to choose from. Magic lamps give you three wishes.

May of 2014 was Happy Cardio Month for me. I started May with an "a-fib ablation" procedure to correct a heartbeat that had, for the previous year, assumed the irregular cadence of a jazz drum solo. It put me at a high risk for stroke. Turns out the a-fib was masking three other conditions: bradycardia, near syncope and sick sinus syndrome. (Don't you wish you could be in charge of naming diseases? I would call congestive heart failure "sweetums," just to soften the blow.)

A pacemaker was recommended. I went through a couple of weeks scaring the crap out of everyone, with my pale, drawn face, blue lips and shortness of breath. At the end of the month the pacemaker was installed. It has a ten-year battery, and every night the device communicates with the Biotronik office in Portland, Oregon. It reports that my pacemaker is needed to normalize my heart rate about fifty percent of the time. If I lived before pacemakers were invented I would already be pushing up daisies.

My heart situation is genetic luck of the draw for my branch of the family. Moffitt males have tended to go *klunk* fairly early on. I think the doctor and modern technology gave me some extra years. Fortunately, I am married to a woman from a longevity family, and so my children's destiny may be improved in this area.

So now I have a store-bought heart. I am officially a heart patient, a cardio guy. Or as we say in my house, a cardigan.

After three big lessons the point is driven home and it's official. I am finite. I am mortal.

Good Larry vs. Selfish Larry

I would like to be able to announce to the unwashed, grubby, predatory, bottom-feeding, immoral world out there that I am closing in on sainthood and that, therefore, they can all kiss my patooty. However, this book is called *Searching for* SanViejo, not *Found* SanViejo.

I can be a selfish bastard. When I travel, I have a well-developed strategy for getting in line first, getting on the plane first and getting as much of the overhead compartment space as I need. And that's in economy class. My wife calls it a "me-first sickness." If you shook me awake at 3 a.m., shouting "Fire!" odds are good that my very first thought would be for my own safety. I hope that very shortly after that, I would shout, "Wait! Save the computer! ... Oh, and my loved ones, of course."

I am like the sheriff of a dusty frontier cow town, facing down a gunfighter in the street. I stare intently at the other man, who's glaring back at me. Only when I shade my eyes with my hand do I realize that the one about to draw down on me from the other end of the street ...

... is *me.*

Therefore, I cannot shoot. Both of my selves, good Larry and selfish Larry, inhabit the same body, so I can't just gun down the bad guy and walk away. That would actually be easy, like severing a gangrenous foot and you're done with it. In this case, selfish Larry has to be restored and absorbed into good Larry.

The way to do that is simple. Every time I am faced with a decision to do the relatively right thing or the wrong thing, I should always do the right thing, take the high road. Then, just do that all the time. Lather, rinse and repeat, over and over. Simple, right?

My wise friends, Pamela and Pat (a former nun), have both said a person should start living eternity now. Live now as you want to live in the next world, so that when you pass over, you simply continue your life. No shocks or surprises, except happy ones, like skydiving without a parachute and birthday parties, and eating anything you want with no worry about cholesterol. Truthful, loyal, generous, unsullied, loving of others—be all those things now, before you croak. That way, when you die, all that happens is that you step across a threshold into the spiritual dimension, as though effortlessly walking from one room into another.

Ben Franklin's attempt to become perfect

Speaking of bad habits, Benjamin Franklin made a serious attempt at attaining moral perfection in his own life. He listed in a vertical column, thirteen virtues that he would strive to embody, with the days of the week in columns across the top. Each night he would check off which virtues he had fallen short of during that day. The idea was to be aware of his behavior patterns and try to avoid unconsciously repeating the same unhealthy practices over and over again.

The virtues were the usual: temperance, frugality, sincerity, justice, moderation, cleanliness, etc. The elephant in the room is chastity, of course, and his admonition to himself was to "rarely use venery (the pursuit of sexual pleasure) except for health or offspring, and never to dullness, weakness or the injury of your own or another's peace or reputation." You can interpret that any way you want.

Ben, who did his best thinking and writing sitting naked in his room for the first hour or so of each day (an "air bath" he called it), admitted that becoming one with all thirteen virtues was more difficult than he had thought it would be. He wrote, "While my care was employ'd in guarding against one fault, I was often surprised by another; habit took the advantage of inattention; inclination was sometimes too strong for reason."

We can all relate to this. I wish I had a mind-reading, sin-monitoring Doberman at my side that would growl menacingly every time I think about departing from virtue. Just thinking about sloth makes me want to take a nap. (*Rrrrrrrrr! Easy boy!*)

Ben knew the problem. You focus on one thing, and another flaw creeps in. For example, I feel no envy when a friend gets the better seat at the table. I look over the menu, being frugal with my pennies. I eat small portions, sparingly, gratefully, drink spring water, waste nothing. I'm doing fine on all fronts; my character is batting a thousand. Then the floor show begins and brown Fatina twirls, and twirls, and twirls, her dress inching up past her upper thighs ... The Doberman starts to snarl. I order a shot of whiskey to shut him up.

The world has more unhealthy distractions now than it did in Ben Franklin's time. Therefore, arriving at the finish line as a person relatively pure in thought and deed requires vigilance *all the damn time*. You can wear a shirt of horse hair in penance. You can put encouraging notes on your shaving mirror to remind yourself as you begin the day. You can keep your snarling, sin-warning Doberman with you at all times. But you will make mistakes anyway. A momentary lapse of attention, a craving you are simply unable to put out of your mind. You will slip up. Either that, or you will tip-toe on eggshells every waking moment, as tightly strung as a piano wire, while outwardly thundering like an Old Testament prophet completely obsessed with moral uprightness—a man without friends or party invitations. If you conduct yourself to such an extreme, you will become a person made of hardened, brittle, dried flakes. Your eyes will stop shining. You will forget how to love.

I think you need to find a middle road you can live with. I'm not saying you should become comfortable with excuses, but you do need to foster forbearance, and carry a big bag of second chances that you hand out as you go around, even if the person you just gave one to comes right back asking for another. And dip into that bag for yourself now and then.

Like I said, I meander, your classic two steps forward and one back. I put a quarter in a blind man's cup, while taking the last donut for myself. I hold the door for people laden with packages, I visualize whirled peas and work on a plan to stop continental drift—while also muttering coarse language, noticing the perfumed maiden crossing my path on the quad, and shoving the elderly aside to get to the fire exit. Helper angels whisper guidance to my conscience, while my friends ask me, "What's with your dog, man? Why is he always growling at you?"

ANT PASSING THROUGH MY CELL

Ant on the lower window bar runs
and then stops.
Runs full speed, then stops dead still.
Then runs. Stops. RunStopRunStop.
Her brain is made of two chemicals,
the run chemical and the stop chemical.
The ant doesn't linger or stroll or savor anything,
never pauses to help an old queen cross the street.
Only runs. And stops.

I did manage to get a word in edgewise
moving alongside. I asked her
to help me watch the sunset.
"NoTimeNoTimeNoTime," she brushed me off
Finally the stop chemical kicked in and she turned,
"Look, I only have time to bite you if that's what you want."
And then she was off.
My God, her eyes were beautiful.

"DOCTOR, THE INVISIBLE MAN IS HERE."

"Tell him I can't see him."

The man was near hysteria. I was in the garden, near wisteria. He was crazed, screaming over and over, "I'm a wigwam! I'm a teepee! I'm a wigwam! I'm a teepee!"

"Calm down," I said, "you're two tents."

We were eating the wisteria in groves. "How do they taste?" my crazy friend asked.

"Ummm, deciduous," I replied.

"By the way," he said, "Robert E. Lee and Stonewall Jackson called earlier."

"Good, how were they?"

"Civil."

Just then a gorgeous blonde pulled up in a convertible with her top down. She asked me directions to Florida.

"What did she want?" craze asked.

"She's going to Kissimmee," I told him.

"Lucky man," he said.

"Nah," I demurred, "And anyway, I'll be in the Middle East."

"Where?" asked craze.

"Is Real."

"But," craze insisted, "Is Real isn't," and added, "It's frightful," his voice shaking with ... fright. "Now, I'm sacred exactly one-half to death."

"Don't be sacred," I soothed. "Is Real is real if your real eyes realize real lies. Here, have a bowl of sugar-frosted Syria. It'll calm you down."

"Ummm, Syria. I like to put Lebanon it, don't you?"

He took a few bytes, but looked only a little better. "You still got fright?" I asked.

"Oman!" he exclaimed, coughing up Qatar, "my Tunisia knocking together. By the way, did you know Iran for Mayor Culpa and lost. Oh, but how I Babylon, don't I? Sari."

Iraq my brain, trying to think. "Just Kuwait, Henry Higgins," I said. "Let's call one of the straights of Hormuz."

"You call. I sold my sell phone," he said, adding, "Oh, Amsterdam! Now I'm really in dutch." He stamped his feat. "Helsinki!"

"You got bad gnus?" I asked.

No, I'm just Tyre, that's all. Tyre of all this Nineveh."

"So you want me to stop typing now?"

"No way" craze said. "Not for all the kangaroos in Austria."

You're stunned, aren't you? You can't believe you wasted your time reading this, can you? And now you want your two minutes back, don't you? Tough. Sometimes I just have to let the dogs out to run.

(Don't) kill your darlings

Albert Camus' novel, *The Plague* is about a deadly disease, cholera maybe, that sweeps through an Algerian city like bran through a colon. The protag of the story, Joseph Grand, a blocked writer living in the beautiful Mediterranean city of Oran, struggles with the opening sentence of a novel he's writing. The writer's efforts to get out of the starting gate is a running subplot in the book and is, today, the main thing I remember about the novel.

The sentence is: "One fine morning in the month of May an elegant young horsewoman might have been riding a handsome sorrel mare along the flowery avenues of the Bois de Boulogne."

Aside from too many adjectives, it's not too shabby as the first sentence in a novel, right? It's no "Call me Ishmael" (*Moby Dick*), and it's no "Ships at a distance have every man's wish on board" (*Their Eyes Were Watching God*), but as opening sentences go it's at least in the ballpark. The thing is, in Camus' novel, Grand can't stop tweaking it. While getting the plague, nearly dying, and recovering, he sweats over every word, rearranges it, rewrites, revises over and over and over again. And that's where Grand's great opus stops dead in its tracks. He *never, ever* gets to sentence number two. I love it. The poor schlub. Anyone who has ever written anything can empathize.

It's like the guy who wants to tell his girl he loves her and rehearses to death the perfect way to say it, rearranging the emphasis: "i *LOVE* you." "i love *YOU*." "*EYE* love *YOU*." He decides to call her instead, and tell her over the phone, so he dials her number again and again, slamming down the receiver in a panic just before pushing the final button that would make her phone ring. Ah yes, high school, been there, done that.

A fairly youngish guy emailed me one day, asking if he could "apprentice" himself to me, and in return I would teach him how to write. After I finished being flattered, I wondered, *How does a writer use an apprentice anyway?*

I guess he could help me watch out for violations of Newton's Variable Predicate Noun Conundrum.[1] Or would he make sure I don't write "that" (a restrictive pronoun) when I should be writing "which" (introducing a relative clause)? Would he sharpen my goose quills and grind the ink stick with water? Or do I get to use my apprentice's blood for ink? That would be something. Blood makes for great ink, plus the sincerity of writing something in blood, and pretending it's your own, is undeniable.

Finally, I told him pretty much the same thing you would have told him, gentle reader. And that's that the only way to learn to write is by writing. You start by writing doggerel, gibberish, crap, I told him. You show it to other writers and receive their respectful feedback: "This is hog twaddle!" and other constructive criticisms.

You must undergo this horrible process while not allowing writer's block to occur along the way. Don't let yourself become like Joseph Grand and his sorrel mare sentence in Albert Camus' novel. Avoid blockage like … the plague. Sorry, couldn't resist.

Never shy away from writing a terrible first draft. You can sit there and mumble to yourself, writing down whatever comes out of your mouth. You don't have to begin your story at the beginning. Start with the climactic fistfight at the end if you want to. Write down any random phrase of stunning brilliance you just that second thought of. Get together with a writing buddy and have a blast thinking up incredibly great opening sentences:

The "Yeah, well I hate you too!" she had been prepared to respond with, got stuck somewhere under her tongue when she saw the car leap the curb and head straight for him, so she just smiled and nodded.

Or …

My imaginary friend stopped coming to meet me at the creek on the day of my first menses.

Or …

Earl bled out on the operating table, refusing the transfusion because the doctor wouldn't promise him that the blood "don't come from no nigger."

I venture that those are first sentences that will entice you to read the second sentence. Try to have a second that causes them to read the third.

Reviews call books "page turners" because the reader is driven by plot lust to claw his way across one page and onto the next.

Be compelling, even if you aren't thriller-and-car-chase compelling, but instead are lyrical-and-languid compelling. "I don't write dime novel trash," my inner snob says. "I write *literature*." Yes, yes, and more power *to* me. So write literature that is deathless-prose-literary compelling.

Go ahead and make the opening sentence compelling, or the very last one, or somewhere in the middle. But write, *damn you, Stella*, write! Always the garbage comes first. The enduring literature comes later, if at all.

So what happens after you write your garbage? First, don't actually bother showing it to anyone to get their opinion, despite what I said earlier. It is hog twaddle, after all. You could show it to a friend whose writing is also hog twaddle, shrug and go grab a beer together. Then you're ready for step two: the rewrite. Rewrite is also steps three, four and five. After those, step number whatever is to show your work to someone who loves you enough to criticize your writing, and is competent enough to offer specific suggestions.

For me and many of my friends, the rewrite process is where the fun and the creativity lies. Rewrite is where hog twaddle becomes upscale premium pig chow and eventually, if you stay with it, nectar of the gods. The rewrites are why I truly love writing. But understand, in honing your work you must be absolutely ruthless with yourself.

Stephen King said famously, "Kill your darlings, kill your darlings, even when it breaks your egocentric little scribbler's heart, kill your darlings." Almost the exact same thing has been said by William Falkner, Anton Chekov, G.K. Chesterton, Eudora Welty, Oscar Wilde and Allen Ginsburg.

I sort of agree with the principle of what they say, but not the tone of it. You don't *kill* your darlings, although you do gently lift them out of the way when the story requires it. It is important to be respectful of creativity as an entity. Your writing is your lover, and people should not kill lovers when a mutually amicable breakup will suffice. Your writing is not a recalcitrant child to be sent to bed without dinner; it's not a wild horse whose spirit you must break; it's not a Barbie doll possessed by demons.

Suppose you have a darling that goes, something like this: *The lilies, dried and lifeless in the dark of the moon, left her feeling like a shadow with nothing to stick to.*

It's an okay sentence; at least it does no great harm. But maybe it doesn't work for the situation. Remove it then, but with some reverence for the invisible creative engine that produced it and the fuel from your imagination that feeds that engine. The umbilical cord of art, that is truly art, runs through you and connects to God. So go ahead and edit, but please don't do it with the heart of a sonofabitch. Be kind to the Muse.

Rewriting and editing is not the act of whipping your story into submission. It's the act of giving life; it's opening up your prose so it can breathe. When you rewrite you are examining the parts and the whole, like a conductor listening closely to the French horns while also listening to the entire orchestra. File the discarded words and letters for later consideration, even if it's only to put them in your mental box labeled, "Stuff I Will Never Say in Writing As Long As I Draw Breath." I have just that kind of box in my mind but it has always been empty except for one phrase "queer as a duck," which has been rattling around in there for a couple decades. I just this second used it, so now the box of things I will never write sits empty.

What about prose that is eloquent, even profoundly so? The danger for a writer is to go beyond eloquence and into the realm of showing off. It's a hazy border but an aware reader will figure out when the writer has crossed the line and moved from expressiveness into exhibitionism. And they won't like it.

Charles Frazier, author of *Cold Mountain*, and Lauren Groff, author of *Fates and Furies*, are writers who are eloquent and you love them for it. The artistry of their storytelling craft raises the bar for contemporary literature. Both authors are able to explain an emotion top to bottom with a nuanced gesture or movement, or a piece of described physicality, without once overtly mentioning that this is what they're doing. Look for writers who have the gift of tucking you into an environment as adroitly as strapping you into a time and place machine that relocates, and ultimately improves on, your body and soul.

But hey, this is the postmodern age of relativism and reality created on the fly. We can do better without formal structure. And did I mention we want it fast? Therefore, if this is you and if you want to just get your book done and you don't mind being a total maniac, let me introduce you to a special kind of pain.

One of the fastest and harshest ways to get your novel down on paper is the brute force method of subjecting yourself to the total immersion and sheer masochism of NaNoWriMo (pronounced: NaNoWriMo). NaNoWriMo abbreviates National Novel Writing Month. It takes place during November of each year. At the stroke of midnight on October 31 you begin writing, concluding at 11:59:59 PM on November 30. Google their website to get in on it.

Every single day of November, including weekends, birthdays, days of illness, days of depression and euphoria, Thanksgiving Day, Guy Fawkes Day, the full moon (even if you're a lycanthrope), you turn out 1,667 words every twenty-four hours. If you heroically take a bullet for the President and are forced to miss a day while the medics jump-start your heart, you have to write 3,334 words the next day. You write even if your plot gets sucked into a black hole and you have nothing to say. You must show up and you must perform. For one month you will experience the closest thing to being married to a nymphomaniac.

You will end up dominating the room you work in. Every surface, including the floor will be covered with folders and notebooks and 3x5 cards with character descriptions and plot twists scribbled on them. Nothing will get cooked at your house unless someone else does it. Ditto cleaned. Your children will complain, while coming to sorely appreciate all the work you used to do for them. Your spouse will likely hate it but knows it's only for a month. Enduring it with love will make him/her a better person. Happy is the person whose spouse is proud of them for being a "WriMo," as we call ourselves.

At midnight on November 30 you will be dehydrated and on the verge of coffee poisoning, your fingers bleeding. You will have exhausted most of your reasons for living, and your marriage will be in tatters, but you will be the proud author of a 50,000-word novel—still unedited, and that quite possibly sucks. But it is a novel nonetheless, a darling. It's a marvelous feeling and you can spend the rest of your days editing, polishing and rewriting your "handsome sorrel mare along the flowery avenues of the Bois de Boulogne."

I have started, but never successfully completed, several NaNoWriMo Novembers. Two reasons: (1) I have to earn a living and (2) my sanity is on a short enough leash as it is.

If all this advice on writing frustrates you, brimming over with wisdom though it is, allow me to further muddle your clarity with this wonderful and time-worn observation by W. Somerset Maugham: "There are three rules for writing a novel. Unfortunately, no one knows what they are."

[1] There is no such thing as Newton's Variable Predicate Noun Conundrum. Really, there isn't, but I bet I had you going there for a second.

Owning your package

The pachyderm in the middle of the room

This essay is a story of hope. This is about men, although not exclusively, and our primal hungers. I include a few work-arounds I have learned over the years for keeping my demons at bay during a period when I was on the road for months at a time, specifically while living in Argentina for a year without my family. In a perfect world, this chapter wouldn't exist. But we're still working on perfect. And so, for you out there in the trenches, with a bad angel sitting on one shoulder and a good angel on the other, duking it out with your conflicted inner self, you may find something useful in this.

Nearly every moment of your entire life, your body will try to boss you around through three noisily urgent channels: your need for food, sleep and sex. Without sleeping, eating and procreating the human race would not exist, so your body has undeniable logic on its side. Regarding sex, some choose to be celibate for various reasons and I respect their choice. Not everyone has to engage in sex, as long as *someone* does. Barring immaculate conception, which doesn't happen very often, sex is the only way to create life. Let me add my own hooray for sex, and not just for reasons of procreating, but for mutual love and comforting.

The religions pretty much all agree on this, but they insist that one's mind must be the one that controls the bodily urges, and not vice versa. Mind and body unity, with the mind's hand on the helm.

I had coffee with Shirley, a dear friend who had served on the grand jury in her town for a number of years. "What's the grand jury about?" she said, repeating my question to her. "It's about rape." Her voice was like steel. "We get so many rape cases. Date rape, family rape. People usually rape people they know, and who trust them."

The daughter of Shirley's nephew, 18, was raped a few months before that in California. She was babysitting for a neighbor. He came home after a night of drinking. His wife was out of town and the kids were asleep. He got affectionate, she tried to leave. He got aggressive. He's in jail.

Shirley's eyes were wet with fury as she spoke, laying the sins of my gender squarely at my feet. "She's the nicest, sweetest girl you would ever meet. Men are shit!" Her voice blew a sharp, desolate wind through me. I must have winced.

"Sorry," she said, "it's still fresh in my mind."

I pulled away from our sit-down at Starbuck's, and resolved to write this essay straight up with no chaser, and put it in the book. As I drove, I recalled something else I heard about twenty years earlier. A friend told me his father had kept porn magazines lying around the house for as long as he could remember. He inherited a sexual addiction that ended up destroying three marriages. He can masturbate eight times a day, which leaves him feeling degraded and used by his myriad demons. He insisted to me, "I *can't* stop; don't *want* to stop." His therapist, of all people, told him at their final meeting, "I feel sorry for any woman who has the misfortune to become attracted to you, thinking, here's a man I can build a life with."

After dithering back and forth in my mind about whether to include this essay in the book, I remembered, *Hey, you wrote this book for your young adult children and their friends—your younger self—right?* My spiritual teacher, Reverend Moon, often discussed the value of one's sexual parts. It's a worthy topic too, because I promise you that right now, this very minute, our beautiful second-generation children—the shining hope of the future of all of us—are getting slaughtered out there in a world gone sexually insane. And yet everyone's silent. It's like the entire building is on fire, all the windows and exits are in flames, and those who haven't already died from smoke inhalation are coughing and choking while calmly talking about the Super Bowl. I told a couple of friends I was writing about sexual integrity based on all the stuff I've learned, and they both tried to discourage me. "Leave it out," one said. "I know you mean well, but just write things that are funny … and nice. Don't write about sexual … you know … urges or people are going to think you're slimy."

Well screw that apparently, because here goes.

This essay is in this book precisely because it's about sex, and acquitting oneself with honor in matters sexual is one of the things that contributes to a person being a good human being. I like to think that most of us wishes we were better people than we are—kinder, wiser, more loving, more mindful, more truthful. There is not one of us who, if we looked at a videotape of our entire life, would not squirm in embarrassment or feel shame at some points.

How do we get the sex part of our lives right when we are so completely interwoven into the fabric of our own flaws? It's like a fish trying to clean the water he's swimming in. The fish may not even be aware of the water itself. I don't have a brilliant plan. I guess we'll just shine the big hairy eyeball on the topic and I will share a few things I have learned along the way. We'll be real and honest, call things what they really are, and see what happens.

This essay is dedicated to my good friend Sean O'Reilly, an Ambassador for Peace and one fearlessly honest individual who wrote a book, *How to Manage Your Dick: Redirect Sexual Energy and Discover Your More Spiritually Enlightened, Evolved Self*, published in 2001 by Ten Speed Press. He sent me a copy when it was published, and it blew my mind. The book is profound on the subject of sexual self-control—the elephant in the room—a topic that is of utmost significance in this world.

It's a tempting planet out there. I have been around it a great deal and have seen how fragile one's good intentions can be, and how treacherous are the waters in which fidelity swims. In the course of three decades of international travels through sixty-something countries I have been approached, sidled up to, and brushed against, by ladies in elevators and hallways from Bangkok to Managua to Moscow—some hired, I'm certain, by the government. I discovered that some Korean barber shops are little more than an excuse for a massage parlor. An attractive woman at the next table in a restaurant in Buenos Aires gazed intently at me all through lunch. Every time I looked up, our eyes met and she would lick her lips. I now know how a pork chop feels. In a Dominican Republic hotel with paper-thin walls, I lay awake listening to a husky-voiced woman in the room next door, entertaining a string of male visitors with loud, groaning, wall-banging sex all night long.

In the face of all this, I have had to create a few rules for myself. For example, when I was alone, I never sat in the hotel bar, even if it was just to eat dinner. I didn't go into the disco in the basement. There are too many honey bears in those places and it doesn't matter that you aren't good looking. Your credit card makes you beautiful. Men with money can always exploit women who worry where they will find that day's meal for themselves and their children. And they do it all the time. In certain African countries I have been in, the elder daughter, walking the streets in the evening, is an unfortunate valuable source of income for the whole family.

In countries like Japan and Korea, and most of Western Europe, I restrict myself to the all-news channel after 10 p.m. Late night television can get very "full frontal." Japan has midnight quiz shows where the cute, giggly young woman has to remove one article of clothing per wrong answer or unlucky toss of a pair of giant felt dice. The questions aren't difficult, but you already know before the first toss that this girl is going to be dumb as a bag of hammers.

"Who's buried in Tokugawa's tomb?"

"Ummm … (giggle) no, wait … umm"

Within two minutes, she's standing there in just her panties, blushing up a storm and feigning modesty on national television.

Once, after unwisely looking over the list of pay-per-view porn flicks on the card that sat atop the television in my room, and seeing one that looked enticing, even briefly fondling the TV remote before finally *willing* the card out of my hand and into the trash can, plastic holder and all, I thought, *Okay, I will be sure to rent this same movie when I get home, and watch it with my sweet wife.* Of course she has no tolerance for such and we never rented it—which I knew we wouldn't— but it gave me something to look forward to in my moment of temptation. Does this make sense? Tricking oneself has its virtues, and sometimes it's your only resource. Not every such encounter with hotel television was as successful at that one.

I know the power of hungers, and am no stranger to the cold sweats. In Singapore, a woman wearing only a towel and a smile awaited me in the sauna at the Sheraton. Of course those benches are hot, and shortly her towel needed to be removed and folded into a square as a cushion for her to sit on. And there she was, long black hair, eyes of luminous onyx, acres of golden-brown skin. "So sorry," she smiled, "okay, yes?" I think I sat there awhile, the longest three to five minutes of my life. I remember her smile was constant and she didn't take her eyes off me for even a second. I was aware of pressure in my ears and the audible sound of my own hot, steamy, rushing blood.

Clutching my towel around my waist, I fled the sauna without taking any of the next steps, but not before the entire Harvard Law School Federalist Society marched through my brain, arguing nuances about which levels of transgression would allow one to approach the edge of the cliff and peek down the slope, without one actually falling over the edge. And etcetera. I rightfully count that episode a victory, but it wasn't pretty. Is there a patron saint for close calls? There has to be, and I owe him lunch. In Asia, I came to the conclusion that every hotel on the continent, from the lobby bar to the fitness center, is designed expressly for the purpose of getting businessmen laid.

Women with powerful urges have sat next to me on the train in Buenos Aires where I lived while helping start a Spanish-language newspaper. I was alone there for a year; my family was back in the States. The women couldn't help noticing the English-language novel in my hands and they wanted to practice their English. Nothing wrong with that. We chatted and they asked if we could get together again to practice more. This happened maybe three times during my work there, and I would always respectfully decline, fingering my wedding ring. With every one of those encounters it was excruciatingly painful for me to abruptly end what could have been a decent friendship—or, in succumbing to the depths of my self-pity, possibly something that might have been blissful, intimate, intoxicating and the absolute ruin of me. An ancient Oklahoma grandmother told me once, "If you don't want to get to that village, don't go down that road."

By far, the most frightening and dangerous close encounters for people to whom fidelity is important are the ones that begin with the most innocent of intent and take one unawares. It goes approximately like this: We meet by chance in a park and strike up a conversation. We talk about our spouses, so all our cards are face-up on the table. I am separated by 8,000 miles from the one I love. My new friend's heart is separated from her husband by an even greater distance across the mere width of their kitchen table. We chat some more and discover we're both deeply interested in the same things. It's a nice afternoon. We talk and an hour passes in an instant. And another hour. We go to a coffee shop to continue. Over coffee and *media lunas* (croissants), she occasionally reaches out and places her hand atop mine as a sympathetic expression of agreement on some mutually felt matter of the heart. I allow her hand to remain where it is, even though the presence and heat of her fingertips burrow a hole through the lining of my soul, through the table we're sitting at, and through the floor all the way to China.

We're both lonely, both more vulnerable than either of us wants to be. A web of intimacy begins to form in the air out of compressed molecules of warmth that slowly inch together and bond in the quiet pauses between words. Invisible chemistry ionizes the atmosphere. What makes encounters like this so extremely fraught with dangerous possibilities is that they are not at all about lust. They are actually about unprincipled *love* that has been given the face of an angel by the power of wretched loneliness.

Around 4 p.m. we say goodbye with an Argentine peck on the cheek outside the coffee shop. It was not a love affair, but a chance encounter that blossomed into what I would call intoxicating friendship over the course of three hours. So, yes, friendship—with more left unspoken than was spoken. As I walked back to my apartment I realized I had scared myself with the reality of my own susceptibility. I never called or emailed her after that, nor did she contact me. We both knew there was no wiggle room at the cliff's edge for either of us to make the slightest move.

Figuring out how to be the kind of man on the road who is not pushed all over the place by a constant barrage of temptations has been a learning curve for me. I did a lot of work for Rev. Moon over the years and much traveling on his behalf. One time after dinner at his home in Seoul, he looked at me for a long moment and then asked, "Larry, you've traveled through just about every Asian country by now. Which one do you think has the most beautiful women?" I understood he was trying to help me realize something about myself. For sure I had been doing some noticing in my travels, and that had to be the worst possible question for me. I turned five shades of red as he just sat there calmly awaiting my opinion, wearing an expression as unreadable as the Mona Lisa's smile. He looked like he actually wanted to know, so I told him The Philippines, with its long history as an intersection of East and West is a beautiful blend that edges out the others. And I meant it.

I have met men who jettison their principles the minute they step out the door, adopting a completely opposite standard of conduct while on the road. It's tempting to do. One fellow traveler said to me, "Why resist what happens so naturally and feels so good? And anyway, if you're reasonably discreet, what does it matter?"

It's self-deception on the level of art, and it matters because *you* know about it. You can repress all thoughts of it; you can insist to yourself, "Hey, I'm my own boss. I paddle my own canoe," or whatever, but still *you* know about it, and *you* always will. In the end, despite the oft-repeated myth, nothing stays in Vegas. Nothing.

But thanks to technology, you don't need to go to Vegas. All you need is a computer and a few minutes alone. Or a cell phone. Of all the juicy temptations available to anyone on the planet, pornography is the most insidious because it is privately indulged in and has never been more accessible than it is right now. One mouse click and there you are with an imaginary human and a comforting, addicting dopamine rush surging through neuron pathways into your brain, down your spinal cord and taking over your face, limbs, breathing patterns, and your helpless control center. The self-induced orgasm stimulated by Photoshopped women (a.k.a. "making love alone") is the new drug, and becomes the death of genuine human relationships.

Technology has led to an explosion of porn—pop-up ads on your computer, cell phone images, television, billboards, lingerie catalogs. Imagination lives on the sharp edge of a knife, and temptation is always within arm's reach, arriving on its own, leaked in from the ozone layer. We become acutely sexualized; without thinking, the head turns to follow the sound of high heels on a tile floor. Magazines and billboards are covered with tits, but we shame women who try to breastfeed their babies in public. Society is telling them, "Cover yourself, woman. Breasts are for men to stare at, not for feeding babies." Folks, that's very, very messed up.

Sex is the most Googled topic on the internet. It's everywhere at once and yet nobody talks about it. That's because so many of those folks who are looking at porn are ashamed of it, and therefore reticent to get into a deep discussion about it. If you're a human being, man or woman, married or single, you're already dealing with lust, porn and/or infidelity directly or indirectly. It's the water in which the popular culture swims. The very immediacy and proximity of it undermines our moral authority and is what keeps us from addressing the big pachyderm in the middle of the tea party.

And by the way, the fastest-growing demographic of pornography users today—is women. Something like a third of porn-addicted people are now female, as of this writing. For many decades, maybe since the dawn of time, it was a non-issue for women, or a silent issue, or maybe a repressed reality. But now, porn use by women is out in the open and is growing rapidly. The need for female mentors is acute.

Like many, at some point I got into the habit of looking at dirty pictures on the internet. I felt like a complete and utter hypocrite. I went to my wife Taeko and said, "Honey, I've been looking at naked women on the computer." She was shocked and concerned but she didn't back away in horror. She moved closer, physically and emotionally. Surprisingly, she said, "Show me." So I did. We logged on and I gave her an eye-opening tour.

I said, "I'm sorry. I won't do it anymore."

"Your apology is accepted," she said. We held each other for a long time.

I realized later that her not reacting with disgust or finger-wagging condemnation at all is unusual for a wife when they find out their mate has been indulging. A wife's revulsion and loathing, the door-slamming and sleeping on the sofa, are natural reactions for a wronged woman, but such things do nothing to heal the problem, and they tend to drive a man deeper into seclusion and comforting fantasies. Women (and men): how you react when you receive a confession like this is important. It can shorten or lengthen the distance to the penitent person's ability to solve their issue.

Whatever she felt, and she feels everything intensely, she squelched it because she wanted to be totally, unselfishly there for *me*. She was interested only in helping me, us, really, get through this. Sometime later when I realized how completely self-sacrificial and unconcerned for her own feelings she had been in the moment of my confession, I understood how enormous is her capacity to give love, and I was overcome with emotion. Everyone who knows Taeko, sees that she is unusual in her ability to connect and to give. There is love and then there is capital-T *True love*. I am fortunate to be a recipient of the latter.

By the way, that admission to her didn't mean my fight was over, but it was an excellent beginning because it cemented the alliance of Taeko and me in dealing with it. It was quite a ride for a few years after that, with good days and bad ones. Episodes of acting out were followed by self-loathing. I prayed about it, fasted occasionally. I experienced a struggle of great effort and personal resolve, endured a few long, dark nights of the soul. Sometimes it felt like I was trudging over plowed earth, or running in place.

What makes the fight difficult is that porn is not a metaphorical drug, but a literal one because of the chemicals it produces in your brain. The flood of dopamine rewires the brain into new "reward pathways." A tolerance to the pleasure chemicals builds up and so the brain needs more intense images—"stronger wine, madder music." At some point, the addiction can become so strong it becomes difficult, and then impossible, for a man to become aroused by an actual living woman. I'm not a trained counselor at all, but I'm a pretty good listener, and I have met people in their early 20s who have told me, "Porn has ruined my life."

Gradually the issue began to fade for me due to the factors I will explain. But for a long time, even after I had abandoned porn, I still live and swim in the popular culture and therefore always know the wolf is crouching just outside the door.

Here's what I have experienced that works in solving self-control issues and that help maintain one's sexual integrity:

1. **First, ask your gut, "How badly do I want victory?"** Then ask it two or three more times in case you're bullshitting yourself like usual. A great sage once said, "If you can't get mastery over your wiener, you should cut it off and barbecue it." One of those pyrrhic "victories," where winning is also losing, so I don't recommend it. But I do understand

the element of do-or-die resolve, even frustration, underlying the words. So how much do you want to win? That was my question to myself. In a very memorable prayer, where I felt God was actually there and was listening, I heard: *If you can't get past this you will never become SanViejo (Saint Old Guy). That venerable title you're searching for will never be more than a pretend thing, your email address. And wouldn't that suck?*

2. **Spiritual support and scripture.** Sacred texts are written by people who at one time have all been where you are now. Read them to learn what they learned. Pull God into the fray. I promise there really is a God out there, and for me, that includes a posse of all of history's saints as well as my thousands of ancestors and kindred folk in the spirit world. (I love you, my guardian whozits.) I have several spiritual teachers, foremost of whom are the True Parents, Reverend and Mrs. Sun Myung Moon. Then there is my community of friends and loved ones. Finally, serving as the voice, arms, eyes and lips of God in my life, is my wife, Taeko. Honey Nim. Maybe someday there will exist words that can describe the place she and I hold in each other's lives. For me, God is a team.

3. **Your articulated set of principles.** Be able to tell yourself in the mirror, in a couple of sentences, what kind of person you are and are not.

Here's a thought: tape your resolutions to your shaving mirror. For example: *Speak to women's eyes and not their chests.* Or: *Cut the flirtatious banter about "taking DICKtation" with Betty Lou from Accounting.* I haven't taped anything to my own mirror, but it occurs to me it would be a really good idea to remember to remove your reminders before having visitors over to your house. On second thought, skip this one. Just wear a hair shirt, put a pebble in your shoe and talk like a Puritan: "What we speaketh, Betty Lou, consigneth both our souls to the hellfires of eternal damnation." That will brighten up the break room.

Seriously, there are a lot of people reading this who are screaming at the pages, "Larry, geez Louise, get over it! Get a life! You're obsessing. It's not that big a deal!" First, don't tell someone who is obsessing not to obsess. It only makes us crazy. Second, men I speak with, who credit porn for their inability to have a deeply fulfilling, full-on relationship with a woman they dearly love, would disagree.

Therefore, articulate your principles aloud to yourself, at least. Also, think about your day in advance, in terms of various triggers and pitfalls that tend to put you back into your old patterns. It's like a guy trying to quit smoking who decides ahead of time to walk with a bottle of water during his break, and not to sit and drink coffee because it triggers a cigarette moment. Or someone trying to lose weight who knows they must never approach a Christmas party buffet without a strategy thought out in advance. (First, fill up on the raw veggies, because next serving dish will contain breaded, deep-fried, mushroom caps stuffed with bacon-wrapped, buttered lump crab and tarter sauce. Game over.)

Likewise, the highly charged sexual imagination already knows certain nominally safe news websites are laced with "click bait" enticers … *Fifteen Most Hilarious Celebrity Breast Implant Failures.* You know where that one's going. Ditto the highbrow documentary, "*Thong Bikinis of the Roman Senate.*"

These things are all foreseeable encounters but we tend to get blindsided by them for the same reasons we fail to drink enough water or get enough exercise. Mastering one's self requires constant vigilance and that's damned hard work, until the new habit is established.

4. **Allies.** You need fellow travelers, a mentor, or a group of similarly suffering buddies who also want to change their patterns. The porn habit is born in isolation, but it dies in community. So find some homies with whom to share the battle. Wives (and husbands), please be your mate's best ally. Your husband is not a scumbag. He's a guy adrift on a raft in a hypersexual culture that is completely devoid of restraint. Unpack the topic and talk about it. Men and women, research the many good, non-hysterical articles on the internet.

So those are four tools that have proven effective for me. Your mileage may vary. Basically it comes down to replacing old habits with new ones, and being mindful of the path you're on. As Abraham Lincoln said, "Just be careful when you're surfing the internet, folks. It's a jungle out there." I guess I should add, be sure to keep a well-oiled sense of humor with you at all times.

There is one more bit of affirmative action you can do. I find that time spent on any kind of unselfish activity that helps another person will improve one's overall spiritual health. The best kind of giving is the kind where you don't expect or want anything back in return. Approach everything with that attitude. Strengthen the component of service to others in your lifestyle. By the end of your life, you will notice that your destiny changed, and was greatly improved.

I had the privilege of enjoying a friendship with President George H. W. Bush that was decades-long, but only occasional in frequency. I was in his Houston office one day. A gentleman and traditionalist, he said, "You know, Reverend Moon is a good man, but why does he always have to talk about 'sex organs' in his speeches?"

"Well, Mr. President," I replied, "what is it that, throughout all of history, has been the ruin of marriages and families … kings—and presidents?" This was at the height of the tumult over President Bill Clinton's Oval Office affair with Monica Lewinski.

He thought quietly for a long moment, then nodded. "Good point."

In summary, all the tools I brought to bear on the self-control issue have bleached out some of the stains on my integrity into faint, residual watermarks of what they were. It gives me a palpable sense of freedom. I made it a priority and kept after it. There has also been an element of dumb luck, like the fact that I didn't die twenty years ago. I am so grateful I could get this far in my quest.

Maintaining God's presence in my daily life has been, and still is, a huge priority, and I'm better at that on some days than on others. But I've found that even God alone is not enough. Cultivating relationships with living people needs to be involved (friends and allies), and I know I would not be writing these words today if it had not been for my wife, her wisdom and selfless nature. And the future? I guess we'll find out. Life is a series of unmapped forks in the road and concealed monkey wrenches, but I'm feeling better about things at this point.

There is a lot more to tell you face-to-face in a coffee shop. This topic really is an ongoing discussion, a sharing of paths. There are some excellent trained mentors out there. I'm not one of them, but I find myself counseling people now and then (listening, really) who seek me out because I first wrote about this back in 2005. My brothers, and increasingly my sisters, who walk the path of gaining mastery over themselves know how tedious the slow and halting, stutter-step journey is. But even slow and halting is progress.

Bottom line: if you believe human life is eternal, and if that's a big deal to you, then you are fortunate because you will probably do everything you can to develop an honorable character while you are still alive on the earth. Will any of us succeed with all our character-related goals? Who knows? But if you keep plugging away, reacquiring the high road when you drift off it, and if you have a strong set of examined principles and a purpose that you reinforce daily with your prayers, mantras, the encouraging words of others and such, there will be improvement you can look back on one day and say, "Well I'll be danged. I somehow got through all this and came out the other end okay. Now ain't that a fine thing." That will be a joyous realization.

A HEART THAT IS ALSO A WOMB

As I stand on Permian Basin geology, amid an ocean of mesquite trees growing out of the sand, the wind comes and swirls around me, making whispering sounds like ancestral voices. Some of us know each other; some only know me in the way that all great-grandparents know the baby long before the baby is aware of them. A few are total strangers who happened to hear the spiritual phone ringing as they passed by, and intuiting a common base, dropped in on my meditation.

I'd like to thank my producer and director and a legion of toothless dirt-farmers and preachers for making me possible. I'd like to thank those terrific wardrobe and makeup folks, the caterers who kept our bellies full of plants and animals. I'd like to thank my eyelids for making sleep possible, and thank my sex organ for love's expression and procreation. Thanks also to Australopithecus, for showing us how to walk upright, and to the Tigris and Euphrates rivers and the Nile for being cradles of life and all. *Muchas gracias* to Mount Ararat for the parking spot. A special shout-out to the one who hung all those sparkly things up there. Stars, I guess.

I seem to have wandered. I ask the bodhisattva teacher, whose ideal is the heart of Zen, to help this unworthy sentient being stay true to my journey toward single-mindedness with a rap of his long bamboo pole. The sting sharpens my focus. How can my mind be so crammed full of that which I seek to empty it of?

There intrudes a random thought from out of left field: There is no value to a semicolon in writing; its use only demonstrates that you went to college. Well okay … it joins closely-related clauses and maybe this creates intimacy in a narrative, comforting the reader and …

… *what the hell? (sigh)*

Is there no hope for me? This time, I don't even have to ask. As if reading my mind, a loving sting from teacher's stick aligns my resolve once again.

I take action to empty my mind. In my thoughts, I tap my knife on the water glass. *Tink, tink, tink.* The sound cuts through the noisy chatter in the intellectual left brain hemisphere, bringing everyone to stillness. "Alright, listen up. I'm only gonna say this once. All you insincere utterances of rote prayer, all you pettyass regulators of rules of grammar, especially you correctly-used semicolons and sentences that must have verbs, all you dry and soulless statements get your smug, worthless butts out of my prayerful meditation right this christbirthing minute!"

I want my sacred time to be chewy. I want to be fully aware of my spiritual teeth sinking slowly downward into the Big Cosmic Oatmeal Cookie, feeling the resistance of each oatmeal flake, the brown sugar, the flour, the raisins, into the bare knuckles of God Herself until tears stream—mine and His … Hers … Theirs. Requiring alternating capital "H" gender pronouns, my God is an anthropomorphic being, a parent, a father-mother. No disinterested watchmaker creator, who wound it all up and walked away. No supernatural bar magnet, please, around whose physical laws the universe revolves. I want a God who howls with laughter, who knows what it means to break wind, and who cries bitterly over cruelty. As do we who are created in His image.

I make a slight motion with my finger, asking the bodhisattva for another cuff on the shoulder. Strike me, my teacher and beloved fellow traveler, that I may concentrate as I have never done before. I'd like to listen now for awhile, in the chewy, visceral silence.

He obliges me and tranquility arrives unseen. I hear no noise, not even the insects that had been chirping outside the window seconds before. I "hear" only the quiet that sits inside quiet. I am in a vacuum, and yet I can breathe. And I am warm. The floor and the walls billow softly inward. I am inside a heart that is also a womb.

Within this tranquil space, which is as large as the world, I see a raven take a single pebble from a field strewn with thousands of them, fly to an adjoining field, drop it and return for another. And then another, another, another. I watch and embrace patience, dedication unceasing.

I see a man and woman making a baby, a daughter, who grows before my eyes, blossoming beautifully, until she is grown and led away by the son of another family. This young new couple makes more babies, infusing into them abundant, limitless love, inexhaustible as the sun's rays. All around them there are wars and revolutions, exploitations and betrayals, political intrigues and one-upsmanship. There is bellicose speechifying and posturing with withering eye-contact—but all this is muted into the background as though the world were just waiting for them to die and turn to dust.

All the attention of existence is focused, not on politics, but only on people making and loving babies. I see the creation of generations and notice they are aligned along a glowing red, vertical spinal column, the bottom of which touches the newest newborn baby. The column runs through the mother and father, then through the grandparents, the great-grandparents, the great-greats and great-great-greats and on it goes, upward and out of sight and back into time, where the topmost end touches the origin of creation. Without any need for argument or convincing, the spinal column shows me that the parent-child connection is the only true axis of the universe.

I am an escaping prisoner of war running past the edge of a village in a foreign land. A child spots me on the path and screams in alarm. I have two options before me. I can quickly and noiselessly kill the child and get to the border, and freedom. Or I can spare this innocent life and be recaptured. I awake to knowing. I understand about terrible choices.

I am standing under a beautiful tree as it spreads its branches overhead. It is tall and stately, and the limbs reach out in a wide canopy starting a couple of feet above me. How perfect it is. How green and how cooling the shade. I stand underneath with a torch, reaching up to brush the leaves. The limbs recoil in silent pain and horror. How amusing. Again and again I touch the lower branches with fire. How fascinating to watch the leaves shrivel and burn, and I have no idea that this is my own Tree of Life, and that I callously cripple it with every pass of my torch. Finally, I shove the fire deep into the leaves, and the entire tree tries to arch upward in a desperate and futile attempt to avoid the flame. At that very same instant, my alarm clock rings loudly and I wake up screaming. I scream for a full minute as I understand the tragic consequences of what one's thoughts and actions can irreparably do to oneself.

All this happens inside the heartwomb. Good. I am just in time to be born. How easy birth is, this kind of birth, anyway. Maybe it only takes a second. My birth comes with no counting, no urgings to push. The "hands" that remove me from the womb are but a sound, no louder than a breeze, a voice soft, insistent. "I love you."

Leaving the heartwomb and out into the foyer of meditation once again, I want to offer some final thank yous, first to Nikola Tesla (history's most generous inventor) for saying, "The day science begins to study non-physical phenomena, it will make more progress in one decade than in all the previous centuries of its existence." A thank you as well to progress, along with whatever credit should also go to dumb luck, for the fact that I was born in a place and a century that allows me to turn on the water tap in my home anytime I want, and get a glass of clean, good-tasting water that won't kill me with dysentery. Furthermore, good night and sweet dreams, Louis Pasteur. Because of you I can enjoy fresh-squeezed orange juice in the far north in the dead of winter.

But with my awareness of these blessings, my personal Father and Mother God, you have handed my conscience a list of the names of every man, woman and child on the earth who does not have these things. In equal parts of my longing, I want to honor this list and I also want to tear up the paper, shred the pieces, and run away and deny it has anything to do with me.

I cannot be proud, nor rest, nor even lift my head before heaven. Another tap of the stick if you don't mind, Bodhi. A good one, this time. I need to go much, much, deeper. Where has the time gone? It's so late in my life, and I have only just begun.

ONE DAY IT WILL ALL MAKE SENSE

Silence deep as mountains on the moon
and the astonishment of loving you
are the separated twins that fill this room.
There aren't enough thoughtful reveries
on the planet to gather all the wool
of longing looks and sighs that fly
from the jars where they're kept
when the heart gets full.
Playful, silly thoughts of you and me
dance when you alight.
I am happy at last
and free to brush the hair from your
shoulders, neck, cling to you from
over your shoulder, gnaw
the lobe of your ear in a trance.

Ripening, falling, bursting at once,
strike rock in a shower of sparks;
your hand cradles my head,
makes my shadows surrender
as the sky grows dark and we drift.
Let the world blather on
like an overcaffeinated talk show host,
going faster and faster, and higher and higher
while we on the ground settled under our shroud
smaller and smaller, share what we are,
whispered half in silence, half aloud.

One day it will all make sense.
Every eye will open and suddenly know
that when black man and white woman
dance with abandon for all to sigh and see,
while in the room old people sway,
knees touching under the table,
that passion will have carried the day.
The goddess of faint-hearted love
will slink back just inside the door to stand
hoping someone will fill the awkward pause
and put a glass into her hand.

FRYING AN EGG ON THE COURTHOUSE STEPS

When I was a 19-year-old intern at the *Midland Reporter-Telegram* in the summer of '69 (twentieth century), our local boy, Steve Souter from Midland, Texas, piloting the "Texas Torpedo" made Soap Box Derby history by having the first lay-down design to win the national championship. As the summer intern, I covered the Derby, and Souter's victory was my first-ever front page lead story. Oh, and someone landed on the moon for the first time.

Also we were in the middle of a heat wave. In a "wet year," Midland gets only about 13 inches of rain, sometimes in just three or four doses, it always seemed. West Texas is hot even during an ordinary summer, but this was *el scorcho*, with a month of 100-plus temps and zero rain. People prayed for rain. It was so hot, even the scorpions got religion.

One day the newsroom was notified that some locally colorful personality was going to fry an egg on the county courthouse steps to demonstrate how hot it was. I want to say it was Wick Fowler (of 2-Alarm Chili fame) who had been managing editor of the *Midland Reporter-Telegram* in the 50s. Wick was theatrical enough, the Kinky Friedman of his day, and if he had been in town it probably would have been him. But I think he was freelancing as a war correspondent in Vietnam at the time. Memory dims; 1969 was forty-seven years ago and I've sacrificed a few brain cells along the way.

Seriously. Nobody wanted to cover this so-called "story," because it meant going out in the hottest part of the day. But not much was happening in Midland, news-wise. Nothing in fact, other than the roads melting. Our one photographer more or less assigned himself to go shoot it. Summer interns are expendable cannon fodder, so Joe the news editor sent me with him to get the caption information and the names spelled right. Besides, we all really wanted to know if the egg would fry.

At two in the afternoon the steps were likely hot enough to give an egg a run for its money without any assistance, but when we got there, a minion had a blowtorch going, focused on the step. KMID-TV Channel 2 News was there too. We all looked at one another, rolled our eyes and made a few disrespectful comments. But everyone stayed because, hey, we wanted to see it. I envisioned the page-one screamer, "Hot Enough to Fry an Egg," with a half-page photo. And my name on the first-ever bylined photo caption.

The torch was removed. Everyone was still laughing, including the aforementioned locally colorful figure as he came out, bent down, cracked the egg and put it on the designated spot. We got the photo and Channel 2 got film and sound of the egg popping and sizzling. The egg fried up and shriveled in about thirty seconds. I think they must have done a prior test run and found that the step, while quite hot, was not the same as a short-order cook's grill. The whole frying an egg on the sidewalk cliché may be an urban myth. Even so, the blowtorch was overkill.

Amusing and pithy quotes were given and we trooped back to the paper. As I wrote the caption for the photo, I told about the blowtorch to a senior reporter and asked if I should mention that. He said, "Why spoil everyone's fun?" The tiny newsroom had about six or eight desks all crammed together with a big, clunky typewriter on each one. All conversations were heard by everyone.

That's when the adult supervision kicked in. Managing editor LaDoyce Lambert looked up, smiled and shook his head. Joe the news editor said, "Gimme that." I handed him the paper with the caption on it. He set it on his desk and that was the last anybody saw of it.

In today's news environment we would call it "Blowtorch Gate," and hound the guy until he groveled and said, "mistakes were made." But as I get older, I increasingly find merit in what my fellow reporter said about letting slide the blowtorch part. Not that we could have entirely, because news ethics requires us to tell the whole story. That said, however, I have learned that not everything has to be of any consequence. Conversations on social media certainly teach us that.

They must have had a similar discussion at Channel 2 because they ran the film as a short feature that night on the late weather. It was too compelling not to. At the end, the weatherman mentioned another sizzling day coming tomorrow, adding, "and we won't even need to prime the courthouse steps with a blowtorch." It was the punch line on a very badly kept, inside joke.

The reason I still remember this little story after all these years is because of what it taught me about the value of occasional gentleness in the news. And fun. The nature of news is brutal, nasty stuff—relentless man-bites-dog and *gotcha*! One day the police scanner in the newsroom said something about a shooting. Our police reporter and I ran out and arrived at a mom and pop deli right after a woman had been shot dead by her boyfriend, who claimed she had put a voodoo curse on him. It was the top story all over town.

It was also the worst day of my summer internship, because later I replayed the whole thing in my head, asking myself, *Why the screaming crud do two print reporters need to drive at three times the speed limit to go watch some lady die?* The image of the woman groaning her last breath as they carried her past me has stayed with me. Clearly, I wasn't cut out for the crime beat. Somewhere along the way in the news business, it was decided "If it bleeds, it leads." I think that was early on, around the time Cain killed Abel.

That was a summer of many formative experiences for me… the moon landing; Vietnam (the war fought on our living room televisions); drive-in theaters; wisdom tooth surgery; love, of course, and pledges; the Charles Manson murders; the Mets; Woodstock and the awakening of my country to a mind-blowing counterculture that would come to be America's blessing/curse stamped on opposite sides of the same coin. In the summer of '69 it was still possible for fierce politics and utopian optimism to inhabit the same person. My idealism had three sheets to the wind all the time.

The events of that summer, including the egg on the courthouse steps, helped me learn there is often more than one reality to choose from. If you're married or have raised children, you've already learned that any number of authenticities can be simultaneously accurate.

On a cruelly hot summer day, most everyone in the news business in Midland, Texas—newspaper, radio, TV—in a rare, collective decision, chose to give the blowtorch a pass or a wink, opting to err as much as possible on the side of fun. We talked about it and laughed. Then we all got on with our lives. Eventually it even rained in Midland.

Still, there was a shared innocence in that dumb little fake feature news moment that has somehow been snuffed out of us and out of the cultural ambiance. Maybe it was Vietnam and the drugs that killed our purity, but either way, for the moment, it's deader than the Peppermint Twist. I wonder if such innocent quirkiness, like the old Midland County Courthouse itself, is gone forever.

THE HEARTBREAK OF LYCANTHROPY

Don't ask me for specifics. Out all night again, that much I know. A lot of running mostly, and rage. Exhilaration. And something about ... slashing. Pulling things apart. But what? Cautiously, I raise my hands from my side, into my field of vision. Okay ... fingernails are caked with dirt, but nothing more.

So far, so good, but please—why me?

As comedian Emo Philips said, there are some days when it hardly seems worth the effort to gnaw through the leather straps. It's obvious last night wasn't one of them. Not when it's that time of the month and the curse arrives on schedule. I can count on there being three nights of this before the unstoppable urge fades for another twenty-eight days. This is far worse than a very bad menses. And this is a blue moon month, full on the first day and the last. So it will be twice this month. Good Christ in heaven!

Why does everything look sideways? What's with ... oh yeah, I'm lying down ... the floor. Shoes gone. Pants gone. Did I feed? Did I mate? I drag myself up to go to the kitchen. No, wait, *this* is the kitchen. Try to clear my head, taking comfort in performing some small act that is undeniably human. I will make coffee. There's the pot, those are the filters, coffee's over there. I can do this.

That's when I look down at my tattered shirt, wrecked, and horribly stained with dried, rust-colored streaks. I begin to shake. I pray my guts out, and it's always the same panicked, pathetic prayer, uttered at the same time on mornings like this. In the kitchen with a coffee pot in one hand.

"Dear God, please let that be animal blood."

WHAT WOULD YOU REALLY LIKE TO DO?

Thank you, Elizabeth Gilbert's Muses

Alma Whittaker asks Ambrose Pike, "I would like to know what it is that you would really like to do?"

Pike replies, "Then I shall tell you, Miss Whittaker. I would like never to travel again. I would like to spend the rest of my days in a place so silent, and working at a pace so slow, that I would be able to hear myself living."

When I first encountered those words in Elizabeth Gilbert's amazing book, *The Signature of all Things*, I whooped and then I tossed the book to the foot of the bed where I lay. I sighed the deepest of all sighs, a sigh profound enough to break the hearts of young girls not yet born. It's like suddenly, from out of the blue, I had been given permission to feel the way I felt. Not that I *needed* permission, but still. Somebody understands!

I was not merely in agreement; I opened the gates to my soul's outer containment wall and let the Visigoths ride in. I whooped again with a resounding cry of acclamation. My shouted *Hallelujah!!* could be heard two gas stations away. I thought about what it might be like to actually do that, to quietly sit somewhere and spend six months working on a painting or a book of verse or the, by-god, Great America Novel.

In my callow youth I would never have agreed with Ambrose Pike's sentiment. I still had the globe to see and savor, I still needed to tread the jeweled crowns of the earth beneath my sandaled feet (like Conan the Barbarian). I had to find a woman to marry and sow her with my mighty seed. There were children to be procreated and raised, empires of chiseled stone to build, enemies to crush. And eventually I did all that. Sort of.

But now, having had adventures in sixty-something countries and having concluded I could find fulfillment living in nearly all of them, I realize that what will broaden my horizons is not to march off toward yet another horizon, and another and another—but to march into my "inner space." I don't need to experience another bleak, impoverished communist apartment block, or see another waterfall when there are still waterfalls in my mind that I have not fully digested. Likewise, I don't need to attend another tango show or tea ceremony. I don't need to hand out business cards to one third of a crowded reception, like marking with my spore, just to prove I was there.

What I need to do is get out and find and realize the SanViejo within me. I need to walk ten thousand steps a day, each one meaningful. And even though I secretly continue to refine and hone my plans for ultimate world domination, that doesn't mean I have to travel. Everything I want to do can be done at home, with my family. It took me a few decades to learn all this, but now I know it to my marrow.

That's why when Ambrose Pike, a fictional character, told me it's okay to not want to travel anymore, a joyous shout escaped my lips faster than squealing oiled piglets out of a rodeo chute. My exclamation bounced across my nightstand, off the walls of my bedroom. It fell back onto the book's pages and into the fibers of the paper and ink, infusing itself with the written body and soul of Ambrose Pike. From there, my unrestrained elation jumped out of the atoms of the ink, back up through Elizabeth Gilbert's computer, out the monitor, onto the keyboard, and from there running up her fingers and arms and into her brain, where it high-fived all the Muses dwelling there, gave each one a hug and a big, fat cigar and told them, "Thank you, Liz's Muses, and your Mr. Pike, for making it okay to love being right where I am."

Years from now, when I finally get old and die in my wife's arms, I hope it takes the undertaker a month to get the smile off my face.

Excuse my religion while it slips into something more comfortable

I was speaking with the minister of a very large Christian church in Houston. We were in his office discussing the enigmatic lightning rod personality that is Reverend Moon, who was still living and quite active. He asked me by whose authority was Reverend Moon ordained a minister? A legitimate question. I replied, "Jesus spoke to him on Easter morning in 1935 when he was fifteen, and gave him his mission. So I guess that was his ordination."

The minister's back stiffened. He glared, making fists in his pockets. "Jesus did not speak to Reverend Moon!"

"I see," I said. "I have to wonder how you could possibly know that." I spoke evenly and without a hint of disrespect. If it's audacious for me to believe that Jesus actually spoke to him, isn't it also audacious for someone living on this side of the veil to be confident about what Jesus does to fill his time on the other side? Does he putter in the garden? Write music? Continue to guide people's spiritual lives? I should have followed up with these questions because at least he knew what Jesus does not do: He does not speak to people.

"Well, God also spoke to him," I added helpfully.

Surely this would clinch it because God has gone on the public record many times. I mentioned as examples, Noah, Moses and John the Baptist, in whose honor this minister's church was named. It's well-documented phenomena, so surely it would be easy for him to accept that God can speak to people if he wants to. But alas…

"God doesn't do that anymore," he said, slamming the door on the conversation.

"Oh," I said, and thought, *Who gets to make all these rules?*

So I did exactly what you, gentle reader, would have done in such a situation. I wrote to the Federal Department of Things God Doesn't Do

Anymore (FDTGDDA), and they sent me their list:

1. God doesn't speak to people to reveal his will. He used to, occasionally, but that was then and this is now.

2. Prophets are old school and God doesn't send them to teach us things anymore.

3. God definitely doesn't start new religions. The religion slots are all filled because we already have all we need, thank you.

So now you know. Our tax dollars in action.

Jesus got into big trouble by declaring that while Moses said "An eye for an eye," Jesus said to turn the other cheek. This was startling new information and the learned elders were properly gobsmacked. The high priests told Jesus as well, "God doesn't speak to people anymore. He stopped doing that after speaking to me and my colleagues." It raises a huge question: How, then, does a living God communicate in real time, issue updates and make course corrections for us, His rowdy, errant children?

Thanks to the experience of Jesus and other prophets, we now know the answer. God delivers updates and reminders through new teachers with either new ideas, or some new expression of existing truth. Every word they utter makes them heretics to the existing way of doing things, and so the new prophet suffers mightily. Think of it as being like a high school where the seniors feel called by God to haze the incoming freshman, usually with death. The new top-dog religion, which has risen up to become large and in charge, develops amnesia concerning the abuses they themselves endured.

What's wrong with this picture?

Well, nothing in America, if you're comfy in Christ. If you're the pastor of a megachurch in upscale Northern Virginia, life is good. But what if you're God? How frustrating that must be. God has been kept in a straitjacket, hammered like sheet tin into man's image by first one linchpin religion, and then by its successors.

Funny hats and costumes

Religions pick up a lot of baggage in the course of a couple thousand years. The beginning is often looked back on as being the best part, something like this: A small group of people, we hold hands in a circle around the fire, getting revelations and one-on-one attention from our young, vibrant prophet. Everyone is brother this and sister that, first names only. We break bread together and share all we have. Then we grow a bit and set up folding chairs in someone's basement. We're still on first names, but with nametags in the larger meetings.

After a long period of fundraising, including checks from wealthy individuals who were told by God to help us out, we finally bolt down permanent chairs in our very own building. Tears of joy flow when we cut the ribbon and dedicate the sanctuary with holy salt. More people join so we get a bigger coffee maker. An inscrutable half-Asian bookkeeper is appointed. She opens a spreadsheet to track donations. We put in some stained glass. We acquire really cool rituals, the best of which are in foreign languages that only an elect few can understand. We establish a priesthood and over the course of decades and centuries the clerical leaders gradually acquire interesting costumes and funny hats. Now we are Reverend and Bishop, and such and such Your Eminence. We are big and comfortable.

Although childlike in our faith, we're not children, and God doesn't expect us to be. Religions come with doctrine, and doctrine requires interpretation and application and some type of orthodoxy enforcement. Keeping everything scriptural is serious business. We usually baptize in the river, but sprinkling on the forehead might be okay too, yes? No? Someone questions the use of musical instruments to accompany worship, citing correctly that our founding prophet never strummed a guitar or was never seen dancing. Although it was a very long time ago and it's hard to really know.

Theological questions are settled and the answers declared canon. Or there is a schism and the group divides and the schismatic members create their own canon. Each faction expresses sadness that the other faction is hellbound. The issues spoken of in the schism revolve around who gets to wear the tallest and funniest hat, while the unmentioned driving force is ego. The battleground is somewhere near the bookkeeper's office.

And so we divide and then divide again, like zygotes and gametes. We do it with rancor, separating bitterly into disparate enemy camps: Church of the Funny Hats vs. the Reformed Church of the Funny Hats.

Again, doctrine and scripture, or is it scripture and doctrine? We love God with all our heart, and we never tire of reminding one another that our own understanding of things is also God's. We fall into the deepest possible divide, a classic Sunni-Shia split and we willingly drown in a black pool of fetid theology clogged with doctrinal deal-breakers, worded such that there can never be resolution. You're either with us or against us, and therefore is it still a sin to kill those with incorrect beliefs? (Of course not, starting with the dung-eating infidels in the Reformed Church of the Funny Hats.)

On a good day religions make us better people, but people come with shortcomings and glitches. You have politics within a church. One's personal biases and agenda creep into their interpretation of God's will. If a religion wanders half a degree away from God's true north, it can end up far afield a millennium down the road. Swish goes the sword. Slam goes the dogma. Boom goes the canon.

The marriage of power politics and our aforementioned glitches have produced the cruelest episodes of bloodshed history has ever seen. Nobody does genocide like a religion.

Now for the hard part

Jews and Christians should be closer than brothers. They both hear God's voice from the same book. And Jesus was a Jew for christsake.

A little patience would help as well. Religion is a 600-year startup. Every one of them endures their "cult" phase—Christians, Mormons, Islam, all of them. They take seemingly forever to settle into a groove and, at best, religions are clunky work-arounds of God and man to help us deal with our awful separation from the Creator. We have to curl ourselves into a ball, focus our minds, scrunch our eyes and pray bullets of sweat in order to commune with God. Prayer results are hard to quantify. Revealed "truth" is open to debate. If humankind had never left its true nature by falling away from God (most religions have their own version of the Eden story), we should be able to see and speak with God as clearly as you and I sit and talk across the kitchen table. It's not natural that our own spiritual selves should be so hazy and indistinct to us.

Why do members of the top-dog religion in charge torture members of the church of the underdog? First of all, because the underdogs are *clearly wrong* and second, because they *can*. But not only because they can, but because they think they *must*. If you're in the One True Church, you may think it's your job to protect the world from heresy. The fact that the people chosen by God to receive and follow the Messiah sent by God Himself, are quite capable of killing that very same Messiah, shows that even the most special of elected people have a spotty record of hearing God's voice.

Don't point fingers at the Jews. All top-dog religions have this failing. It helps explain why, after all these millennia and after all this religion, we still don't have a very good world. Many would say things have gotten worse.

We should have learned to expect that God needs to shift gears now and then. He sometimes has to punt, approach us from another angle, re-explain things, send a new prophet who can speak the lingo. The coming of Abraham and then Moses were tweaks of the status quo, as was the coming of Jesus. Heavy flack was likewise encountered by Muhammad, Siddhartha Gautama Buddha, Bahá'u'lláh, Zoroaster, En no Ozuno, Confucius, Pythagoras, Adi Shankara, Basava, Hamza ibn-'Ali ibn-Ahmad, Joseph Smith, Ann Lee, Jakob Ammann, Ellen G. White. And many, many, many more. Precedents abound.

Since human nature shows no signs of improving, we should expect further tweaks from on high will be needed, and we should not get so bent out of shape when a new prophet emerges who may sound a teeny bit heretical. Oh, but you know we will. I'm not saying you have to drink the Kool-Aid offered by everyone who shows up applying for the job of New Prophet. It's just that being slower to act in opposition than we usually are, would be a big help. And stop disowning your children who bring home a stray messiah now and then. Talk to your children, love them, keep the door open. And pray for your own understanding.

I never thought I would say aloud that I am grateful to be a member of a persecuted faith, because the day-to-day of it is certainly no picnic. But I am. I used to send Godward this daily prayer:

Lord, if Jesus and Mohammad and Buddha are really in favor of a movement to get all the faiths working together in harmony (such as ours), why can't they have a word with their followers who are daily beating the crap out of us? Thanks, it's me again, Larry. Amen.

I doubt that the top people in the most influential religions are bored with their power and influence. One gets used to being in charge. Who doesn't enjoy attention and advantages? But we know what absolute power does absolutely, don't we?

Therefore, I no longer pray for God to fix the contest for me, to magically place my chosen faith in the winner's circle. While I have no wish to spend my entire life suffering for my choice in religion, I do see a certain value in this "walking a thorny path" stuff. It's a conundrum. There's no question that having your prophets martyred, the followers scattered and hunted down, being hounded by the IRS, or merely being spat upon while street preaching in Times Square does strengthen one's character and resolve. Persecution actually improves religions and even helps them grow. Go figure, but it's true. Personally, I have been fire-hardened into a man with a clear sense of who I am, and I can flip the middle finger (with a loving heart) at anybody who might benefit from that.

Being a member of a pariah faith also has great theatrical shock value. When I attend a wedding with friends I haven't seen in decades, I get to watch their jaws drop open, one-by-one, as I tell them, "… and that was in '74, when I had this profound epiphany experience with God. I gave away all my cocaine and joined Reverend Sun Myung Moon's Unification Church." An eerie silence settles over the room that is actually kind of soothing, like the final stages of hypothermia, where everything is peaceful and warm, and nothing hurts.

Occasionally someone will light up and respond, "Really?! Wow, what's it been like? What kind of person is Reverend Moon when you get him alone?" People this unafraid to avert their eyes, and who are that plugged into what's going around them, are quite rare, and I love it when I encounter them.

The burden of being the new top dog

What happens when my religion becomes a numbered item on the short list of top dogs? What will happen when my religion finally becomes comfortable and gets a seat at the table. Or yours does, and you obtain that coveted country club membership that signals your arrival?

One day, after this happens to us and we're running the show, my great-great-grandson will come to his father to utter the words he has long dreaded to hear: "Pa, God spoke to me last night."

His father tries not to show how startled he is. "We'd better sit down, Son."

With his eyes on high-beam, radiant skin and heaven's own smile, the boy tells his father, "I was praying at the Holy Ground, and God spoke. She said we need to start doing such and such. She also said it's okay to marry outside our faith as long as we don't drift away from God. And, by the way, she's really tired of our hats."

"Um … *she*?"

Persecuted faiths are truly blessed by God. I believe that. And with that blessing, one day many others will be attracted to their teaching as if the truth of it had been blatantly obvious all along. People will just stream in through the door. The way it is with Christianity today. This is what blessings are about.

Let me address all of you—you Unification Churchistas, you Latter Day Saints, you Baha'is, you Jews for Jesus, you Quakers, you Falun Gong, you Buddhists, you Ananda Marga, you Nation of Islam, and the rest. You know who you are.

What will you do when you finally become comfortable, when your phone calls start being returned? Are you already there now? Will your religious institution and the way you've always done things loom so large that it disallows God to reveal to you some new expression of his or her eternal self, perhaps from some little nobody in the back row of your congregation? When your ship comes in, and blessings arrive in such abundance that you are unable to even list them, and your leadership becomes calcified by the perks of privilege and the adoration of the flock, what will become of you? And importantly, what will become of those who had opposed and persecuted you?

Will you try your own hand at outdoing the excesses of the Inquisition? Will you burn at the stake, the Joans of Arc of your age? Or your era's Edward Wightman, the heretical English Anabaptist minister who insisted that Jesus was a man free of sin, but was not God himself?

Religious institutions, after they get comfortable, don't have a very good record of patience with the mavericks within their groups. And that's the shame of it, because these mavericks have included the various founders mentioned earlier, and scores more. Love them or hate them, it's your call, but whichever religion you adhere to, it's pretty certain the founder of it had to color outside the lines—and then redrew the lines to fit what was needed for a new age to be born.

They were human beings, with their own issues, but each one contributed pieces to the big puzzle. And then there is the Reverend Sun Myung Moon, now deceased, with whom I have the most familiarity. His appearance coincided with the digital Age of Information, and so there aren't many who have not encountered him in the press and formed an opinion about him. Nobody would disagree that he is a maverick amid the comfortable status quo. I don't know about you, but when my religion becomes top dog, the rest of you infidels are toast.

Just kidding. Will you take a pledge with me to tolerate new ideas within and outside your faith tradition?

I hereby promise to hear out the mavericks within my church, and those who walk in off the street or crawl out from under the Holy Rock. I will listen with a prayerful heart to try to hear God's voice in what they say. In either acceptance or rejection of their message, I will still love them.

Some religions envision the eventual end of the need for even religion itself. I am seriously, totally one with them. In some future time when enlightenment is universally attained—maybe there will come a kingdom of heaven on earth, when all the tears are dried, the lion lies down with the lamb, and in the words of the prophet Merle Haggard, "We'll all be drinkin' that free bubble-up, and eatin' that rainbow stew."

But for now, we're pretty much stuck with various churches and temples clogging the landscape. Ditto our rituals, our divisive costumes and funny hats. And I would say that for now, in advance of the coming heaven on earth, we actually sort of need religions and churches. What we really need, though, is for my religion and your religion to work together in harmony without each one trying to suck the other into our voracious maw.

There are things we can do to improve the situation. For example, let's park the hats at the door and use our institutions, dogmas and tax-exempt statuses to create more unity and less division between the faiths. And between the races, please. What is a racist? A racist is the poor dumb bastard who thinks humankind is made up of more than one race. Let us all slip into something more comfortable. Like respect for one another.

Postpartum

Along with our national deficit, I leave the problem of religious conflict to my great-great-grandson to solve. I chipped away at it but with few results. I'm sure he will come up with something perfect that will unify all humankind, even though his life will be made hell by jackbooted thugs in top-dog clerical garb. He will be martyred for it, of course, and I won't be able to meet and thank him in person. So let me do it now.

> *Thank you, Zebadiah Q. Moffitt (for surely that will be your name) for never being comfortable with the idea of men and women of God hating one another, and for sacrificing all to finally help everyone realize the universal loving reality of God. I'm sorry you were (fill in the method of execution) in the village square at dawn.*
>
> *Love, Gramps.*

JALAPEÑOS NEXT TO THE RUTABAGAS

I will plant jalapeños next to the rutabagas. Beanstalks will climb the tomato trellises. In the garden there will be a minister, an attender, an activist, and a brother or sister. The feeling of siblinghood will permeate the air of heaven and earth, the way smoke infuses itself into the clothes of people around a campfire.

Go ahead and put the Thai Kang Kob Pumpkin in with the Pacific Purple Asparagus, and both among the super elongated mutant grapes with the cotton candy taste. No reason the ingredients for Jicama Pineapple and Black Bean salad can't grow in the same row *before* they arrive at the table together, with Andean Oca and Kaffir Lime to squeeze on them.

Ujikitsu Citrus is already an orange and lemon half-breed. The separately podded peas of the Camachile-Korkalikka are a diabetic's dream, so helpful to subdue the rampaging sugars of the Cherimoya and Blue-Berried Honeysuckle.

Egyptian Walking Onion stands astride the garden like a colossus.

It's time for some frank talk. "So tell me," I ask them. "Which one of you is certain you're better than the others? Which of you gets to lord it over the rest? Who's on top and who's oppressed? Which one gets to *enjoy* being the world's cheap labor market for the time being? Who brought the beer and chips?"

They act like such ideas had never crossed their minds. I don't believe their silence because everyone I know wants to rule the world. But these guys, nobody's talking. They just sit there like vegetables.

Different circumstances, different feelings, different looks and smells. They ripen at different speeds. But there are no ideologies among them, nor ideals to bandy about. I see no map lines drawn in the dirt to mark their borders. No trash talk or arrogance. Not one of them says to another, "Go compost yourself!"

And wondrously, they seem to have accomplished all this without the guidance of missionaries.

NEVER LET SCHOOL STAND IN THE WAY OF GETTING AN EDUCATION

Ask and you shall request, receive and you shall have

This is an interesting theory, and there may even be something to it. Generally speaking, and except for the exceptions.

But first, some background. I did my master's thesis on cross-cultural communication while hitchhiking through Mexico, Central and South America. It was an audacious undertaking that began with a Broadway-quality song-and-dance sales pitch to the grad school department head and my fellowship supervisor at the University of Texas at Austin.

My travels produced, now that I reflect on it, a rather lame excuse for a thesis that still makes me cringe to think about. But what a glorious spasm of scholarship it was. This was the 1970s, a brief window in time when *touchy-feely* worked in academia. Fueled by intuition and a wisdom-seeker's vague and dippy guidance system, I ping-ponged, not only between cities and countries, but between premises, propositions and topic ideas. My thesis changed on a daily basis as I worked out of my backpack. I was on the road and that was all that mattered.

That was an era that paid homage to the esoteric personal trip. I felt like I had the world at my command, even though my thoughts were so diverse and random, I could have been "eclecticuted."

Each day at dawn, I set my determination, announced it into the oncoming breeze, then rolled up my tent and tattered map and stepped into the sunshine to see what would become of me.

For example, one morning I sent a thought to the invisible fixer-uppers:

Hi, it's me again, the seeker. Today I want to meet someone who will make me forget all about my inability to find love that doesn't turn to ashes. I would like understanding, please.

Always good to say please when making an ethereal request. Also, regarding "love," I didn't necessarily mean romantic love (but didn't rule it out), but rather love that is superior, whole, un-mundane, exquisite and perfect. The kind of love that, no matter how special a person was, he would feel unworthy in its presence. A bit demanding of the ol' Cosmos, I know, but at the dawning of the Age of Aquarius, such requests were pretty much routine among certain people of my generation. And we got fairly dependable results, as long as one was open to broad interpretations of the outcomes.

That afternoon, on a promenade in downtown La Paz, Bolivia, I saw a man painting beautiful pictures on plates, holding brushes between his toes. One of his brushes had only one bristle, which he used for painting the eyes of infinitesimally tiny figures. *The painter had no arms.*

He worked patiently, asking no one's assistance, and with evident joy. Clasping the small plate between two toes he painted, holding brushes in his other toes and mouth. He opened jars with his toes, gripping the bottles with the other set of toes. His paintings were gorgeous. I was instantly judged in the presence of someone who had smashed a hole in the fabric of what's possible, and was weaving beauty and love out of thin air, held together with the spit and bailing wire of his own spiritual grit. I had encountered exactly the love I had requested to find, and it was perfect.

A family adopted me for a day. I met them at Monte Albán, amid the ruins of the pre-Hispanic Zapotec empire near Ozxaca, Mexico. They took me to mass at the cathedral, and then to a late (for me) dinner. Afterward, with mom and the kids walking behind on a dark trail, the father gave me a tour of the nighttime sky, explaining every visible star and constellation in detail. They took me to their home to sleep, fed me breakfast the next morning, and sent me off with fruit and corn cakes wrapped up in paper and tied up in a cloth.

Every day was like that during that magical summer. It seemed like any type of person I wanted to meet, and everything I needed to learn, was placed right under my nose with a neon arrow pointing at it. Nobody (including me) ever has the continual good fortune I experienced for three months. I wondered aloud, sitting on a hill above Lake Titicaca, "Somebody out there is taking care of me. So who are you?" I missed going into Chile by one day in September, during the 1973 revolution when my fellow hippie backpackers were being rounded up and detained. Quite a few people in Chile simply disappeared during that time, courtesy of their own government.

Over the course of that summer I began to see that the barrier to happiness is not that real love is incapable of lasting a lifetime. The problem was the utter vastness of my ignorance of the composition of love. My immaturity and hormones had confined love to a small corner of my already tiny, insular universe. I had set out on an exercise in cavalier scholarship, not looking for life's Big Hairy Answers, but I was changed in many small ways for the better by the events of the summer of '73.

The molecules of existence really do try to help us and teach us. I have found this to be true even when I have been ardently seeking, but with barely a clue as to what for. For *understanding*? How does a random universe process such a request? It doesn't; it can't. Ask a person, "Please teach me stuff" and that person would have to know you even more intimately than you know yourself to avoid teaching you things that are tangential scattershots to your central needs. You will learn how to crochet potholders and sauté slime creatures in cream sauce, but you won't learn the essentials you need.

But when I sought for, asked for, prayed for *understanding*, with little elaboration on my part, I was led into profound experiences that were not always what I wanted, but were exactly what I needed. Every time. I was guided by an intimate presence that knows the molecules of the past, present and future me.

What Larry Moffitt Learned in the Year 1973: I am not alone.

My graduate thesis, written when I got back to Austin, reflected this theme. I graduated with an MA in Communication. Today I feel an energy similar to what I felt at the time of my grad-student odyssey. Forty years have passed and I feel the mojo has somehow returned. It's the same illogical optimism riding in on a thickening of the air.

It's more than "Ask and you shall receive." It's "Hold out your hand and catch the stars that will fall into it."

Mortal Coil I:
It's odd we rarely talk about the afterlife

We spend more time shopping for lip gloss than thinking about the eternity that comes after physical life

L et's do the math. You were born. Ninety-nine-point-some-high-number of you will live between zero minutes and 110 years before you finally go ka-BLOOEY. Game over. You will lay down your burden, bite the big one, kick the oxygen habit, get traded to the Angels, etc. And then what? Two choices: there will either be something waiting for you after this life, where you will have consciousness and further existence

Or ...

There will be nothing over there. There might not even be an "over there" over there. Nothing. No consciousness. Not even white noise. You will become part of the anonymous electron stream of the big creator bar magnet.

Or perhaps something lies between those two extremes, a purgatory of sitting on hot rocks while your beloved on earth offer intercessory prayers on your behalf to get you through the pearly gates. Personally, I think of purgatory as a tedious existence, like an afternoon spent accompanying someone who is shopping for lip gloss.

"Do you think this is too red? Which is better, this red or that red? What about this color: Drama Girl Doorslam? Do you think this makes my lips look fat?" An afternoon of this is the closest I can come to imagining a hellish twilight that knows neither life nor death.

Whatever it may be that comes along next, you know that you have approximately 80 years of adventures (if things go well) and then you're outta here. Life happens to everyone, although your mileage may vary. And sooner or later everyone one of us will croak.

Then there comes a long, long, long, long, long, long time of—what?

An outstanding question, because many people will proclaim with absolute dogmatic certainty some assured post-death scenario, while having very little hard evidence. If they're a king with an army that has some free time, they might even mobilize the troops and go kill the king next door who has a different certainty about what happens after death—and likewise zero actual proof. Ironically, the king who gets killed will have the satisfaction of finding out first what actually does happen.

If it's oblivion, then so be it.

However, the long record of human culture going back at least as far as the Neanderthals indicates some awareness of the spiritual world. The body of literature of near-death experiences shows a consistent narrative that crosses all nationalities, races and cultures. The global consensus throughout human history favors there being something over there besides oblivion, and by a huge margin.

Almost everyone, including me, assumes or claims to "know" there is an afterlife for every human soul. My question, then, is why don't we talk about that more than we do?

It's because we don't know what comes next and we are nagged by doubts about our readiness for the next phase of existence. People say, "Sure I will die of course, someday. Just not right away." We always add that qualifier, "but not now." The thing is, few people die someday. Most of us die suddenly, unexpectedly, and too soon—and with a full schedule of plans on our plates. You are hit by a truck on your way to propose marriage. Or you're in a chainsaw horror movie, in the prime of youth, but you have just uttered the words, "What's that noise? I'll go downstairs in my underwear to check." Some of us die on schedule: we have a date with the hangman at dawn. But for most death is a big, shocking surprise.

The vague someday we use as an excuse to avoid facing reality, suddenly becomes the only reality we have. It goes like this: "I'm not gonna die ... I'm not gonna die ... I'm not—click—okay, I'm dead."

We know it's coming for all of us eventually, but we studiously avoid talking about it. So don't expect to see the Grim Reaper honored on a postage stamp.

Until now.

Of course it's a "Forever" stamp. How could it not be?

The process of crossing the River Styx, buying the farm, passing your best-if-used-by date, going the way of all flesh, and so on, is something we drown in euphemisms when we aren't showering it with aversion. There are way more Tupperware parties than there are conferences about the existence that follows this one.

And yet, the idea of there being an afterlife began with earliest man. Some caveman, but most likely a cavewoman, noticed that people sometimes fall over and stop breathing, which begged the unavoidable question, "Where did Leroy go?"

There is indication that Neanderthals had occasionally practiced burial of the dead, based on arms folded in positions that indicate meaning, and some funerary artifacts. But that was 50,000 years ago. There is much more available evidence for the Cro-Magnon people, a mere 28,000 years ago, having some notion of an afterlife. Their elaborate interments with tools, ivory tusks, small carvings and art, offer indisputable evidence of spiritual awareness and religious experience.

At some point in our discussions, someone will generally raise the timely God-or-no-God question that everyone loves so much. I think most of us presume it's a binary either/or proposition. God either exists or not.

The odds and common sense favor an intelligent and benevolent creator. I'm just saying, the what-happens-next questions are excellent topics to mull over and discuss with others while you're still alive, if you get my drift. If the earthly life really is preparation for the eternity that follows, then there might be things you can do now before you find yourself taking a dirt nap, living in a pine condo, picking turnips with a step ladder, etc. Like, for example, don't be a dirty, rotten scoundrel.

We are alive a paltry hundred years at best, give or take. But Moses who lived a full life 4,000 years ago, is still dead. I assume he's doing something useful to advance God's Providence wherever he is. So c'mon, people. What's it like there? Do they have mountains and rivers in the spirit world? Are there cities? Can you own a house with a lake view? Do people walk around; do they fly? Do they have hobbies and pets? Do they get involved in earthly politics? Is there a heaven and a hell? And the big question everyone wonders about, but few ever voice: can we still have sex?

Aren't you curious, especially about that last one? Of course you are. So how can you spend more time shopping for lip gloss than you spend in serious inquiry or prayer about the life after? There are spiritual mediums who receive glimmers of what's what over there. Consult with half a dozen of them and compute the average. Over time you'll begin to triangulate on the spirit world and get a sense of the look and feel of that aspect of life.

I could avoid the whole topic altogether if I were certain there was no God and no afterlife, but I don't have enough faith to be an atheist. An atheist is not some fence-sitting agnostic; an atheist knows with unshakable, absolute certainty that nothing comes next. That takes incredible faith.

We segue from life to the afterlife. Question: Is it the Afterlife or simply Your Life Volume 2? Or, more simply, is the fundamental change between the physical and spiritual so minor that it remains just Life? With no further clarification needed.

Mortal Coil II: Atheist guys and spiritual guys

An atheist friend says the existence of a spiritual realm is horse pucky. And he may be right, at least in that be-careful-what-you-wish-for kind of way. My friend is both an atheist and a scientist, the poor bastard, and when he insists there is no God, he may be creating his own self-imposed reality. I haven't been on the other side of the veil, but it might be the case that if you insist there is nothing there, then, for you, there is *nothing*.

For most, the physical realm and the spiritual realm exist completely apart from one another. Over a beer they might acknowledge that the two worlds can overlap in some ways, like people seeing ghosts, but not normally. And of course for some, there exists only the physical. The spiritual realm suffers the enormous disadvantage of not being visible or quantifiable in measuring-cup terms, even to the most devoutly religious. Unless you're a mystic, in which case, unless you are a very, very capable one, chances are 50-50 you're also insane.

So for most of us, nobody can know what's over there. You need to have determination just to believe it exists in the first place. It requires telepathic communication (which is what prayer is actually), and that most illogical of all human concepts—faith. Faith is *knowing* things you can't possibly know.

It's possible for the spiritual part of one's mind to harbor an unseen metaphysical state, but not everyone is in touch with that aspect of himself or herself. I'm saying all this to ask you to cut some slack for our atheist brothers and sisters. I am a believer, even a "knower" if it comes to that, but those of us rooting for the spiritual team are on shaky ground, in the eyes of those who call themselves rational. That's why we can't nominate God for president or even get a Christmas manger scene going in the park.

It is easy to imagine the physical world as a self-contained sphere. Everything inside it responds physically. You tap on it and it makes noise. It sizzles when you fry it. If it looks like a duck, walks like a duck and quacks like a duck—it's a duck. A person can be born, raised, educated, get the coveted corner office, have scads of friends and find love and happiness completely within this realm, with no immediately perceivable need to even think about a supreme being.

How did our concepts of the physical and spiritual parts of life get so separated in our thinking? Who did it, godless liberals? Well, yes of course, but really and truly it happened long before God even created godless liberals. The separation is unfortunate. Every spiritual person alive is painfully aware of the barriers that exist between humans and God. Most faiths have an understanding that originally, God was easily perceived by the first created beings in an idyllic Eden-like setting. Howevever there was some kind of disobedience or betrayal way back at the beginning. As a result, our spiritual senses shut down, we can't hear God anymore, and now all we can see around us is physical stuff.

But there is considerable circumstantial evidence for the existence of God: (1) an extremely complex, consistent and orderly universe, (2) tied for second place—nurses, school teachers and adoptive parents (3) tied for third—puppies, autumn foliage and fresh, hot blueberry muffins with butter. And seriously, way more than that.

Take Earth, for example. If the Earth were only a little bit smaller, its gravity would not be able to hold an atmosphere. If it were only two or three percent closer to, or farther from, the sun, we would freeze or burn up. As Earth speeds around the sun at 67,000 miles per hour, it rotates at a speed that evenly heats and cools the surface each day. The moon is the precisely the right size and distance from the Earth to create tides that move the oceans enough to prevent the water from stagnation, but not so much that the oceans inundate everything.

If the Earth were any closer to the center of the galaxy than presently, the clusters of neighboring stars would make it impossible to see into the farthest reaches of deep space. Our planet's location is ideally suited for exploration.

The characteristics of water, including its freezing and boiling points, surface tension and chemical neutrality are ideally suited to support life. Two-thirds of the earth is covered with water and two-thirds of the human body is made of water. The human brain, the eye, our opposable thumbs, the ability of the human voice to mimic every other animal and bird on earth, are all too perfectly constructed for any of this to be unplanned.

The evidence piles up and up and up. Scientists wax poetically about the uniformity of physical laws throughout the universe. Many insist that the universe is the result of, not just intelligent design, but love. Someone who cared an awful lot about the outcome, including the health and happiness of you and me, was driven by extreme compassion, to dive into, and ponder, every infinitesimal detail to manifest such incredible perfection in the creation. There is nothing random about it.

Now think of the spiritual world as its own sphere. In it are God, heaven with angels, and hell with boogeymen. You can also include the spirits of the dearly departed.

The advantage held by spiritually-oriented people is that they also acknowledge the existence of the physical world because they live in it every day. For them, the physical and spiritual worlds are two spheres that overlap (either a little or a lot, and either sometimes or continually), and people are both physical and spiritual beings at the same time. For such people, there is little or no separation between the physical and spiritual realms, and many have no problem reconciling the compatibility of religion and science.

It seems logical to me that spiritual people, who acknowledge both realms, must have the most resources available to them and the widest range of options. In my life I have seen, felt, touched and otherwise tasted the spiritual. I know that place; I know those guys. We interact all the time. My intuition tells me that my life on Earth, no matter how brutal it is to my sensibilities, is preparation for that spiritual world. I know that realm to be exquisitely beautiful. It is also exists eternally. Most important, it is real.

On the other hand, my hidebound friends say they are the ones who have the advantage because they are not hampered by the sky-pie delusions of spiritual folks. Seen on the internet: "Being an atheist is kind of like being the only sober person in the car, but nobody will let you drive." Heathens have always had the best one-liners. I would offer this correction: Being an atheist is kind of like being the only *blind* person in the car but nobody will let you drive.

Debate utterly fails with people on both sides of the God-or-no-God question. However, what each team can do for the other is apply love. At least do that much. I will try to love those who deny what they can't see, touch or taste, and have no faith in. And they will attempt to love me in my naïveté, my dewy-eyed perkiness as I seek support in my spiritual superstitions like Tiny Tim leaning on his Christmas crutch.

Everyone has a lifetime lasting between zero seconds and a hundred years, give or take. That's how much time each person has to come to their own freely arrived at decision as to where they stand on existence's big-ticket item. To go *poof* into oblivion, or not to go *poof* when it's all over, that is the question.

Personally, I think you will get pretty much whichever your consciousness and soul demand. You will judge yourself and choose your reality. The comedian Rodney Dangerfield (who is currently dead) said, "I had a friend who was an atheist. He died and I went to his funeral. There he was, all dressed up and no place to go."

MORTAL COIL III:
WHERE SURVIVAL OF THE FITTEST FAILS

Is living for the sake of others a good philosophy, since there is no apparent evolutionary advantage for altruism?

I have a fondness for certain spiders in the Amazon rainforest. The ones that are so big and fast, they make their living eating birds. I like that they set the bar high and challenge themselves. Darwin didn't study them, but he would have agreed. They eat birds, find mates, make baby spiders and die—the more fleet and cunning among them, living longer to make more better, badder spiders. It's not give and take. It's just take. Survival.

Nature is pretty dependable in this way. From the top of the food chain to the bottom, everyone is pretty much onboard with the program: the biggest, fastest and fittest survive. But the weak and slow also serve a purpose. They become lunch. The only creatures not completely in sync with this are humans, whose voracious appetites are mitigated by other factors such as conscience and religious teachings. People have been instructed to "turn the other cheek" and believe "It's better to give than to receive." Not every person operates this way, but enough do, so that a wolverine observing our species would roll its eyes and shake its head in bewilderment at the fact that humans don't just go whole hog on the dog-eat-dog thing. Every culture of humanity has some version of the Golden Rule that admonishes one to treat others the same way you would like to be treated. Jesus even goes so far as to say there is no greater love than to lay down your life for another person.

But again, try to explain this worldview to the next pack of hungry wolves surrounding you, closing in step-by-step, in the snowdrifts of a deep Carpathian Mountain forest. For that matter, try explaining it to John D. Rockefeller or John Jacob Astor during their ascents to legendary robber baron status. The fact is, John D. would tell you, as he chomped his cigar, that if tigers turned the other cheek, there would soon be no tigers.

There is no easily apparent evolutionary advantage for altruism or self-sacrifice. There is no survival-based reason to put a nickel in a blind man's cup. If you take a bullet to protect the President, you'll get a high school named after you, but you will not survive to pass on your genes.

There is no reason, based on continuance of the human species, for a starving prisoner to divide his handful of rice and give half to a fellow inmate. There is no reason for a missionary to work in a leper colony. There is no reason to volunteer your time to work for free in a soup kitchen, feeding the homeless. "Oh but I'll die and go to heaven," you say. Perhaps so, but that's not a survival reason. There are, in fact, many reasons to avoid doing these things. Ask any rainforest spider.

To help us bridge the gap between the spider and ourselves, let us look to the Austrian neurologist and psychologist Dr. Viktor Frankl, who survived the predatory environment of Auschwitz concentration camp in Nazi Germany. Under the most brutal conditions of soul-crushing dehumanization, he discovered this three-part premise for survival: 1) We are born to love and be loved; 2) the highest act of love is service to another less fortunate; 3) the only true freedom we possess is our choice of response to any given situation. What Frankl speaks of are aspects of existence that imbue life with meaning, no matter what the conditions, and that therefore even suffering has meaning. His famous quote: "What is to give light must endure burning."

Life is full of stories to demonstrate that humans revolve around an imperative of love that can function equal to, or stronger than, the need to survive. To be fair, we need to acknowledge that animals are also capable of sacrificial love. Penguin fathers stand around all winter straddling an egg to keep it warm for hatching, and salmon swim upstream to lay their eggs before dropping dead from exhaustion. One can argue that such devotion on the part of animals exists only to ensure continuation of the species. But who can really know what goes on in the mind of a rabbit leading a coyote away from its den to protect its young?

Sacrificial love may help your children survive, but it is not strictly necessary for continuation of the human species. For example, more human beings would be created through rampant pillaging and rape. Bouncing children on your lap, cuddling, remembering birthdays, love poems and sharing the last donut are nice and they promote harmony and a sense of well-being. But they are not as conducive to one's own prosperity as buying low and selling high, or grabbing a company by manipulating the board of directors through backroom politics.

According to Jewish and Christian tradition, the very first human beings were in communication with a supreme intelligence who told them to NOT do something "survivalish" in order to maintain the unblemished parent-child relationship between the creator and the created. Prevailing tradition says that *something* was a commandment to not eat a piece of fruit, but the survival imperative would command exactly the opposite. Do eat fruit. Eat lots of fruit, then make some into jams and jellies, and dry and preserve the rest for later. The survival imperative would even instruct Eve to kill, cook and eat the talking snake.

And seriously, fruit? The Book of Genesis couple eats fruit and immediately covers up their sexual naughty bits. Who are we fooling? God tells a couple not to do something that has an element of temptation to it. They do it anyway and immediately they both cover their sexual parts. It's not hard to figure out that the commandment from God had something to do with the proper circumstances for sex. Many assume they had sex before they were sufficiently mature to deal with it. By the way, being emotionally developed enough to handle the complex territory of sexual relations is another huge differentiation between humans and other animals. All this is a lovely can of worms for another essay.

We intuit that the immediately obvious reason for the difference between human beings' altruistic nature and animals operating on instinctual autopilot has to do with a special consciousness on the part of humanity. Along with our tools, language and fire-building skills, our consciousness and reasoning ability, including altruism, have put us at the top of the food chain and will keep us there until we wipe ourselves out with super gonorrhea.

Reverend Sun Myung Moon spent some time in prison and, like Dr. Frankl, found survival by creating meaning amid the most brutal of circumstances. In Reverend Moon's case, in a North Korean prison camp where death by cold and starvation was the standard fate of prisoners, he distributed to other inmates the warm clothing and precious bags of rice powder he received from his family. He was compelled to care for those around him, not making his own survival a priority. And thus he survived.

Again you have to ask why a person would behave in such a counter-intuitive way if he wants to preserve his life. Sooner or later, discussion of the self-sacrificing love in human consciousness necessarily moves the conversation Godward. Not only that, but it moves some of us into the awkwardness of discussing God's nature and personality. If humankind is created in the image of God, as we are told, then we should look for clues about ourselves and God in both the hard sciences and the humanities.

Reverend Moon has some startling views on the nature of God and man, and he refers to the Creator as having "no choice" but to instill into human consciousness some kind of unselfish quality, "the principle of living for others," he calls it. If there were no such thing as an impulse for unselfish love in people, every person would be either a conqueror or conquered. Predator or prey. There would be nothing in us to mitigate our defensive urges, and therefore, there could never be peace, nor ever a chance for deep happiness to exist on Earth. Even with the existence of human altruism, peace is in very short supply.

Reverend Moon, offered three reasons for God instilling in human nature, the imperative of living for others. The Creator's motivation is related to the understanding that humans have a fundamentally different consciousness than animals. Reason one is that, in a civilized culture, when someone does something for you, he says there is an innate sense of gratitude that manifests as a desire to return what is owed, plus a little extra if your circumstances allow it. For example, your car won't start and your next door neighbor, seeing you lift the hood and scratching your head, brings his car and jumper cables to where you are. It takes him all of ten minutes. In gratitude, your wife bakes him a pecan pie at Christmas, and when your garden comes in, you take him some tomatoes and cucumbers and corn. Such behavior is a subset of our natural desire to reach across the divides that exist between all of us, and it is an inclination that is part of our inborn software.

Of what value is this inclination? We naturally love our own families, but this quality of reaching out to strengthen bonds by going the extra mile helps make it possible for us to build extended families among people who were formerly strangers. If you take the social risk of organizing a block party for the "strangers" who live up and down your street, you're creating an extended family. You've created a group of people who will watch each other's backs—who will keep an eye on each other's houses when they're on vacation, or who will mobilize to petition city hall to put a stop sign on the corner.

This quality in us, of reaching out to the other, eases the process of diplomacy between nations, races and faiths. Humans are the only animals that confront racism within our species.

Reason two for God having no choice but to establish the principle of living for the sake of others is that human societies exist in ordered hierarchies. You have a king and peasants in society, and a hierarchy of eldest to youngest within families. If the youngest child in a family is the one who takes care of others more than anyone else, that person will naturally rise to a leadership position over his or her brothers and sisters. That person will be made the leader by the others. Whoever lives for the sake of others, becomes the central person, and in doing so, helps create a united, peaceful environment—an unselfish trait with results that actually do mitigate in favor of survival. And happiness.

Reason three is that we were hardwired by our creator from the beginning, to respond to love. But more than love originating from above, we respond to love originating from below. A parent can be moved to make a decision by the sincere request of a two-year-old. In that sense, the one below is more precious than the one above. This is not what we might usually think, but it makes sense if you consider that God created humankind because God wanted—even needed—children with whom he could exchange love. Man's awful history of brutality and cruelty has been painful for us, and I think we have no idea how much more excruciating our existence has been for God.

God, being parental in nature, invested everything in order to create us. And because we were created in that kind of image, it is we who become sparkplugs of love in that relationship by inspiring God with the creative artistry of our love for one another, and by the care and protection we give to the animals and plants put into the world by a loving Father and Mother God.

But then again, it is possible for a person to have a fine life of wealth and health even if they ignore the principle of living for the sake of others.

In this world, you can lie, cheat and steal, and even take pride in your superiority and craftiness. Certain important textures will be missing, but an abundance of wine, women and song can mask a great deal for a long time. Maybe even the duration of your entire physical life. But then you die. Then what? If the importance of living for the sake of others isn't all that apparent in this physical earthly life, it could be a very big deal when you arrive in the life after this one, if the combined faith traditions of the world have gotten it even partly right.

Religious traditions inform us that developing one's capacity to love completely and unselfishly is, if not important on Earth, essential for existence in the spiritual world. This follows the pattern of your life in the womb where you grew legs even though there was no place to walk. It's accurate to say you are born twice in your existence—once onto the earthly plane, and again onto the spiritual plane when you depart your earthly life.

The principle of living for the sake of others may be the most important survival trait you need to embody before you die.

I was happy to find out that John D. Rockefeller and John Jacob Astor, as well as Andrew Carnegie and many other ruthless robber barons, spent the last years of their lives donating their wealth to the arts and other causes that benefit others. Tears welled up as I imagined that near the end, they came to understand the survival imperative of doing for others. My friend, Pam, squashed that notion. "Lars, they didn't realize a damn thing. They got old and guilty and were influenced by women who cared about their own children and the future."

Yikes! Note to self: Be sure to die *after* Pam so she doesn't show up at my funeral. And speak.

Blue is the Color of Consolation

He was drawn to the ocean with the soul of a poet and the heart of a lover.

I sat on a boat with Sun Myung Moon a few times, fishing at the tuna grounds, a certain spot off the coast of Gloucester, Massachusetts, designated by depth, water temperature and topography of the bottom.

He usually went out around dawn, fished all day and boated home in the dark. As the sun tracked across the summer sky, he sat on the boat's bridge with his fishing pole in hand. Occasionally, he would change his bait, or move the boat to another spot. When a big tuna was hooked, there would be a crazy scramble to raise the anchor, haul in all the lines and maneuver the boat to keep the propeller from severing the line.

Sometimes, I was on a different boat nearby. More often, I was on the water the days when Reverend Moon was elsewhere, and I was a guest of the people who fished every day. Being "occasional" like that meant I never fully got past seasickness. I never acquired my sea legs, and could never assume I would last an entire day without "blowing chunks."

My best day on the water was the time the ocean was smooth as a sheet of glass. Usually there was at least a light chop or a smooth, undulating roll. But on this particular day, there was nary a ripple. None of the fishing veterans on our boat had ever seen it that calm, and they remarked how eerily quiet it was. The others on the boat were so in awe of the stillness that nobody wanted to speak above a whisper. Here were six grown men standing on a boat, gazing out into the Atlantic, everyone whispering. Then we drifted off into silence, each one lost in his own thoughts.

In the midst of profound awe, I briefly thought if this were a movie, Godzilla would suddenly burst upward, with a pants-wetting roar, rising ten stories above us and then squashing us flat before sinking below the mirrored surface once again. Seagulls would return and resume circling peacefully in the ironic silence as the credits roll. My reverie was broken by the sound of low conversation and quiet laughter on a boat a half mile away. We were becalmed in an extreme of quietude and bliss.

There was the morning a storm appeared out of nowhere and waves towered twelve feet above us when we were in the trough. On the peaks of the waves, the prop buzzed angrily against empty air. Waves broke against the sides of the boat, or on top of us, bringing us perilously close to being capsized. My knees hurt from the slamming of the boat on the water. I fought panic as fishing gear flew out of the cabinets, and breakfast flew out of the people.

The ocean, which gives us life, can take our lives back with a flick of Neptune's trident. Nothing humans can build is stronger than nature. On the ocean, we are quickly stripped of all swagger and pride. Comforting hubris is instantly replaced by the constant reminder that we are soft flesh, easily ripped to shreds and tossed over as fish food. If you go out daily onto the ocean for a living, abandon your foolish thoughts of desperately clinging to this material world. Out there, you are bait.

The weather and water between these extremes are what passes for normal, to an ocean's thinking. Reverend Moon spent many hours sitting on the bridge fishing in solitary contemplation. I liked to fish from the bow, where my trick to prevent seasickness was to fix my gaze on any stable land in the distance. Or the water's horizon, if land wasn't available. The few times I was on his boat, I watched him sitting there and wondered what he was thinking about. Sometimes, when we returned to land, he would share his thoughts with us late into the night.

What follows are some of the things Reverend Moon has told us about the ocean, about fishing, and why he thought God set things up the way He did. I am indebted to Karen Judd Smith, a capable and respected fishing captain who spent several years on the water in the 1980s, and Marilyn Morris, for compiling many of his words about the ocean and publishing them in the book, *God's Will and the Ocean*.

I didn't encase the excerpts below in quotation marks, but know they are his verbatim spoken words. In one or two places, I paraphrased very slightly, only for the sake of clarity.

The ocean gives off a blue hue that an observer would never grow weary of over thousands or tens of thousands of years. God was thinking of humankind in creating the color blue. You never tire of looking at the ocean, no matter how long you gaze at it. Blue is the color of consolation. Once you are immersed in God's love, everything including people and the world of nature become your friend.

However, if everything were blue, you would quickly begin to hate it. You would suffocate. The ocean may sometimes look silver, but it also takes on a jade color. At other times, it takes on different hues. There are many colors in the soil as well. The color of soil is usually close to green, and so it's logical to say that we, who were made out of the soil, would like the color green as well. Green, another color of consolation, is in harmony with the blue of the sky and the ocean.

The ocean, when calm, is mystifying and has the power to draw people in like a captivating, beautiful woman, a queen of mystery.

When the gentle breeze rustles by, the beauty of the ripples takes my breath away. No splendor comes near to that.

Although we can compare the beauty of the ocean to a woman, once it becomes angry it can be more frightening than a tiger or a lion rushing toward you in the wilderness. When waves tens of meters high are upon you, you do not stand a chance before their majestic vigor. You just sit, wagging your tail and shaking your head, tossed about by the waves as they come. You have no power over them. That is why people who love the ocean cannot be arrogant.

The freedom one has when sitting with a fishing rod is beyond description. There is no place to go. You can't even listen to music because you must be silent. All you can do is gaze at the ocean and talk with the sea and the heavens. It is the greatest feeling to be at sea alone in the very place where the ocean and heaven become one. I constantly go out to the sea to benefit spiritually in every way.

Air and water are just like love. When you look at the ocean, you should not regard it simply as water, but should consider it a gift from our Heavenly Father. A great revolution can begin in you from the moment you begin to reconsider the ocean from that perspective. That's why you must love the ocean.

I like salmon. Why do I like them? Salmon are brave fish. These fish travel through all the five oceans. I have another reason for appreciating salmon; it is the quality of their sacrificial love. Four to six years after they are born, they return to their birthplace. How do they know their way back? As if they had promised each other long before when they were young, the salmon of both sexes meet each other and consummate their love within a two-week period. It is as if Adam and Eve engaged in lovemaking after returning to the original Garden of Eden they had left so long ago. And that is not all. These salmon then die for their young. As soon as they have mated, they die. Indeed, even in nature, love is greater than life.

Think about a married couple having intimate relations in the middle of a tranquil ocean. Would the ocean complain? No, all of creation longs for that kind of love. You should have the heart to understand and feel that everything in the natural world cries out for couples blessed in marriage, and true to one another, to make love in their midst. In the world of love, you have access to all places.

Water is the ancestor of life. You should love the ocean while thinking about that. Water creates harmony. The ocean embraces the universe, and loving water is the same as loving all of creation.

No matter how vast a continent is, it is but an island in the ocean.

Unless you have been on the ocean, you cannot imagine how horrifying are waves that are tens of meters high when a storm brews. Even the strongest wind fulfills a mission, for without it there would be no waves to oxygenate the water, and the fish would not survive. Water never dies when it is moving. But without movement, it soon stagnates. Water circulates. It becomes vapor that condenses to become fog and mist. It then evaporates, becomes clouds carried by the wind that circulate around the world. This vapor follows the sun's rays in the summer, and then it becomes rain

Moisture is absorbed to create many things. The moisture in the air and on land can be used to make boiled rice and bread. Consider how much toil was involved in that process and how valuable these things are. The universe is engaged, is in motion and cooperates to make that bread. A piece of bread is not easily made.

There is something that breathes and thinks throughout the five great oceans and six continents. It is invisible, like voice waves or electric waves. That something can lead to the path of liberation for future humanity through untapped resources for food and energy. As long as there is land and the ocean, people will not starve.

You hear all sorts of sounds on land—the sound of the wind blowing, the sound of the tree branches swaying. The sound of people and the sound of mice running around. But the only thing you hear at sea is the sound of water. Even though it is a sound, there is a sameness about it, so it does not bother you. When you go out some distance, you no longer hear the sound of flies buzzing. You no longer hear human sounds. There is no better place to practice spiritual discipline. Spiritual discipline is the practice of meditation and self-discipline. Through spiritual discipline we can enter a state of harmony in the mind. That's why I do not stay at home, but go out to sea where the wind blows on a small boat called One Hope. *It is not comfortable being on the boat. However, it helps me find the center of my inner mind.*

I go out to sea with such passion, feeling that today must be better than yesterday, and tomorrow must be better than today.

BLUESERS

John Lee Hooker singing Boom Boom
is heard in the folds of your belly fat.
When the Cotton Mouth Man blows The Creeper
his blues harp slithers, takes over, grows as
ever-lovin' kudzu along the doodle of your noodle.

Big Maceo plays Chicago Breakdown
bringing on visions of a piano
lighter than your honeysuckle,
steppin' round the floor.
Thank you White Lake Blues Festival
for headstoning his grave,
unmarked since fifty-three.

Thank you Janis Joplin
for doing the same for Bessie Smith
thirty-three years after she went.
Two months after that, you followed her
didn't you?

At night when it's all done
I can still hear John Coltrane
riffing on This Little Light of Mine
going on and on
I'm gonna let it shine.

It never don't make me cry.

Hunting Bambi's mom

Best shot in the family with fixed iron sights, at least when we were young, was Mom. She could still her breathing and heartbeat to mimic a cave dweller frozen in a glacier.

When we were younger our whole family went on shooting outings as a family. We set cans and cereal boxes against a hill and trudged down and up another hill to peer seventy-five yards across a small valley at what now became microscopic Campbell's Pork & Beans cans and Snap, Crackle and Pop on the head of a pin.

Mom took a deep breath, let half of it out, held it, slowly squeezed the trigger and nailed Campbell right through the weenies.

I don't have blood in my veins. I have that red clay and sand. I grew up in a family of hunters on the high plains of Wyoming, in Oklahoma's red dirt country and West Texas desert. We always had rifles and shotguns leaning in the corner of my dad's closet, and plenty of ammo for all of them on the shelf above.

We learned how to clean the guns and how to safely cross a wire fence with a shotgun or rifle, passing it unloaded over the fence from one to the other. We learned when to shoot and when not to, always thinking about anything that might lie directly beyond the target. Dad said, "A bullet goes for a mile." Some go much farther than that, but a mile was the ultimate distance for a little kid.

We went hunting in the fall and winter for doves, pheasants and deer. With deer it was almost always a buck, but sometimes not. Seeing a doe stretched out across the hood of the Jeep unsettled me. I thought of Bambi's mom. It's perfectly legal to shoot female deer, but still, to little children, there is no difference in moms between a human being and a beloved cartoon fictional animal who thinks and feels and talks. I never asked my dad about it; I didn't have the articulation to formulate my question. But if I could have, my words would have emerged as, "Why did you shoot a mommy deer?" That unquiet image has remained to this day.

Dad never needed to explain that you hunt for food, not just to kill something. We didn't kill "trophies" to hang on our walls. We just knew it. Never shoot an animal you don't intend to eat unless you're protecting your chickens. Then it's okay to go after possums and rats, and defend the sheep from coyotes. I do recall shooting a crow or two in the garden on the farm in Oklahoma. Somehow, the arrogance of crows just pisses you off.

Then one day when I was in high school, without becoming "anti-hunting," I simply stepped away from it. The hunting urge, and me, went separate ways. I knew and respected the environmental value of hunting. Culling the deer herd harvests the older males, allowing the young bucks to mate sooner. It also eases overpopulation and their impact on the surrounding habitat. I'm okay with all that. Why hunting's thrill dissipated from me is a bit unknown. I still eat meat that someone else kills and I benefit from medical procedures that were tested on animals. Some years later I agreed to go dove hunting, and shot a few. The experience confirmed my feeling that I am not a hunter.

Therefore, you'll find it oddly inconsistent that in my late 40s, when I was invited to go deer hunting in West Virginia—I accepted. I really liked the guys in the group. And besides, lots of people go deer hunting and don't see any deer. Also, there are many reasons for not taking a shot when you have one. Maybe I just didn't like the cut of his jib; he moved behind some trees as I was philosophizing on the nature of existence; he claimed to be vegan. (I never shoot vegans as a personal policy).

I do enjoy walking around outdoors with a bigass gun, blasting the hell out of things. That, and blowing stuff up, are primal urges I still harbor.

I ended up on a wooden platform in a tree fifteen feet up, holding a deer rifle. It was a sunny, chilly late-November dawn. I had been in the tree since before sunrise, but I had a jug of hot coffee, and the sun that slowly lit the horizon to embers and then poked through the branches made it well worth the chill.

Numbing cold gave way to a world rimmed in gold and an austerely beautiful fog that lasted only long enough to help me envision the ghosts of Civil War soldiers tramping through the cane and milk thistle.

The sun warmed only the places it reached. Moving my hand in and out of the shade, I could feel twenty degrees of difference. My rifle rested in the crook of the tree. Deer passed by now and then, only one or two hundred yards away. I glassed them through the scope and could see the muscles of their shoulders and haunches rippling beneath the fur. They were lean, healthy. Close enough, through the scope, to reach out and touch. God, this was beautiful.

Then I heard a rustling close by. A magnificent buck and three females came strolling and grazing into my field of view. They stood directly in front of me, twenty feet away. His females stood next to him inside his sphere of protection, and I thought, *Well, you're a lucky man.*

He reminded me of a 19th century mega-stud power broker, an invincible decision-maker, a railroad robber baron with a cigar and snifter of brandy. Only this was the younger, muscled Yale wrestling team version of that. And then I realized …

Omigod, it's freakin' William Howard Taft!

William Howard Taft, the last U.S. president to have sported facial hair while in office, had reincarnated as a white-tailed deer in West Virginia. It had to be him; look at his self-assured stance, his women. I'd know that face anywhere. Surrounded by his entourage, he was at his winter estate with Bambi's mom and his secretaries. And there he was, calmly munching winter wheat not two dozen feet away.

I stayed quiet, motionless, stilling my soul, like Mom would have, giving off no signs of life, devoid even of self-awareness. I was dressed in brown camo, a nut-brown scarf and wool hat. Peering through the crotch of the oak, I "became" the tree. A winter tree. The kind of winter tree that wears glasses, holds a rifle and badly needs to pee.

The rifle talked to me, as they sometimes do when they feel free to speak their mind. In a prehistoric voice I heard it through my hands, my chest, my loins. It said, "Hunt, survive, feed your family, live. Other deer will grow strong where this one once stood." The rifle added as a reminder, "This, too, is love."

There is no way to fathom this if you don't hunt, but I know the truth of it to the last corpuscle of my body.

I comforted the rifle, saying, "I have learned much from you. You have given more than you have taken. But I don't need this buck to feed my family. I have other ways." Mine was a view one acquires after having lived a certain number of years. The young archer, his blood hot and racing, cannot think this way.

The buck, an ever-watchful sentinel, looked up from chewing the grass. His gaze wandered farther up the tree. He saw me and stared, thought, *This is a tree … and yet … something is way off here … but what?* A tuft of grass hung comically from his gaping mouth.

Then it slowly registered on him. *Holy crap! Where did you come from?!* The look on his face was priceless. I'm sure his gentleman friends at the club still razz him about it over brandy and cigars in the off-season.

I grinned at him, waved, and in a respectful voice, said quietly," Mr. President."

All four of them must have jumped ten feet in the air. Without ceremony they simply vanished. Their hooves made almost no noise, and even then, only for a second. Instantly they were gone. I poured myself another cup of coffee, unzipped and peed an earlier cup off the platform.

Hunting is a partnership, a relationship between human beings and the creation. What was essential to do at one time, is somewhat less so now, and is therefore a topic of heated debate. Through greedy excess, through wanton slaughter, through killing game from the back of a goddamn pickup truck driving down the road for christsake, through hiring someone to shoot your animal and bring it back to the lodge so you can have something to mount on the wall of your man cave—through all these things we disgrace ourselves and the gifts creation has given to us.

To hunters who do the work and who honor the process as sacred, and yes, sometimes necessary, who feel in their souls this covenant for which the creation holds us responsible, I respect and salute you. There aren't that many of you still out there, but to those who show reverence for the eternal nature of this love, I give you my blessing.

At some point, poetry stopped being about the journey

Enjoying poetry requires slowing yourself down first. That's hard to do and that's why so many people loathe the stuff.

Rings of the Lord by Sunhwa and Larry Moffitt/2008

Poetry helps us learn how to think about what we are already feeling.

The thing is, poetry has never ceased to be vital for the human spirit. Poetry, "vitamin P" is an essential nutrient that enlarges our capacity to put the world into perspective, to digest woe and be tolerant of the flaws of others, and to relieve stress through the appreciation of beauty. Poetry makes people live more richly, however few and brutal may be the years one is actually allotted.

Verses by William Shakespeare are mostly about love. He did his sonnet writing in the 1590s when all the theaters were closed due to the black plague. And somehow his thoughts turned to love.

He used a lot of iambic pentameter, as his linguistic sound pattern which is a line of verse with five metrical feet, each consisting of one short (or unstressed) syllable followed by one long (or stressed) syllable, for example. It looks like this:

da DUM   da DUM   da DUM   da DUM   da DUM
when I   do count   the clock   that tells   the time

His Sonnet 18 (of 154 total), has a melodic quality that rolls effortlessly off the mind and tongue. Each of his stanzas follow an ABAB rhyming pattern where the rhyming lines in each stanza are the first and third, and the second and fourth. At the end, his sonnets have a two-line couplet that rhymes.

But you don't read it aloud in anything resembling a marching cadence, even though you could. You read it evenly, and naturally, and it makes the sound, and creates the feeling, of something happening that is perfectly in sync with your calmer, happier self.

First, slow down your mind and heart. Read aloud this first stanza of Shakespeare's famous Sonnet 18. Read it two or three times, as though speaking to a lover.

Shall I compare thee to a summer's day?
Thou art more lovely and more temperate.
Rough winds do shake the darling buds of May,
And summer's lease hath all too short a date.

It's not just beautiful, it's perfect temperature beautiful. The imagery, along with the rhyming pattern and meter make it smooth and rich—a lyrical hot knife through butter. Below is a stanza from a poem I wrote a few years ago. The rhyming pattern is ABACDC. The first two lines are not strictly iambic pentameter, but the last four are in the sweet spot.

Each letter, no, each wine-dark drop of ink
squeezed from tears of broken love and forged
into a chain with blood in every link
becomes the only thing we have to hold
when all other hopes turn to rot and dust
and death lays down its fingers in the cold.

That so many of us have let the poetry appreciation gene atrophy in ourselves impoverishes the future.

Poetry is an unusual art form because far more people today write it than read it. Perhaps, more than being read aloud by others, poetry is your higher self communicating with your glandular self. Here are two things about poetry that I have decided are true: First, poetry is a spiritual window to the soul, same as one's eyes for the tactile senses. I think that's obvious and understood by you who have kept reading this far. And second, the best way to absorb poetry at the visceral level is to read it aloud to yourself. And that's where it's important to perform an internal metabolic downshift. Slow down your overstimulated twenty-first century inner Speedy Gonzalez—your breathing and heartbeat, your fight-or-flight reflex, even your toenail growth. Slow to a crawl, way, way down, almost slower than it's possible to be in this social media world. Become glacial. Modern life has outrun the contemplative pace of poetry, and you need to touch base with the Edgar Allen Poe in you.

Poetry matters, but the reason we have stopped making poetry important in our lives is the same reason we have stopped reading *Pride and Prejudice* aloud to the family by candlelight in the evenings. Technology has made us hyper. For example, I typed this entire piece with lightning fingers in less time than it took Bill the Bard to grind his ink stick, slit a goose quill and scrawl, *"Wherefore art thou, Romeo?"*

I sip the verse like sacred droplets of winter harvest ice wine. And then in one second, from lingering stillness to warp-speed, zippity-bang, I grab my bagged lunch, kiss Honey Nim and I'm running out the door, launched officeward with a damn tie around my neck—the symbol of my slavery.

I'm onto the next reality. Subduing syntactical demons, I word-process a memo from regular understandable English into unfathomable business babble: "… prioritizing outcome-based methodologies for capacity bandwidth, maximizing precision accuracy boogely boogely bippity bum."

Lunching at my desk, I inhale white bread and aphrodisiacs, before rushing the finished memo into the corner office of a stock-optioned Kahuna authority figure.

The secretary of his outer defense perimeter looks up. "Who goes there, knave?"

I use my power stare on her, through eyes as dark as volcanic glass. "This memo is *mission critical!*"

She backs off, a hint of fear and confusion in her eyes. "Awright, give him room, people!" And then I'm in.

But I digress, don't I?

The upshot is I wrote and delivered that memo, transforming life on earth as we know it, in less time than it took Lord Byron to pen a note to the milkman. A note that, today, would auction for a million five, by the way.

To help you appreciate poetry, you should meditate on what it takes for the brain to become poetic by embracing that mental space. Get away from ambient sound, turn the lights low, put a paper pad in front of you and a pen filled with sepia-toned ink in your hand. Put on a cape, grab a raven, do whatever it takes for you to rein it in, Bubba. Then write one. Expel yourself from the modern space-time continuum and into a rhythm we haven't experienced in a widespread way since gifted orators addressed large crowds without microphones. A time of, say, Lincoln's speech at Gettysburg, or Johnny Bap at the River Jordan anointing his cousin, Jesus.

You need poetry for life's giant events—for the passing of heroes, or to commemorate battles, or for recovering your equilibrium after being ambushed by forbidden love. Also for bullet-point moments of personal clarity, such as realizing the immediacy of something for which you are willing to give up your life

You need poetry every day. You need it like you need veggies. You need it to water the bougainvillea of your boogie wagon, to cool your magma and unfold your brain wrinkles, to cleanse the colon of the troposphere. (*The what?!*)

Anyway, you need it, trust me.

Here are a few emotions with which poetry can help. Just snippets, for flavor. Look these up. Read them all, and more. You can thank me later when you recover.

World War I blew William Butler Yeats' mind, as it did everyone of that time after having seen the entire world destroyed. He wrote "The Second

Coming" in 1919, possibly trying to come to terms with the carnage of what had amounted to global suicide.

> The darkness drops again but now I know
> That twenty centuries of stony sleep
> Were vexed to nightmare by a rocking cradle,
> And what rough beast, its hour come round at last,
> Slouches towards Bethlehem to be born?

There is the rage of the beat poet, none angrier than Allen Ginsburg, expressed in "Howl." To properly read this work, lock your door and shout the entire poem as loud as you can. Then go out and burn down the mission.

> I saw the best minds of my generation destroyed by
> madness, starving hysterical naked,
> dragging themselves through the negro streets at dawn
> looking for an angry fix …

Like Ginsburg and Sylvia Plath, sometimes I can't decide if I want to see the whole town turned upside down. Or if it already is and I just feel the need to take notes.

Don't stick your head in the oven. Read the poetry of Plath and then lie down with a cold rag on your forehead.

Keep your sodden tiramisú. I get will get merrily drunk on Emily Dickinson. For I am besotted of "The Belle of Amherst," my beloved recluse.

> Because I could not stop for Death
> He kindly stopped for me
> The Carriage held but just Ourselves
> And Immortality.

Yes, Emily, oh yes!

I'd better stop now. Once I let my spirit be taken by Miss Dickinson and her contemporary, that rake Walt Whitman, I will not stop for death nor dinner.

His fingers brushed her cheek

It was our thirty-first wedding anniversary several years ago. Me and Honey Nim had blown through the years in a meteor fly-by. Her Japanese palate likes anything from the ocean, so we chose a nice seafood restaurant for our commemoration.

A day earlier, I had finished reading a new book by Phyllis Edgerly Ring called *Snow Fence Road*, a beautiful, expressive novel about complex relationships and the restorative power of love. Novelists say the secret to writing is to make the reader care about characters that are so true to life that the reader walks around all day having imaginary conversations with them. Set in the fictional coastal town of Knowle, Maine, this is that kind of book. It's a great read, which I ingested in huge gulps and dealt with "book hangover" for several days afterward (the feeling where you don't want to start a new book because you're still enjoying living in the one you just read).

At the restaurant, as we sat there talking and laughing about truth, beauty and life, I recalled a description in Phyllis' novel where the man "reached out and lightly brushed her cheek with his fingers."

At that point we have only been married a third of a century, so the juices are still fresh in us, and the lightly brushing fingers thing seems like the perfect romantic expression for a moment like this. There we are nicely dressed, with the ambient light, the wall tapestry décor, sitting toe-to-toe in an intimate restaurant. I reach out and bush my fingertips against her left cheek. My caress is light, confident.

She smiles a "thank you," spoken so softly it cannot be heard beyond the few inches between us.

It was like a time-machine replay of our love's first awakening three decades earlier. I am inspired to try a variation on more of the same. I ever so gently reach up with my right hand to brush the back of my fingers down her right cheek. "I love you," I tell her.

Her face flickers in the candlelight. Her eyes twinkle.

And now for perfection—I reach out both hands, brushing my fingertips down both cheeks. And finally this: I gently cup the side of her face with one hand. She reaches her hand up to take mine, move it toward her mouth, and kiss my palm.

Still, she's starting to think this is a bit odd. She looks at me with a quizzical smile, "What?"

That's when I tell her about the romantic book, the hero, the pretty girl, a blossoming love similar in many ways to our thirty-one-year-old kind, and how I was inspired to brush her cheek with my fingers. As I explain the whole thing to her I find myself once again, rendered adorable in her eyes.

The way she looks upward and to the left, tells me she is leafing through her mind's Japanese-English dictionary. It's housed in the foyer of her cerebrum, a large space lined with shelves. I hear wheels softly grinding inside the right hemisphere, as she quickly grabs a verb off one of the shelves, then sorts through some nouns, a preteciple, a purgatory, an interrogative doodlebug. The gears finally catch with a click. A bright shimmering smile spreads across her face, lighting her up as she hesitantly says, "I am a peaceful … shining … rabbit."

A *peaceful, shining rabbit?* Why not? Maybe this is why we've never become bored with each other in three-plus decades.

Ours was a very typical courtship and marriage. She came from Japan, and I from West Texas. We were introduced to each other by the Reverend Sun Myung Moon and were married on July 1, 1982 along with 2,074 other couples in Madison Square Garden, where we covered the floor of the arena in neat rows of alternating grooms and brides.

One might think a mass wedding is not romantic, but it was. So very. The room was filled with love. Love times two thousand. All I saw was her. When we exchanged rings, I also slipped onto her finger my great-grandmother's gold wedding band. I carried pictures of my parents, grand and great grandparents in my suit pocket. The whole family, past and present, was there in the room as we were sprinkled with holy water.

Like I said, your typical wedding.

On any other night the Garden's arena floor is covered with a slab of ice, and hockey players knock each other's teeth out. And thirty years earlier, Marilyn Monroe stood where we stood and sang "Happy birthday, Mr. President" to JFK, while wearing a dress so tight she had to be sewn into it. So who's to say what's normal in the world?

A great many friends in our faith community also celebrate their wedding anniversary on the same day. Each one's marriage and life is, of course, unique, with a unique book to be written about it. Certainly one common aspect in a group of thousands married at the same time is that there is not a chance of any of us ever failing to remember our wedding anniversary.

WHAT LOVE IS PART I: HUNGRY LOVE

Puppy love is much more than just a test of your gag reflex

This train of thought began on a literal train stalled in Philadelphia Station on the way to New York. A super-cold patch of winter, a rare "polar vortex," the news called it, had downed some lines north of Trenton. A conductor strolled by and I heard his radio say, "… squawk … crackle … sixty to ninety minutes …"

"We're gonna miss our meeting," a guy across the aisle says into his cellular. The thought of an entire train full of people, hundreds, missing meetings, made me go weak in the knees. New York City is going to come in way short on meetings today. Attorneys will go to bed hungry tonight. Curse you, polar vortex!

However, on a dead train you can hear things that are normally drowned out by the rumbling wheels. One of those things—two in fact —are directly behind me. A man and woman in the grip of the onrush of love's intoxication, are giggling and kissing up a storm—kisses that sound like Tom Sawyer slapping a loaded whitewash brush against a plank fence. It's quite evocative. In my mind, skyrockets explode in the air above me, waves crash against the shore, locomotives go rushing into tunnels. Sigmund Freud sticks another cigar into his mouth.

Insatiable, hungry love builds a cocoon around a couple and time loses all meaning. The continuation of our species will not be denied.

The guy across the aisle glances back at them, then looks at me and rolls his eyes. I don't commiserate. I am in the presence of love's "ground zero" and I must be respectful. Yes, passion is messy, lacking in dignity, and not for the faint of heart. But don't shout at them to "get a room." They'll get one soon enough. We are privileged to be witnessing the dawn of creation, which, on this particular train, went like this:

"I love you, Honey, so much!"

"I love you too, Chewy." *(Chewy? seriously?)*

"How much do you love me?"

"Umm ... this big" (I was dying to look back to see what he was measuring.)

(shriek, giggle) "Oh, stop."

As a detached onlooker, this kind of thing can challenge your gag reflex. And not only that, but the more illogical and storybook-like it is, the better.

Picture this, ladies: You're at a farmer's market. You spy a beautiful apple atop the pile. You and he, on opposite sides of the fruit stand, reach out and in slow motion, your hands touch the same apple at the same time. You look up, your eyes meet, and you *just know*.

Here's another for the gents: You're the owner of a rare dog, an Appenzeller Sennenhunde. It's a misunderstood breed, a loyal, working dog, very protective but often hostile to strangers. Your employer, the CIA, has given you an impossible mission that will keep you out of the country for six months. (You're being sent to Australia to get the Ozzies to stop telling American jokes. Example: Why was war invented? To teach geography to Americans.) Your dog has already bitten all your friends and nobody will take care of him while you're gone. Your heart is sick. In the quiet of a stalled train in Philly Station, you strike up a conversation with your seatmate, a nice-looking fresh-faced girl. At some point, you tell her about your dilemma (careful not to mention the CIA because then you'd have to kill her).

Her eyes light up. "Hey, I'm a *Sennenhundista* too," she says, using the inner-circle code name of lovers and owners of the Appenzeller Sennenhunde breed. She shows you a dozen pics of her dog on her cell phone. "I love the little fur-butts." I'll be happy to take care of him for you."

She gives you her digits. Turns out she lives in your same apartment building. You're both single, and looking. You both have a tattoo of the same mythic goddess on your left cheek (not a face cheek). You both failed shoe-tying in kindergarten. Incredible coincidences: you both have left hands; she bakes her own bread, you eat bread; you were both really small when you were born. Oh, my God, the coincidences just go on and on!

I think God is driven by the impulse to love. I believe that He (She) is a willing prisoner of outrageous, selfless passion. I think God cannot

not love. Which is why we, in our best moments, are that way as well. I'm telling you, God lives for this stuff and never does it halfway, never phones it in. Every time you encounter God, the sleeves are rolled up, the ball cap is on backwards, there're sweat stains down the front of the shirt and dirt under the fingernails. Love is all God thinks about, and that's why love jumps up and bites people a zillion different ways every day. You think you're hungry for love? Your Creator is famished.

Big, fat hungry love actually has a function. But it's high-octane stuff, and learning how to manage love takes a lifetime. What separates a saint from a selfish bastard? Somewhere along the line, the saint learned how to love others before loving herself. Putting others first is the secret to taming and riding the big, fat, hungry beast of love. You put her convenience and pleasure before yours; she puts hers before yours. That's the most fertile soil for love's growth.

Giddy, stupid, puppy love (where big, fat, hungry love starts out) is another story. It's not merely a joke being played on people by the universe. Although basically unworkable, the puppy-love phase operates in the same way as the first stage of a rocket. It is the most powerful because it has to overcome inertia and gravity in order to put the payload into orbit. Loveologists (love scientists in white lab coats) tell us the "in love" phase burns hottest for the first 18 months or so, at which time a more solid, steady-state love takes over to smooth out the hills and valleys your couple will encounter from then on. Loveologists also warn about the pitfalls, potholes, landmines and shoe-sucking swamps that love encounters, but nobody ever listens to that.

Furthermore, loveologists believe love jumps out of the starting gate with someone risking all, confessing to the other, "I love you." The one who initially took the leap now holds breath, waiting for the essential four-words: "I love you, too." It is important that the response be delivered within a few seconds of the initial declaration in order to complete the circuit. A delayed reply to "I love you," or worse, silence, muddles the magic and confuses the universe. But when the connection is made with the ideal sequence and timing, it's *BAM!* Lady and gentleman, start your engines! Ignition, lift-off! Each one lives and breathes for passion and "true love's kiss" because, well, *that's the story of, that's the glory of ... love.*

What an exquisite time of stars and rockets it is. If you're young, it's the one time in your life when you can listen to a song like "Teen Angel" without wanting to puke. I'm not kidding, check it out:

That fateful night the car was stalled
upon the railroad track
I pulled you out and we were safe
but you went running back.

What was it you were looking for
that took your life that night?
They said they found my high school ring
clutched in your fingers tight.

Teen angel, can you hear me ... etc.

There's a brief time in your life (if you're fortunate) when you are fully alive enough that this song makes *absolutely perfect sense*. That's your passion-crazed, high-school-ring-rescuing, slicing-your-own-ear-off phase. Without it there would be too few stupid poems in the world, because nobody would care that moon rhymes with June. There would be very little giddiness, and no need to listen to a bunch of danged songbirds and crickets chirping. There would also be no people spray-painting marriage proposals on highway overpasses, and fewer Saturday night gunfights. Zero chick flicks.

But more essential, if love's tsunami were not the most powerfully motivating force in the world, then other and higher forms of love would also not be able to exist. Love's driving engine not only promotes mating, but it impels people to rise to new heights of sacrifice for things that are right and just and true in the world. Because of love, some will devote their lives to healing. Others to comforting and fighting for oppressed people who have no voice of their own. Passion has many expressions and some of you among us will continually put your lives on the line, on the road to becoming Mother Teresa or Spartacus.

Therefore, while freezing in a train stuck in South Philadelphia Station, don't scoff at the sloppy, schlirpy, syrupy couple in the seat behind you. Raise your glass to them. Those two are on the ground floor of learning how to master the strongest of earthly emotions. Don't worry, they'll grow out of the Teen Angel phase someday. Odds are they will become grumpy, jaded and beaten into submission by life. But for now, God bless them. May they never forget what it is to have thought their love was more powerful than the need for food or air or a warm train. My two cents is that if you can be on good terms with puppy love, you will more closely resemble God.

I think it's also important for everyone to try their hand at writing a love poem or two. It doesn't have to be great, or even rhyme; it only has to have all of you in it. Steel yourself, because I'm going to conclude with a poem that many people think is great. I want you to do something for me. Like other forms of poetry I wrote of earlier in this book, this sonnet works best if you read it aloud quietly, maybe a couple of times. So do that now, please. Do I really think you're actually going to do that? Of course I do. And you will, too, if you know what's good for you.

How Do I Love Thee? (Sonnet 43)
by Elizabeth Barrett Browning

How do I love thee? Let me count the ways.
I love thee to the depth and breadth and height
My soul can reach, when feeling out of sight
For the ends of being and ideal grace.
I love thee to the level of every day's
Most quiet need, by sun and candle-light.
I love thee freely, as men strive for right.
I love thee purely, as they turn from praise.
I love thee with the passion put to use
In my old griefs, and with my childhood's faith.
I love thee with a love I seemed to lose
With my lost saints. I love thee with the breath,
Smiles, tears, of all my life; and, if God choose,
I shall but love thee better after death.

WHAT LOVE IS PART II:
WITHOUT LOVE, ETERNITY FALTERS

It's like this. You're in your mother's womb. It's wet, warm, cozy. You hear sounds outside, someone chopping onions, listening to Boz Scaggs, muffled conversations, the near-constant sound of someone peeing. You don't know what's going on, but it's cool. You're a little bitty fetus, about the size of bait. You have a heartbeat and that long bellybutton doo-hickey that gives you food and oxygen. Life is good.

Then you start to become larger, and what's worse, you start to acquire all this equipment you absolutely don't need. Things like legs, arms, eyes, a mouth, and other, you know—"parts." You grow fingers and toes and you're thinking, *Yikes, more stuff I don't need. I'm all over the place! You start to grow lungs that take up more space, and they don't even do anything. It's crowded in here. This is not good!*

The space issue gets worse every day until one day you start to feel really squeezed. Then everything suddenly gets tighter and tighter and tighter—then *megatight.* You didn't even know there was a drain in here until the plug gets pulled. The warm water disappears as the room collapses. Your head and face are squished. You start sliding … down—or is it up? You're sucked out of the hole and suddenly it's bright, and cold. It's not just different; it's *scary* different.

Someone smacks you on the ass. You scream your head off and everyone seems very pleased about it. You're surrounded by giants, all laughing, slapping each other on the back and handing out cigars. This nice lady with tears in her eyes gets her face real close to yours and starts talking to you softly. You recognize her voice, but she's speaking gibberish, like you're an idiot.

And lungs! Omigod, they start working now, doing the job your belly button used to do. You're sucking air and it feels good. You also discover the other parts come in handy now, as well. You need the arms and legs, hands and eyes. Now you can ride a bicycle, shuffle cards. You can insult an entire nation with just one finger. You figure out something else, as well. In the womb there was just you. But out here you're bouncing off a lot of other people, and in doing that, you can come to care deeply about some of them. You learn about love, first from your parents and then from your brothers and sisters and friends. You start to feel like you can't live without it. As you climb that learning curve, there is a truckload of trial and error, and love is not easy to master. But you do your best.

Or not. You might think, *Screw these people. I'll just take care of myself. I don't need 'em anyway.* And you're correct in one sense. It is possible to grow up big and strong, and become filthy rich and a giant of industry, without ever lifting a finger to help another human being. You think: *Oh sure, I can love other people. I'm not a heartless fiend. But first I need to get my attorneys to secure the mineral rights to western Montana. That pristine wilderness is loaded with silver and jade, and uranium, and that land is not going to strip-mine itself.* When you're on the fast track to becoming a robber baron, loving and helping others only slows you down and gets in the way. *Take time to stop and smell the roses? Gimme a break.*

Some people are Gandhi and some are Attila the Hun. But most of us are in the middle somewhere. Where you end up has a lot to do with where you begin. It starts in your home; that's where you receive your first how-to-be-human lessons. Around the cooking fire, with what you experience and see others doing, you learn love, intimacy, sharing, giving and taking. I watched the grown-ups to see how they did things. For some reason, I remember my father always jumping up to open doors for the elderly or anyone with a big package or on crutches, or who just looked like someone that would benefit from suddenly having a door pop open in front of them. He was guided by consideration for others.

Life's big-ticket issues were explained to me with love and clarity one snowy evening in 1956 in Casper, Wyoming. I was nearly six years old and we were at the family dinner table when my father solved the mysteries of race and gender relations for me, for the rest of my life, *in just one sentence*: "Don't treat people different just because their color is different, and don't you ever, ever hit girls." That was pretty much everything I needed to know from that point on, even if the waters did get muddy again when I hit puberty.

The racial topic from the newspaper (thank you, Rosa Parks) was somehow thrown in with me having punched a girl in my class (who richly deserved it). That moment was like being handed an engraved stone commandment, and it has replayed itself in my mind countless times throughout my life. I remember it like I'm watching it on video. I even remember we were having canned creamed corn at dinner that night.

Other lessons followed. Don't steal, don't lie, don't make fun of someone's name, and don't rub poison ivy on your arm. In the third grade, when I wanted to take a classmate to a grade-school square dance, my mom called her mom to set it up. Dad drove us to the church where the dance was, and coached me ahead of time about opening the car door for the girl.

My parents were a nurturing tag-team, switching off roles of good cop and bad cop as needed. From my two brothers I learned how to fight, how to get my butt kicked and how to negotiate. Our family enveloped us as we jostled against each other like stones in a rock polisher. I knew who I was and where the boundaries were. Within the boundaries there was a lot of freedom. I'm aware today how extremely fortunate I was.

Together, all these flowing rivulets of input helped me create my *whoness* and *whatness*. Oklahoma Granny says, "Your character is made of all the things you do when they ain't nobody lookin'." Granny nailed it for sure.

Religions can be useful because they directly address the issue of character development, and they also tinker around with what happens in "the next life," after our bodily parts dry up and fall off. We might be thinking, *After this life there is nothing. No God, no heaven. Just empty oblivion.*

But be careful, because that's what you were thinking when you were in your mother's womb, and you were wrong then too.

But either way, you'll be walking along one day, and you'll croak. No big deal, you just croak. You fall down on the ground, your phys-bod goes to room temp and you find yourself in the next world all dressed in your spiritual birthday suit. "Hi, everybody!" And it's really, really *different*. People there are laughing, same as when you were born. They're slapping each other on the back and passing out cigars.

You discover that your spiritual body is made up of whatever character you have developed during your lifetime, and that your ability to love unselfishly, which was technically not necessary for physical survival, is suddenly the currency in the spirit world. If your physical lungs didn't develop in the womb, you would have huge issues upon birth. Likewise, your capacity to love in the spiritual world will be just as crucial as having healthy lungs is on earth. Love is the stuff you breathe there.

I think that's the reason every culture has a version of the Golden Rule, why the family became the first primary school of love in every society on earth, why every religion came up with a similar set of basic rules. They all intuit along similar lines.

WHAT LOVE IS PART III: THE JOURNEY OF COUPLES

Marriage is a hard thing to get right

The Platters sang "smoke gets in your eyes," about how you can get fooled by love—thinking it's the real deal when it's not. "They asked me how I knew my true love was true," the song goes. "I of course replied, something here inside cannot be denied." It's a song of heartache and woe that underscores the problem of distinguishing *garden variety* romantic love from true romantic love.

There exist many shades of yearning. If you read Song of Solomon (Song of Songs) in the Bible, you know you are in the presence of a master of erotic poetry from around 900 BC. When he lauds her "pomegranates," he ain't talking about fruit. Since it's in the Bible, I assume the book is allegorical reference to one's original God-given desire for a spouse. It's steamy stuff and it inspires me in all kinds of good and meaningful ways.

Then what about Helen of Troy, owner of "the face that launched a thousand ships?" True love for sure, right? When Paris stole Helen of Sparta from King Menelaus and she became Helen of Troy (one of those women whose last name is whatever city she lives in), it was hugely insulting to Helen's original owner, and so he had to send a huge army in a thousand ships to get her back. But was she really *that* beautiful? Did she have such a cute little nose? Twinkly eyes? Inspiring pomegranates? I suspect Menelaus may have been one of those men for whom his woman is turf. It's good that he wanted her back, and that he sent out an army of swarthy guys with girded loins to do the job, but sorry, I don't necessarily count this as true love. It could have been about the king's pride.

Okay, then what about the Age of Chivalry? Was that all about true love? Well, let's look at the culture of the deep south in America, pre-Civil War. You have granite-jawed manly men, and the tradition of women fainting when the swordplay got too intense or the language too coarse. Those girly girls would seize up with vapor lock, faint and hit the deck— *ka-clunk*. Then the local Bradley would spring into action.

"She's fainted! You go get help, Hezekiah. I'll loosen her corset."

[Fade to the next scene as Belle awakens.]

"What… where am I? Oh, Bradley, thank you. I must have fainted. Umm… so where's my corset?"

"Now, Missy Belle, don't y'all go and worry that purdy little head of yours."

Can we agree that chivalry is sometimes about something other than true love?

Wait, I know. Romeo and Juliet—world's first chick flick. A beautiful romance with an ever-rising body count.

It ends this way (spoiler alert in case you haven't read it): Finding Juliet drugged, and thinking her dead, Romeo quickly chugs a vial of poison. She wakes up, sees he's dead and then stabs herself with his knife.

Bada-bing! bada-boom!

What a stupid mess, and was it really true love? Actually it sort of was, or at least it was in the ballpark. But the emotion I feel most is that I would just like to smack them both upside the head. I would counsel Romeo not to let impatience and grief blind him. Why not wait a bit, like even half a minute, to make sure Juliet is really dead? Feel for a pulse maybe. Use your head, boy. How about a last kiss? *Hmmm… her lips are warm. That's odd.*

What we can learn from all these examples is that popular culture and literature are clueless about what true love is. Ditto for most of us. How does this translate for we who are in the thick of the fray, who aren't gods or saints but are expected to live day after day, year after year, decade after decade with the same man or woman? How do young couples get to become old couples without calling it quits or murdering one another?

The things you find cute in one another when you first meet can become enormously irritating over the course of decades. For example, I will tell the same interesting-slash-amusing story more than once. Even a lot more than once.

Honey Nim told me, "Actually you repeat yourself all the time. But sometimes I still laugh. I'm not laughing at the story. I'm laughing because I can't believe you're telling it again."

I think I would never, ever put up with me.

Another major obstacle that needs to be overcome in a long-term marriage is petty bickering. I'm not talking about screaming and throwing jars of fruit preserves. This is an insidious, sabotaging erosion. Like the death of a thousand cuts, it eventually becomes irreversible.

Her: "That was last summer, when the mayor bought that strawberry ice cream cone for the little kid."

Him: "It was cherry vanilla."

Her: "No, it was strawberry"

Him: "It was cherry vanilla. I was standing right next to the mayor."

Her: "Strawberry. I remember the little red bits in it."

Him: "Those were the cherries."

It never stops. When you've been around such a couple, just reading this puts your teeth on edge. If it's not ice cream flavors, it's the day of the week of last year's Veterans Day parade, or the song the band was playing six years ago when the drunk guy fell into the punch bowl.

Listening to a couple bicker about this kind of thing, I pray for strength, but not the strength of patience. I pray to be strong enough to throw them both at escape velocity into a decaying orbit around the sun.

Taking constant pot-shots at one another creates hairline fissures in the coffee mug of your marriage. Then, at age fifty-five, one of you will leave the other as the last child leaves the nest and the mug falls apart in your hands.

Here's what to do instead. Forget the strawberry vanilla ice cream or what song the band played. Both of you should decide at the outset not to give a rat's ass about anything less important than the house being on fire (and only if you're in it at the time). Each of you becomes dedicated to helping the other person win every argument. Life is too damn short for pointless disagreements. Don't make me throw you into the sun.

Be good friends with your spouse. Enjoy each other's company and like each other's stuff. If she likes cooking, like it too. If she likes English Premier League soccer, like it too. If she likes shopping for antiques, go antique shopping with her. Touch and caress each other frequently throughout the day, even if only to maintain the transfer of skin cells and electrons between you.

It is your God-given right to observe anything about your spouse and think it's lovable and sweet, instead of stupid and lame. Even though it may actually be the latter. You have the right to see or hear something from your husband that could easily irritate the living crap out of you and find it comfortably familiar instead. Honey Nim does this with me sometimes, and occasionally I will even appreciate in the moment, that she is exercising superhuman self-control. It puts me into an introspective space and I realize I owe her one. This kind of weighing and assessing exists as a continual undercurrent in a relationship that both people care about and want to do the work to maintain. It's about give and take. She works two jobs to support the household and put you through medical school. When you graduate, you buy her an endless stream of used cars so she can pursue her passion for demolition derby.

What do we really know about love? A lot, actually. It's organic, for one thing, and interwoven seamlessly into daily life. You walk up behind her as she stands at the sink doing whatever, and you brush the hair to one side so you can kiss her on the neck as you move in beside her to help do whatever. Or, outdoors, she takes time to look at you and smile as she hands you a freshly loaded musket while you're shooting Visigoths from the ramparts.

You don't "fall in love" like tripping over a tree root in the dark. It's more work than that. You grab love by the scruff of the neck and wrestle it to the ground until it yields up to you its secrets. Tenderly of course, with flowers, soft lights and music, although cleaning the kitchen works best. Foreplay begins in the kitchen. There is the need for patience. Science will acknowledge there is also some luck involved. Sometimes the dice come up snake eyes and you lose, no matter how hard you try. Despite your best efforts, the chemistry may not be there. For those times, the radio has sad songs.

But sometimes chemistry comes through for you. You've seen it, an elderly couple walking along together. Each one is an ancient bag of bones with nothing even remotely attractive or sexy about them in any external sense. They are wrinkled with halting steps. But there they are, holding hands, smiling tenderly at one another. Letting the cane take his weight, he slowly bends over toward her. She waits patiently for her kiss.

He reaches her face and tenderly plants one where he has kissed her a thousand times before.

Watching it, you're amazed and inspired. It occurs to you, *Dang, it's possible after all*. When I was a callow young man I thought I would never understand that kind of attraction in a thousand years. Today, not even fifty years have passed, but now I understand it. Some of you reading this will be among those fortunate enough to be in that old couple's shoes one day.

Having an enduring love like this is my goal, and I saw it in action up close as I was growing up. It was the love my dad had for my mom, Peggy of Noman, Oklahoma, and she for him. But it was no fairytale. Nobody ever said marriage is a cakewalk and they rode out the same storms every couple endures. But ultimately neither of them sank, or drowned.

She was bedrock country, raised in rural Oklahoma. Salt of the earth. Smart and strong for anything she believed in. Pretty in a wholesome farm girl kind of way, her face launched just one ship. His.

LOVE ITS OWNSELF

Set the sunrise beside the road
and give the clouds a raincheck.
I came to find you, Doodlebug
to feed you a la mode
We will bargain fair and square
my chaos for your train wreck.

I lick my veiny, speckled nose
reveling in perfunctory.
It is my love
which is like a red, red rose
and like France
which is actually another country.

CZECHMATE

A Czech Republic mortar-forker loves an Irish fairy.
They tarry not, and marry. She is smooth and he is hairy.
My daughter favors me, said she, for she is fair and frail.
Their son looks like a beast, you see, the Czech is in the male.

THE SPRING, SUMMER, AUTUMN, WINTER OF FAMILY

Me and Honey Nim have five children. Or we *had* five children. Now we have five adult friends to whom we gave birth, then raised.

I live in a faith community where five offspring don't even raise an eyebrow but in the general population of our fellow sojourners on earth, the thought of having five children can be a jaw-dropper. Folks want to know, "Wow, that's a lot. What was that like?"

It's an unforgettable journey, that's what. Five children is not a lot; it's huge. It was between child number four and five that we finally figured out what was causing them. Someone sent me a pamphlet with some diagrams. I was gobsmacked! *Omigod, sexual intercourse! Who knew?*

The last two times we found out we were pregnant, we stood there looking at each other dumbfounded, looked down at the drugstore test strip again, then back at each other. Always we came to the same conclusion: *Hey, what the heck.* The ones we already had were pretty interesting people. We were sure the new ones would also amaze us in many wonderful ways. We embraced and celebrated. So, by way of the exact family-planning science of *que será, será,* we grew to become a tribe with five children.

Those who warned us it is expensive to raise five children today were right, of course. But this size is what we are. A family is not several individuals. A family is "we." It's a big "us." "Family bamily ramily," as we sometimes call ourselves, makes up a large part of the definition of each of us individually. When any one of us is away for too many days, the others begin to seriously feel the lack.

But the one single fact that continues to surprise me and Honey Nim every day without fail is how different each child is from the others. (Child is an odd word to use for people who now have children of their own.) What continues to amaze us to this day is that five personalities, so diverse from one another, could come from the same two parents. It seems impossible.

Each one of our children contains a bit of me, some traits of her, and then this huge third other aspect of their personality that seems to have simply appeared, as though it came in through the air conditioning. No two are alike. They have characteristics I associate with the four seasons, and that have nothing to do with the time of year they were actually born. For example, a child with a winter personality can be born in July or any other time. The classifications are my own, but you may recognize some of these traits in your children, or in yourself.

Spring is a tempest, often the baby of the family.

Carried around in arms from birth, they can be as adorable as an internet video of sleeping puppies. But Spring is also indulged and given license to be hot-tempered. Daughter Sunhwa (forever "Hwa" in the lexicon of the family bamily ramily) is grown now but still a Spring. If Hwa and our dog sat down to play a game of chess, there would be no rules and the game would never end. She will be a wonderful mother because she will never forget how to understand her children.

Autumn is talented and complex.

Autumn is where life and death meet amid great drama, where art and intellect make another foolish attempt to share space within the same human being. There is a fragile intensity and brilliance there. Autumn can die young, or turn bitter in late middle age, or can live long, happily, wise and fully realized. Nobody forgets Autumn. Daughter Theresa ("Treegy" in the family bamily ramily), is a classic Autumn. She's a chef in Seattle. She also works the boarding gates for an airline, which allows her to fly free, anywhere in world the airline flies. And she does. Her motor runs hot, and one should never trifle with a person who uses knives for a living.

Summer has the open spirit of a blue-eyed blonde.

Summer, loving life and people, is barefoot and happy to live in the woods and eat squirrels. Being a born romantic, Summer can be the best child or a parent's worst nightmare. Never in between. Son David ("Captain America" in the family bamily ramily), of dark eyes, music and healing—lives for high ideals. Doctor Dave, the physical therapist, will re-pop the dislocated shoulders of the world. Thank God his wife keeps him organized.

Winter is easy to dismiss, to put off to one side.

That's because what a Winter person offers is deeply held and hard to fathom. Everyone hopes Winter will not destroy the world. They say what they think and can leave wreckage in their wake. Speaking truth to power can cost them dearly. But Winter is fiercely loyal. Winter will stay by your side long after it's unwise to do so. Daughter Kathy ("KatP" in the family bamily ramily) will hold your hair back for you when you puke. She will take a bullet for you. If she doesn't shoot you herself.

Son John (formerly "Phish" in the family bamily ramily, but now just John), is a Winter-Autumn blend, intensely private, somewhat mysterious. However, it's as clear as glacial melt that God is training him, pushing him through various trials with great love and attention to detail. He is a nurse right now, and may always be involved in healing. He's also an excellent cook. I doubt even John knows this, but there is a hero inside him that grows year by year, and awaits only the tapping of God's finger on his shoulder and the whisper in his ear, "I need you to go and do this for me, even at the possible cost of your life." Whoever comes to occupy the position of John's wife will never feel un-cherished.

Can a Winter love a Summer? Absolutely. In the ice-bound depths of February, don't you long for May? In the two-season tropics, a Dry Season can surely love a Wet Season. Likewise, the seasons next door to one another such as Summer and Autumn. That's because the lines blur and people change. It is possible to be all four seasons at various points in one's life. One can start out bright and become grumpy, or vice versa; begin selfish and evolve into loving unconditionally; begin interested in nothing and grow into being interested in everything; begin hating to sing and turn into a person who loves to sing; begin indifferent to children and evolve into the nurturer and parent of all the children in your corner of the planet.

Having witnessed such fruitions within people I have known over the years (including our own children) I observe that, just as a person can inhabit more than one season at the same time, so also can one person be a member of more than one race and more than one faith tradition at the same time. There are no boundaries or barriers within us or outside of us, except those obstacles to our own peace and happiness with which we insist on strewing the landscape.

THANK YOU FOR WATER THAT DON'T KILL ME

The greatest revolution of the twentieth century is that the people reading this can turn on the tap and get a drink of water that won't kill them.

I still can't sleep normally. (I know in my innermost heart that trans-Pacific travel at jet speeds is an unnatural act). I had returned home that morning after a 14-hour flight from the land where the sun rises, and took a long nap when I got home. Mistake. Now, the big green numbers beside my head read 3:34. My head on the pillow sees them sideways. I sigh, lift my head and scan the floor in the dark for my bunny rabbit slippers. There should be two of them. I see Flopsy; where's Mopsy?

I get up and flick on a lamp. It lights up, and the room that was toe-barking dark is suddenly glowing, safe and embracing. The light is my friend. Darkness loves me, as well, and always has, but it's a metaphorically tougher love. Light is the right tool for the job at this moment, and so the lamp stays on. I grab a sepia tone pen and a yellow pad, and go out to sit on our yard-sale sofa, my bare toes resting atop a luxuriant yard-sale throw rug.

The air around me has been processed by my home's central heating system thingy and I am perfectly comfortable. I could boil water and make tea in an instant if I wanted it. Or coffee. I could build a small fire in the woodstove and roast chestnuts, or dig around in the fridge for strawberries in January.

Surely I am like a god.

I find myself staring, as if in a trance, at the lamp switch, at the pen in my hand, while observing the air swirling around me at just the right temperature. What miracles these are.

Just two hundred years ago, the biggest king in the biggest castle would be sitting in a cold draft all the time, too hot in summer and too cold in winter, before dying at age 34 from sepsis caused by an abscessed tooth (if not the contents of Ms. Borgia's poison ring). I am middle class, which in modern terms is higher than a menial domestic and lower than a nobleman. But I am much better off than Good King Wenceslaus of yesteryear. I don't need twenty servants stoking the fireplace, trimming goose feathers for my pen, grinding ink, lighting tallow candles and melting the bottoms to make them stand upright on a plate.

Gadgets are my servants.

Little Red Goldilocks, who broke into those bears' house said, "This porridge is too hot. This porridge is too cold. But this porridge is just right." What a whiner.

My porridge is always just right, and I can heat it in two minutes by exciting its molecules with a bombardment of electromagnetic rays of the microwave spectrum that polarize, titillate and thrill its little molecules. *You're sooo hot!* Or I can blow on it to make it cooler.

I can even put fresh blueberries in my porridge in the dead of winter. They're flown in from wherever in the world it happens to be mid-summer.

However, none of these miracles can hold a tallow candle to the fact that even the poorest person in the industrialized world can turn on the kitchen tap and get a glass of water that won't kill them with dysentery. If you're reading these words from the spiritual world, and if you've been there for, say, three hundred years, you probably died from dysentery. But don't be envious, because whatever kind of heart disease ends my life will not exist either, in 300 years.

You (currently living Earthlings, my younger selves) are reading this essay because you're a seeker on a journey of discovery. I presume so, anyway. Even if you have already found what you are looking for, inside you beats the heart of an adventurer. Now and forever, your journey will never end. You will always desire to find out which ideas and things are the most true, and which answers are the best solutions for every soul on earth. That, by the way, is why you were created.

You're probably conscientious about things on some level. You try to help out where you can by turning off lights you aren't using, or refusing to buy water in plastic bottles (of which everyone one of them seems to end up in the Pacific Ocean). But even if you recycle, and you always tell the supermarket check-out guy, "paper" (instead of plastic), your efforts are a drop in the bucket.

Even if you do all that, and even wear hemp-fiber sandals, will you save the planet? Sadly, you won't. The reason you won't is because you're way out-numbered by *the entire world*. The entire, disposable plastic dependent, money grubbing, rainforest burning, genetic food modifying, chicken breast hormone injecting, ocean polluting, mercury dumping, carcinogen eating, sex trafficking, power hungry world. That's why.

Stephen Hawking, the theoretical physicist and cosmologist, said recently that the human race faces extinction within the next thousand years unless mankind finds a way to inhabit other planets. A couple of problems with this are (1) he's way too optimistic. We don't have a thousand years. We can easily make our world uninhabitable in just a couple hundred, being the creative geniuses we are. And (2) if we go to other planets, we will be taking ourselves, and our exploitative ways, with us.

We may also be taking some of the newly-discovered viruses, or mutated stronger versions of viruses we've known for a century but which are "reawakening" in strains completely resistant to the antibiotics that used to kill them effortlessly. Our old friend, the sexually transmitted gonorrhea for example, has emerged as a super gonorrhea that laughs at quinolones, penicillin, tetracycline and sulfa. *"Hombre, we doan need no stinkin' badges."*

I call it super gonnorhea fragilistic expialidocious.

Everything mentioned in this essay so far is why, when you tell the supermarket check-out guy "paper" instead of "plastic," it's about as effective, in planet-and-mankind-saving terms, as switching deck chairs on the Titanic. If the world thought the way you did, we would have a shot. But it don't.

The only answer, and this is going to sound really naïve and stupid, is for we human beings to change our very nature from selfish to unselfish, from partisan to bipartisan from right or leftwing to headwing. How do you do that with 7.4 billion people (as of this writing) in a world made up of cultures who have hated each other for one or two thousand years?

This is a topic that needs to fill another essay. A series of essays, many, many international conferences and many, many books. I need to be granted a new, younger life so I can do better next time. How do we get success when some people would rather see their own grandchildren dead than give a break to the enemy?

Was it jet lag or thoughts like these that woke me up this morning? That compelled me to get up, locate the missing bunny rabbit slipper, stumble to the kitchen to make coffee, then to turn on the tap and watch the beautiful clean water pour out of it like magic. And just stand there and stare at it.

A CALL FROM THE UPSTAIRS PHONE

I got a call from a friend today, someone I had not spoken with in some time. He's a wonderfully kind individual, one of those people who is always thinking of others and reaching out to them. He has a good word and thought for everyone.

He found himself driving on the highway past the building where my office is. He thought of me in that moment and called. Or rather, he said, God told him to call me. He said, "Larry, I am driving past your office and God spoke to me just now. He asked me to call you and tell you how very much he loves you, how much he needs you and how happy you have made him." My heart overflowed with gratitude and I was warmed and moved to hear such sentiments. I have people I need to call right now.

I believe God must be Irish. Not because it's blarney, but because the God I've met can be overly effusive at times. Am I creating God in my own image? My golden gut says no, and I will bet you a chicken pot pie with heavy cream and a crisp, flaky crust.

My friend also said that if you love many people, then when you go to the spirit world, you will be able to be fully present in many places at the same time. This is why God and the great saints can appear to many different people in visions and in their dreams, all around the world, and at the same time. That's a lot to meditate on, so take your time and don't rush to judgment. I'm still mulling that one over myself.

It is important for your future if you can love people. Love many, many people of every type, nation and race with all your heart and soul. If you can do that, then you are really and truly free.

Whoever has loved the most people by the time they die wins. But paradoxically, bragging rights don't come with the victory. The best thing about meeting a bodhisattva is that he or she is usually unaware of being a bodhisattva. Humility is the very reason for their stature.

PAY ATTENTION IN GEOGRAPHY CLASS

Driving up to daughter Theresa's graduation from culinary school, we stopped in Lancaster, PA, to eat at one of the Amish villages (tourist attractions). Each one has a restaurant, a market, souvenirs, etc. The actual Amish people live their lives away from the tourists, which is the way they want it. These theme-park-style attractions make money and so everyone wins.

We stopped at a convenience store and sent son John (19) inside by himself to ask directions. It went like this:

Lady: "You can go down two miles and take a right at the Shell station, unless you're looking for Intercourse."

John quickly, "No! Not that."

Lady: "Blah, blah, blah more directions, etc."

John got back in the car but didn't have any kind of clear information for us. "She acted kind of funny," was all he said. He looked a bit shaken and perplexed.

A half-hour later, sitting in the Amish restaurant, the waitress extolled the various tourist attractions, mentioning that we might want to drive over to Intercourse. After the waitress left, John looked relieved. He leaned in and told us what had happened when he was asking directions. John said, "After she asked me if I was looking for intercourse, I got so rattled I didn't hear anything else she said."

John had been keeping all this bottled up inside him until the waitress let it be known that Intercourse, PA is a nearby town. Only then could he share what happened. Until then, he had been thinking so that's what the attraction is with the Amish—intercourse. And then he was wondering why his parents wanted to come here, and bring the whole family. That's why he had been looking so weird.

It took me and Taeko twenty minutes to be able to stop laughing.

Advice from God's friend in Manila

Anyone who is one in heart with God is one in heart with everyone else who is one in heart with God.

I was in Manila fighting sin. My own, of course, as always. But that's not why I went. My purpose in going to the Philippines was to look after some details related to an upcoming international conference—logistics stuff, hotels, catering, ground transportation.

The thing is, God is pretty much everywhere and most people are quite happy with that thought. That's why God is easy to think and converse about. Or can be. Many of the people who would be at this conference were themselves spiritually oriented, coming from a wide variety of faiths. Lots of Catholics, this being the Philippines, but everything else too. So I ended up speaking with people about God all day long, and over dinner at night. I was having the time of my life.

Like you, I'm a seeker. Or at least I hope you are, and that you remain so all your life, even after you've found "Life's Great Big Hairy Answer." There is still a lot of seeking and improving most of us can do within our great big answer, so don't get too comfy.

My back was bothering me one morning, so an associate suggested we go to a spa and get ourselves worked over by someone reputed to be a highly skilled massage therapist. I was lying on the table, covered by a towel, my head on my arms as I was about to fall asleep. A woman roughly my age walked in and introduced herself as Lucille. Her fingers were knotted and twisted like gnarled branches brought to life by a special-effects artist.

She laid her palm in the middle of my back and said, "Ah, okay. Yes." It was as if I was hearing her end of a phone call with my spine. She moved her hand. "Yes. Un-huh. Okay, yes." And then she hung up. She asked me, "Are you a writer?"

"Yeah, I do some of that," I said, "but today I'm helping organize a conference"

"A meeting for religious people," she said. It wasn't a question.

"Have we met before?"

She ignored me, saying only, "Those who do not live in trust with God are foolish people. I have no time for them." She said other things on the same theme, but I'm not sure what, because my ability to form coherent thought suffered a power outage as every corpuscle of my soul rushed over to my back to see what was going on with Lucille's mahogany thumbs. My stress points were being hunted down like dogs and personally mangled by her bare hands.

After a certain amount of moaning in dire agony, I gasped, "Lucille, can I ask you a question?"

Apparently not, because she ignored that one too, while quickly heating the air inside glass cups and placing each one upside down on my back. About a dozen in all. I couldn't see how she did it, but I smelled the fire and felt minor heat. As the air cooled in the cups a strong partial vacuum was created inside each glass.

"I'm taking out the bad blood," she said, adding inexplicably, "Never fight with God."

"Okay, I won't."

"I know you don't."

The glass hickey-makers sat on my back for 30 minutes, rearranging my blood. I had lots of bad blood still in me from my car accident the year before, and plenty of new bad blood from the stress of organizing this conference instead of being at home writing, like I should have been.

But soon my bad blood was good blood and I had 12 large red circles on my back that, in the event of a strip search going through customs, would identify me as a guy who had been in a fight with a giant squid.

After she made another brief phone call to my right shoulder, Lucille announced, "This is where you were injured."

She meant in the car accident. She was batting a thousand. The thinking of normal people is that injuries are left alone, or touched only tenderly at most. Lucille leaned on my injury with the pointy part of her elbow.

My shoulder was screaming silent, shoulderly obscenities.

"Ahhhh, you're killing me!" I told her. Loudly

"I'm not killing you. I'm loving you," she said, applying even more pressure to the ligament muscle thingies, my *triceratops ob-la-di ob-la-da*. If she had been a professional wrestler, we could call her The Manila Folder. Hahahaha. Really, I crack me up, sometimes.

Most of us have experienced situations when life looks like certain death. When what seems counter-intuitive is actually the correct course. Like when you're disarming a bomb and your brain is shouting, "Whoa, don't cut the red wire!" But you cut it anyway, and everybody is saved. I love it when that happens.

This was like that. As soon as she stopped leaning on my shoulder, the being-on-fire feeling stopped and went away—*utterly and completely*, leaving behind only the deafening silence of *no pain*. And anyway, isn't it one of life's ongoing literary archetypal scenarios that you do something difficult, and it's painful, but it's for your own good? Or that you look down the road toward a fork where the signpost holding the direction arrows pointing toward "Good" and "Evil" has fallen over and you can't tell which road goes to which destination?

Did I tell you I love the Philippines? I do. The people, the culture, the mangoes, the geckos—it all works for me. I don't know where Lucille came from, but God bless her. She would be a magical saint in any culture.

Paper towels

The good kind

T rue life adventure. Honey Nim sent me to the store for some sliced turkey breast. Or kale. (I get the two mixed up). Anyway, I get a pouch of mac & cheese, which I know she'll like much better. Just add a little water and nuke it in the pouch. How awesome is that? I'm searching for the shortest checkout line when the cell rings. It's her.

"Hi, Honey."

"Did you get what I asked?"

"Even better …"

"Okay, I need you to get some paper towels, too."

"I'm on it."

She says, "Get the good kind." And then hangs up.

Wait, what? There's a GOOD kind? This is paper towels we're talking about. I'm thinking those are as generic as butter. Or tampons. You would think so, right?

Au contraire mon frère.

One entire side of an aisle in a 60,000 square foot Super Giant store is devoted only to paper towels. The aisle recedes into the distant horizon. It has its own zip code. I'm about a third of the way in, looking a little bewildered. One-ply, two-ply, 48 two-ply sheets per roll (or 29.9 meters squared.) Maybe there's a brand labeled "Good Kind." Nope, none of them are. Or maybe it's assumed that all of them are.

A store lady about my age appeared behind me to ask if I needed assistance. Apparently I had been standing there quite a while, frozen in time.

"Yes, thank you. I need paper towels. The good kind."

"The good kind," she repeated.

"That's right, the good kind."

"Such as … ?"

I thought for a second, then said, "Well, paper towels that don't have original sin."

Almost without skipping a beat, she gestured to the dividing point between two brands in front of us and said, "From here, down to the end, they've all been forgiven."

And then she walked away. True story.

Honey Nim liked the paper towels I ended up with. Was less enthusiastic about the mac & cheese in a pouch—not a substitute for kale, apparently.

THE WHOLE MEGILLAH

Lobsters, mangoes and Maria von Trapp's curtains

Near the end of the last century when CAUSA was inaugurating its new headquarters atop the Tiffany Building in New York, Father and Mother Moon and some of the kids attended the ribbon cutting and banquet.

(CAUSA, besides being the Latin and Spanish word for "cause" is a rare acronym that works equally well in English and Spanish: Confederation for the Association and Unity of the Societies of the Americas. And also, *Confederacion de Asociaciones para la Unidad de las Sociedades de America.*)

A caterer took over one hallway of offices to put together a feast, the centerpiece of which was a big Maine lobster on each plate. Father and Mother Moon, being the founders of CAUSA, were the honored guests. They and the other pioneers of that great organization were seated on a raised table at the back of the room, facing the stage where the entertainment would be. Several hundred others were seated at round banquet tables in the auditorium

I was working backstage helping with the entertainment, enjoying being part of it. I didn't have to entertain that night or emcee the proceedings, so it was a relaxing evening for me. A few of us hatched a conspiracy to grab Father and Mother's plates on their way back to the kitchen. We would eat their leftovers, whatever was there, as an act of love and bonding. This time in the early 1980s was a golden age, and that's how close we all felt to them and one another.

And so we stood in the doorway to the kitchen and waited patiently. Finally the waiter carried the plates back to the kitchen, and as he passed through the door, two of us gently lifted away both their plates as he passed by. "We'll just take these for you," I said with my big Texas howdy smile.

Their plates each had a lobster shell; the whole lobster, including tail, middle part, claws, head, etc. Mother's plate had few bits here and there, but not much—some lobster, a couple of broccolis, maybe. Father's plate was clean, but what was shocking was the lobster shell. There was nothing in it. When I say *nothing*, try to imagine the vacuum of deep space.

There was not enough lobster left for even an ant to find and carry away. The lobster shell was cleaned out head-to-tail as though it had been dipped into an acid bath. Most of us have eaten lobster and some of us take pride in getting all the meat out of the claws. The hard-to-reach pieces that hardly anyone ever gets all of, the very tiniest leg joints, had nothing left in them. After Father finished that lobster, there was not enough left to find with tweezers and a magnifying glass, including the eyeballs.

Seeing this impressed me in a way that no sermon of his ever could. Many times I heard him speak in person about honoring the heart of God's creation by letting nothing go to waste. Use the whole *megillah* in other words. If I were a lobster, and assuming I was at peace with my place on the food chain, I would want to be eaten by a good person, who lived for others, and who used all my nourishment to that end. If it were my lot to be eaten in order to sustain the energy of someone working on behalf of all creation, I would not want any of me to be unused and tossed out.

That was many years ago. This afternoon, Taeko and some of the kids and I stood in the kitchen eating beautifully ripe mangoes Taeko had just bought. She sliced them on either side of their unreasonably large, flat seeds. Then she expertly scored the soft fruit with a knife, just down to the peel, but not cutting the peel itself. She inverted the peel so the fruit stuck up scored into cubes by the knife. This is just about the only way to eat a mango without having to take a bath immediately after.

Not only was it easy to eat, but it was possible to get pretty much every bit of the mango. There is always some left on the seed and we scraped that off with our teeth, getting hands sticky up to the wrists and our faces messy between chin and nose. A certain amount of wash-up is inevitable.

I leaned in and licked a piece of fruit off just below Honey Nim's lower lip. "We eat the whole mango," I reminded.

While this was happening, we had the soundtrack of "The Sound of Music" going in the living room. It was something of a Moffitt family favorite when the kids were growing up. Maria von Trapp, played by Julie Andrews, had a small household budget so she took down the bedroom curtains and used them to make matching play clothes for all the little Von Trappitos.

That was Julie using the whole mango.

We human beings are wasteful, living on the edge of planetary burnout. Perhaps we could be forgiven for not being aware of overconsumption back when the earth's population didn't go much beyond Noah's valley. It didn't dawn on us when humankind first began causing animal species to go extinct. The European bluebuck was hunted to extinction in the late 1700s. The last California grizzly bear was killed in the 1920s. Even when travelers in the American West shot buffalo from trains just for fun, killing millions and leaving their carcasses to rot in the sun, alarm bells didn't go off in the public consciousness. There were still vast open lands and plenty of stuff out there, and complex ecosystems were not well understood. To the extent collective humanity registered the connection between slaughtering entire species of animals and plants, and the eventual destruction of ourselves, the articulation of it was muted or lip-service.

We humans have always had an instinct to be selfish and wasteful. What impressed me so much about Father is that using the whole lobster is his own private standard. He just quietly did what he always does.

In the late 1940s, early 50s, Father was sentenced to nearly three years in a communist North Korea slave labor camp for the crime of preaching about God. The Heung Nam death camp was all about slow starvation and controlling people with food. If, weakened from illness or a lack of food, prisoners failed to complete their quota of filling bags with caustic ammonium nitrate fertilizer, their nightly ration of a bowl of rice would be cut in half. Not meeting the daily quota then became self-perpetuating because the prisoner would become weaker and sicker still, until finally they would literally crawl and stumble the four kilometers to the fertilizer factory and back at night. While eating his handful of rice at night, a prisoner would suddenly stop with the chopsticks not quite reaching his lips, and would die. Even before his body slumped to the ground, the other prisoners would grab his rice bowl and force his mouth open to pull out and eat the rice he had not yet swallowed.

On that CAUSA evening, if we hadn't been standing in the doorway, waiting to ambush his leftovers, I may never have learned viscerally how that experience shaped and honed his relationship with not just food, but with the oceans, the land, the air, and all the things that people need in order to survive, feel love and then deliver love to others. I was imprinted by that experience and when I told Honey Nim, she was impressed as well. The heart of gratitude was in our thoughts when we ate the mango. I hope one day to be as thoroughgoing a steward of the environment as Father and Mother Moon are, but at least I was blessed to be able to see the standard and be judged by it.

A TREE FALLS IN A FOREST

The Tao of firewood

A tree was visiting our driveway. It just dropped in. Several trees actually. Karl's friend, Troy, said he had a truck full of wood to give us—hickory, cherry, maple and oak. I took counsel of my Inner Paul Bunyan. The trees had already been felled by pave-the-earth developers, and the dismembered trunks had already been loaded onto the truck, so I said okay. Otherwise it would have gone into a landfill.

They delivered and dumped it while I was out and suddenly I was the proud owner of a driveway full of tree parts, ranging from trunks three feet in circumference to rotted hollows that would burn with the heat value of a damp straw voodoo doll. Nearly three cords of it overflowed into the street, what scientists call "a bigass pile of wood," and only a couple of days to deal with it before the City of Bowie's code violations people started papering me with nastygrams.

Normally I like to spend quite of bit of time contemplating wood before splitting it. I bow to its spirit and its unfaltering immensity, strength and nobility. I love wood, and it loves me back. But this time there would be no opportunity to *get to know* the wood. No time for late-night brandy and cigars, and pondering the infinite in the company of the steadfast soul of venerable and ancient trees. I had to rent a chainsaw and power splitter and just get it done.

The best wood for splitting can look anyway it wants on the outside— ugly or pretty or whatever. But inside, the grain is true and vertical and unblemished. It splits easily and in its innermost heart, desires to warm the hearth of true-hearted heroes. Firewood sometimes has to settle for warming the hearth of arrogant bastards, but that's never its first choice.

Just the act of burning fine hardwood judges a person's character severely. For example, I checked the age on a cross-section of log after sawing it. I counted its rings: 75 … 100 … 150. This mighty oak was a sapling in 1866, the year Jesse James robbed his first bank, taking $15,000 from the Clay County Savings Association in Liberty, Missouri. This was the same year Andrew Rankin patented the urinal. The stories that tree could tell.

When I think of firewood in general, and this tree in particular, it shames me to consider that this oak tree lived a century of hardship, enduring droughts and floods and fires, so that I can heat my home for one cold evening. It is not an equal trade by any way of looking at it. In a just world, it would have been crafted into flooring in a house that would last another hundred years. Hardwood manifests unconditional endurance.

I have identified a cast of characters in the wood I chop. There is "honky-tonk angel wood," whose logs are smooth as a baby's butt on the outside. But inside, they're hollowed out, powdery and infested with bugs. It falls apart under the axe but produces little in the way of heat. You burn it just to get rid of it and kill the vermin inside.

"Wife beater wood" is completely twisted inside—like a wife beater. The grain runs every which way. You can chainsaw it into round sections, but splitting those sections—forget it. It will laugh at your ax, and will sneer at your tenuous hold on your foolish "manhood." So you set it aside next to the woodpile. In five years or so, it will still not split, but it will rot just enough so that yellow jackets will build a nest inside and gang-sting you when you get close with the lawn mower.

At the noblest end of the spectrum, there is "lovely wood." This is often hickory. It's not that impressive externally. When it's old, the bark falls off easily and it looks even more nondescript. But when you heft it, the density is heavy, substantial. It is strong against the ax, complicated and multi-layered inside. When you split it and let it season through a summer and into the following winter, it burns long and fully and will warm your house and your family corner to corner.

As hard as I and my family had to work to harvest and move and stack it, I am happy this hardwood found its way to my house to be properly used rather than rot in a landfill. The process of wood rotting is exquisite, by the way. Rotting things are broken down by nature and contain the entire universe in a microscope's eyepiece, but that's another essay.

The ordeal of having way too much wood plopped into my yard has been analogous to a spiritual trial. In five days I had to chainsaw it into woodstove lengths, then split it. Finally, I had to haul and stack it. This was back-breaking work. Me and Honey Nim were joined on day two by the Korean and Chinese boys who lived with us that school year. The Moffitt kids helped a little bit between school and work.

When I went out to finish splitting early on the morning of the third day, autumn's frosty dew made scattered diamonds on the grass and the sun promised a warm afternoon. That, along with the feel of the leather gloves carried in the palm of my hand, made me recall what it was like doing early morning chores on my grandfather's farm in Oklahoma. *It was exactly like this*, I thought, *except the chores were different*. We had cows to milk in those days, and sheep to be let out of the coyote fence and back into the pasture. The murmured "ba-GAWK" of chickens awakening, the splendid smell of glorious cow shit when we opened the barn, the crunch and feel of gravel under my work shoes, fused together in a mosaic of images.

All this was happening in my mind, the entire picture in a few seconds, as I walked over to the log-splitter in my backyard to crank it up. I began to notice that as I split the last of the big logs over the space of an hour, my motions took on the cadence and mannerisms of my granddaddy Brown. I bent over in that slow way like him, moved at his pace, and even conversed quietly with the dogs the way I remember him doing when I was eleven years old, as though the dogs understood every word I said and wagged in agreement.

Over coffee afterward with Honey Nim, I wondered aloud how I got that way, how I saw snatches of things as though watching a movie. And in thinking of such scenes, from what headwaters do these vivid images come? What makes me personify and romanticize firewood, of all things? Where does this come from? I don't think I have an artistic heritage. As far as I know my forbearers were mostly Christian dirt-farmers who toiled from sunrise to sunset, busting their backs trying to build something out of nothing. Most things in life were black or white for them, wrong or right, with not much gray area. Honey Nim said that in Japan the warrior class, spent their days slicing each other up in rivalries. It was the artists, from whom she descends, who became farmers. Farm life in Japan was hard like it is here, but while the crops were growing, they studied calligraphy and ancient beauty.

We felt the shared bond of both our families having worked the soil. We are made from soil, and in us breathes the spirit of wood, water and fire. All that day she and I hauled and stacked, laying the logs for optimum drying the rest of the summer ("loose enough so a chipmunk can run through the pile, but a rabbit can't.") At noon, we started a small fire in the fire pit using last year's wood. We cooked two steaks over the fire, roasted some garlic bread and ate hungrily with knife, fork and fingers. Sunset came and went as we enjoyed the Indian summer warmth. We were outside the whole time. Our work finished as the last of the light faded, we sat side-by-side in the twilight, and finally, the darkness lit only by the embers that remained. Stars were scattered all over the domed sky. Under Orion's three-starred belt, I distinctly heard the honking of geese flying south in the dark. I had no idea they flew at night.

Eden, a couple days post-apple

August and worst August
the smell of dry desperate sin,
hot biting fire ants and warm beer.
Sweaty underslip worn as a housedress,
sticks to the skin, the dirt and history.
So crazy jealous, damn you anyway, Rhonda.
Head against the inside of the screen door,
I would kill for a breeze.

We gots to dig in the dirt for groceries now.
Sweathog angels from two heavens over
who musta rose up from the ashes of Dixie,
look askew and quizzical this way and that
smirking, "Which of you knows how to work a shovel?"
Grace don't get handed to us no more, do it?
We even gots to dig for the right
to respect our own selves,
dig for love that don't up and quit on you.
She looks over. "Bubba, dontcha leave me."

"Stay with it, Bubba honey." She strokes his hair.
"You got to hang in there, do what I could not.
Don't fall no more than I done already.
Redemption will be hambone in our poke salad.
Jes' don't fergit me when you're called home
to Jesus, trailing clouds of glory."

EVIDENT MERIT

The "Shouts and Murmurs" section of The New Yorker magazine emailed me a nice rejection slip:

> Dear Mr. Moffitt,
> We're sorry to say that your piece, "I Awoke This Morning in Need of a Latte," wasn't right for us, despite its evident merit. Thank you for allowing us to consider your work.
> Best regards,
> The Shouts Dept.

Ha! You see that?! "... despite its evident merit." That's right, *evident merit*. That means my submission contains real, by-god merit that is also evident. Which means any fool can see it. Just sayin' that's the kind of quality you're getting in this book as well.

Of course they still rejected it flat. Like Betty Lou Grinder did with my offer to take her to the Senior Prom those many years ago. But still, "evident merit" is a better deal than I got from Betty Lou. She never said, "Larry, despite the evident merit of your offer to take me to the prom, it isn't right for me."

And let me say, even though I'm grasping at straws in the fight for love and glory, I really admire my attitude in all this. I gotta hand it to me.

As you must have guessed, this is by no means the first such rejection I have received for things written. I have a small, but enviable, collection. And of course I will keep on sending things to publications because ... well ... because evident merit.

I just wish some publication would write me a rejection slip that truly says is like it is. For example, as follows:

> Larry, I know someday we are going to be flogging ourselves with a wet, knotted rawhide whip for rejecting your unspeakably breathtaking submission to our mediocre rag. And damn it to

crud, Larry, I know we're going to fry in hell for it, but we are just too freakin' braindead to view your writing in the historical context that will elevate your work to the stratosphere one day, while we and our stupid, scum-sucking little magazine will lie rotting in an unmarked pauper's grave, and you will have a bridge over the Hudson named after you. A bridge that everyone will love because of you, despite its godawful traffic jams.

I AWOKE THIS MORNING IN NEED OF A LATTE

I awoke this morning in need of a latte. I briefly considered upping it to a macchiato, frappe, then pondered it and thought, *Nah, just a latte.*

Did I mention food? Something from the biscotti phylum would be nice to munch during my poetical, mystical, long walk on the beach. Oh, and at sunset of course—or dawn. Anyway, one of those.

Putting it all together in my mind—a long walk on the beach at sunset, with a latte and my dog. I'm wearing Birkenstock loafers and biodegradable hemp fiber shorts that run half on electricity, half on gas. The dog isn't actually "my pet," per se, but a companion animal who belongs to herself. A golden retriever named Dakota, or better, Aragorn.

That Indian on television who cried looking at litter along the road, he's there too, on the beach, looking at more litter. At his feet lies a half-full can of Sherwin-Williams Peach Blossom Whisper interior, oil-based latex paint. "We cover the earth," the label says.

A discarded newspaper called *The Answer* is blowing in the wind.

A few loose pages catch around my leg and I look down at the classifieds. A light drizzle begins to fall as the personals section gets my attention. Tangled in my legs are four broadsheet newspaper pages of "in search of" ads (ISOs) in six-point type. The drizzle intensifies into a full-fledged summer shower. Raindrops fall straight down from a windless sky. Just before the pages are turned into paper-maché, I manage to read one of the ads.

"ADJPNSCSCND (Asian divorced Jewish professional non-smoking Christian street car named desire) in search of like-minded man for LTR (long-term relationship). Must enjoy quiet walks in the rain. E. Rigby"

I look up and there she is. The author of that very ad is just fifty yards up the beach, walking quietly in the rain. I look around and see others. A lot of others, in fact. Why hadn't I noticed them before? All the lonely people, where do they all come from? Where do they all belong?

There are now hundreds, maybe thousands of solitary individuals, all walking quietly on the beach. Nobody is speaking to anyone. There isn't a hint of rain gear or an umbrella in the bunch. Most are deep in thought, gazing down at the sand. A few are facing the sea while, metaphorically, facing the latency of their unrequited hopes as a harbinger of humanity's ultimate desolation amid love's inability to deliver the goods, forthwith.

Or, whatever.

The only sound on the beach is unison sighing.

A nice-looking youngish guy, yet somehow old in acquired wisdom, catches my attention—thin, with blue eyes, thick black hair, killer abs. He walks in low jeans and a shirt left unbuttoned, through the intermittently spaced lost souls, feeling his way as much with intuitive radar as with his eyes, searching, sifting. He approaches a young woman carrying a mocha java grande made from aged Sumatran beans. Full-bodied, smooth, spicy, complex. As is her coffee.

He gives her a quiet, "Hi."

"Hi." She nods back and a moment of silence settles over them.

"You know," he finally says, "I climbed cathedral mountains. I saw silver clouds below, saw everything as far as you can see. And they say that I got crazy once and that I tried to touch the sun. I lost a friend, but kept the memory."

Though alarm bells of warning are going off in her head, they are like a ringing in the far distance, as removed as an Amish farmhouse fire bell two counties over. She looks at him with her head slightly tilted. Her delicate, soft mouth, shorn of all defenses, can utter only, "Gosh."

He gazes sagely toward the horizon. "Now I walk in quiet solitude, the forest and the stream, seeking grace in every step I take. My sight is turned inside myself to try and understand the serenity of a clear blue mountain lake."

She intones a long "wowwww," way too subdued for her own good. Her eyes are wide, undemanding of anything.

With dark, sloe eyes, and flashing an irresistible shit-eating grin, he takes the mocha java from her hand, downs the rest of it and tosses the cup. "Name's Lucifer. I like long walks on the beach."

"Jennifer. Virgo. I like quiet walks in the rain."

"Cool."

I watch them stroll away together. The summer shower abates, and as it does, the walkers in the rain fade one by one. Nobody actually goes to their car and drives away. They just fade, literally, unmindful that it is also happening to everyone around them. With the cessation of x-amount of raindrops, each one grows increasingly transparent until right near the end when they suddenly poof into nonexistence. The imploding air makes a tiny plinking sound as each one disappears. *Plink. Plink. Plinkplink ... plinkplinkplinkplink.* It was like watching a video of popcorn popping, played in reverse.

It seems these personals ad walkers can exist only in the rain. Only at the beach. Their loneliness was foretold by the fact that none of the ads said, "Love loud, boozy socializing on the beach in the rain." Just quiet walks. Intimate, confessional statements from people trying to end their solitude by proclaiming a love of solitude. How strange, I thought. Once again here is a need for the existence of a font for irony.

Go ahead and judge me, if you want. I have come to accept that I can't be everything to all people. I am learning to be happy with myself, to love me as I am. I often surprise myself with little gifts. I need a latte.

My biodegradable hemp fiber shorts are half-filled with gas as I *"go placidly amid the noise and haste, remembering what peace there may be in silence."*

Also typed in "ironics" is my sworn statement to the Environmental Protection Agency on the unfortunate demise of a school of dolphins accidentally electrocuted in the preparation of this report. The printer, plugged in, fell off the table and bounced off the pier into the Club Med cove. The little Flippers never knew what hit them, and I'm sure they didn't suffer.

Your own North Star

You remember exactly where you were and what you were doing when the World Trade Center towers fell. Do you remember where you were when you got your marching orders from life?

The instructions may have arrived incrementally, so maybe you don't.

When you were a kid you may have intuited a goal line out there, or several (to be in medicine, to raise cattle and children, to be a musician, or a revolutionary). "Not all who wander are lost," says daughter Hwa. This simultaneous beautiful philosophy and famous last words, causes her to radiate life-affirming energy, while putting her in some peril.

Fortunate are they who have opened early on, the Welcome Wagon Basket life handed them. In it are some indistinct maps, a compass that works part of the time, packets of good and bad luck, a box of gumption and a handy middle finger for explaining things to people of bad will. But not everyone receives that basket at birth. There are so many folks out there who seem to perceive nothing, drifting on wind and water ripples from the moment the umbilical is cut, until long after they croak. They walk around with a vague feeling that someone cheated them.

Your fate is whatever happens to you along the way, for whatever reasons. Fate is fluid, subject to whim … taking a right turn instead of a left … two ships passing in the night with destined soulmates leaning on the rail of each one, who may or may not see one another, and who may or may not connect their two eternities … People like to say there are no coincidences, but I've never believed that. Sometimes stuff just freakin' happens.

Ah, but your destiny. Your destiny is guided by your personal North Star, which never budges from its fixed position above you. Your destiny is bigger than the stuff you do. Your destiny lasts longer than your lifetime and it's always there waiting for you like a familiar beast in the trees, in this world and the next.

Whether you're a bronco buster or a Buddhaboy, does a crisis of faith make you run and hide, or do you stand fast, even if you're scared as hell, and stare into the fog until it parts, no matter how long it takes? Either way, when the fog finally clears, your destiny, your North Star, is still there. Where it always was.

Your original understanding was not wrong. Stop roaming the room with your eyes in search of easier destinies. Don't look for the cavalry to come to the rescue. *You're* the cavalry. Grow a hump to carry your water supply. Find oxygen in the examples of others who have had to stand utterly alone, against great odds. Read their words. And while you're at it, write your own words. There is always someone who can learn from you.

Be even steadier when the deck beneath your feet grows ever more unsteady. When the ship is rocking back and forth and the waves are slamming the sides sharply and unexpectedly at every moment, and people are heaving up the groceries, and the nets are dredging up new messiahs, faint hearts are fainting and crazed souls rampage through the streets—there is only enduring. Ride it out, babydog, and don't expect to be thrilled by what's going on. It could be that the darkened cloud is so vast it takes a hundred years for its silver lining to finally appear on the horizon.

Well, I guess there is one small, tiny positive thing. Being on a ship in a raging sea means never having an uninteresting day, and never having to stir your coffee.

AUGUST 1955

When I grow up I want to be an imaginary friend. In the summer of 1955 I am six. Every summer is the summer of wasps. And dogs and chickens and feral cats on the dirt farm of Clyde and Kathryn Brown three miles outside Fairland, Oklahoma. Grandparents.

I walk down the red dirt road every afternoon, slipping out after lunch in the heat of the day to get out of taking a nap. If I am not there in the house, bothering anyone, no naps are needed.

The dog and I converse as we walk. I don't speak to the dog; we converse. Duke is fine and happy with being a border collie, and would I like to throw a stick anywhere? Duke rattles on incessantly, making little sense. I'm fine with that. The air is so hot it has its own smell and humming sound. The rocks of the county-graded road enter through the hole in my sneaker.

Loneliness lies silently upon my shoulders. It slinks upward and sits on my head, squashing my cowlick flat. Then it covers my head, hanging down over my eyebrows. I, and the pain of my aloneness, are inseparable.

At the creek, she waits in blue. We talk and play games. Skip stones and sing many, many songs. Her, me, Duke. One day she said, "Next year you will be seven and I will not be here anymore."

DEATH BY TOASTING IN BEIJING

Y ou can fly from Washington to Beijing on a United flight leaving
Dulles at 10:00 a.m., arriving at 3:30 in the afternoon the next day,
without the sun ever setting across your bow. You will make a pit stop
in Chicago to take on fuel and honey roasted peanuts, and sometimes
another stop in Anchorage if you've had strong headwinds over Canada.

Sixteen and a half hours will have elapsed and you will have crossed
the International Dateline, which adds the extra day, but you will also
have been hugging the trailing skirt of the sun. Your so-called mind will
tell you it's still the same day. However, you will have flown a total of
7,162 miles and will arrive a grubby, foul-tempered basket case. You
will feel the way a desiccated king found in an unearthed Egyptian
pyramid looks.

If you want to take the scenic route, Northwest will get you there
in just under 24 hours with stops and waits in Detroit and Tokyo. The
mileage is 8,202, an ideal flight for people who have a thing for airport
transit lounges. Do it economy class, in the middle seat of a jam-packed
777 and you have a real travel experience. However, you'll have to pay
extra for the pleasure. This flight is $300 more than the other one, for
reasons nobody knows. Nobody. I've done it before in a pinch, but never
without drugs.

Transglobal flight may be man's most unnatural act. It violates the terms
of service of our circadian software and that's why we are punished for
doing it. Flying against the direction of the sun (from Orient to Occident)
messes you up even more than going the other way. For example, if you
take off from Tokyo to DC on a Tuesday morning, you experience a series
of 4-hour days, arriving on the very same Tuesday you left—a half-hour
earlier than when you took off. You will have traveled backward in time.

I have a theory, lightly held, that if you could fly against the sun,
around and around the world without stopping, you would continue to
travel backward in time and would grow ever younger all the way down

through infancy until you curl into a fetal position in your seat, shrink into an embryo, a zygote, a sperm cell and then—*poof*. As soon as I get enough frequent flyer miles, I'm going to do just that. But until then, having a spherical earth actually presents a lot of problems for everyone and has no real advantages I can think of. It makes me wonder if some aspects of the creation weren't handled by committee. Round planets. Good grief, what could they have been thinking?

On this particular occasion, we were on Thai Airlines, flying with the sun to Beijing. Thai Air is not a natural fit for a China destination but was necessitated by our schedule and the availability of 20 seats. The "we" in this trip was a delegation of high-profile policy wonks and former assistant secretaries of state, now in private practice. We were going over for a look-see and meetings with counterparts in the foreign ministry and Chinese think tanks.

My traveling companion was Ambassador Douglas MacArthur II, namesake and nephew of the famous General, and a dear friend and mentor for many years. In his 80th year, he was spry. He had been a U.S. ambassador to four countries and the lifelong husband of Laura Barkley, daughter of Truman's vice president. A student of the old school of gallantry, he was blessed with a diplomat's twin muses—dignity entwined around one arm and charm, hanging on his every word, around the other. When he unsheathed his wit, it did the work of a demon barber's straight razor.

We left Washington on American to connect with Thai Air at Dallas/ Fort Worth. From there we went to Tokyo and overnighted in an airport hotel, but got very little sleep due to jet lag. From Tokyo we went to Bangkok, where we hung out for two hours in a transit lounge featuring a malfunctioning air conditioner in a land of perpetual August, windows that wouldn't open and a hundred passengers from an Indonesia flight, all of whom were apparently on their way to a chain-smokers convention.

By the time we touched down in Beijing, to be greeted by deputy ministers in dark suits and one ribbon-spangled military official, we were blithering. Greetings were exchanged. A skinny interpreter was shoulder surfing beside and slightly behind his boss, hovering like a hummingbird, moving when the boss moved, all the while seamlessly transforming one language into another for our conversation. He had been well chosen.

He was named Gao, and his English was colloquial which indicated schooling in the U.S.

Gao asked us to call him Chuck. He had chosen his western name in honor of karate master and actor Chuck Norris. A couple days later, he mentioned he had attended the University of Texas at Austin. I gave him the high sign of our shared alma mater, a raised fist with the index and little fingers extended, and uttered the requisite "Hook 'em, horns." Chuck beamed. His days at UT were obviously a golden time for him, too.

The assistants handed us typed itineraries for our meetings and activities. They asked if the schedule was to our liking, and it seemed to be so, but then again our critical faculties weren't engaged at the moment. A group of lesser assistants solicitously requested our luggage tags and went off to gather our bags and put them on a separate truck to the hotel. We would find them waiting for us in our rooms when we got there, one of them said. Only then did someone absorb the itinerary sufficiently to realize we would not be going directly to our hotel.

I think if they had pushed back the welcoming reception a couple hours and had taken us to our hotel first so we could freshen up, then maybe what happened next could have been avoided. I'm certain of it, in fact. But even the sinewy legions of Sparta never had marching orders as inviolable as a Chinese Foreign Ministry's visiting delegation schedule, set in type. Just our luck to arrive at the cocktail hour.

The bus pulled up to a large gated compound and we offloaded in front of an expansive building with a marble front. Two flag poles stood on a landing halfway up a set of wide, ceremonial steps. The flags of the People's Republic of China and the United States flew next to one another. We were at a friendship hall, a facility used by government ministries to host receptions and dinners for foreign delegations. The plan was to have a drink with a few high-ranking diplomats and Foreign Ministry leaders, exchange toasts to our continuing friendship, to make what Ambassador MacArthur liked to call "agreeable noises."

We filed into the room trying to look brighter and more spirited than we felt. We had worn suits and ties on the flight from Japan because that's the kind of delegation we were, and we had shaved that morning so we looked basically human. There were around 150 people in the room, men and women of officialdom. No out-of-the-ordinary rancor existed between our two countries at this time and they were pleasant and genuinely welcoming. The space was like a large hotel ballroom, only better. It had a high ceiling, three robust crystal chandeliers and plush carpet where a large Chinese character for "friendship" dominated the center of the pattern. Running half the length of one wall was an enormous and exquisitely done tapestry of maybe 30 feet in length, depicting a mountain valley and a flight of cranes. Except for the portrait of Chairman Mao at one end of the room, of a tasteful size and location, there was nothing political about any of the decor.

Plush couches and doilied chairs ringed the walls. At one end, two large yellow chairs sat side-by-side with a low table of beautiful hardwood in front, inlaid with ivory carvings. A small interpreter's chair sat between and behind the two larger chairs. This is where presidents and prime ministers sit for photo opps and pleasantries before the real back-room stuff begins. We could see they had laid on their best room for us, and in a culture where courtesies are carefully weighed and extended according to stature, this meant something.

Waiters in bow ties and red blazers circulated with trays of drinks, and a light buffet of dim sum (steamed buns filled with seasoned pork) was set off to the side. They smelled good and, contrary to what some say, the best dim sum, or *bao zhi*, in Mandarin, are not found in Hong Kong or New York, but in Beijing at state receptions. But that would have to wait.

The ambassador, as the delegation leader, and myself as the organizing *daibiao misu*, were led to an open space directly in front of the presidential chairs. All the king's men and their shoulder surfers stood in cheery expectation. I could see that the honor of meeting the nephew and spitting image of General Douglas MacArthur, in addition to the ambassador's own distinguished diplomatic accomplishments, was something to write home about. Hands were shaken. How is everyone feeling? We're all fine, and you? Excellent, and how was your flight? Just splendid, thank you.

The room grew quiet and conversations stopped as everyone turned toward the center in amicable silence. Our host from the Foreign Ministry said something in Chinese. His surfer interpreted his thanks for our having traveled such a prodigious distance and that it was a distinct honor and great pleasure to have this distinguished group as their guests.

Our host informed us that his formative years in diplomatic service had been spent at the embassy in Washington and seeing us made him nostalgic for those days. He invoked pleasant memories of Washington, the cherry blossoms around the Jefferson Memorial in the springtime, the good-hearted people of America.

He complimented Ambassador MacArthur on his youthful vigor. And he meant it. China is one place where 80 years old isn't thought of as "old" as much as it's thought of as revered. Anyone able to outlast his enemies long enough to arrive at age 80 is given due credit for his wisdom and cunning. He looked forward to the meetings of the next few days, which would be joined by U.S. Ambassador Winston Lord. He made nice all over the place and concluded in English, "Welcome, dear friends" and raised his glass. We raised ours, clinked our glasses together and drank.

And now it was Ambassador MacArthur's turn to render a responding toast for our team. He stepped up to the plate as he has done maybe a thousand times in his career. "Gentlemen, ladies," he said, "it's wonderful to be here in the Republic of China."

Nice beginning. The only problem is that the Republic of China is Taiwan, a China that officially doesn't exist in the place we were in now, which is called the *People's* Republic of China. A silence bigger than The Great Wall fell over the room. The ambassador caught himself immediately, adding, "… the *People's* Republic of China." Okay not perfect, but neither was it fatal. The ambassador continued unflustered, "… here in Taipei."

Ah, yes, now *that* was fatal.

The cadre of shoulder surfers was immobilized, but even officials who didn't understand a lick of English heard "Republic of China" and then "Taipei." The earlier silence had grown to the size of Kublai Khan's unwashed Mongol horde. He caught himself once again and said, "… uh, rather Beijing."

But now it didn't help.

In the People's Republic of China it was required at that time that anyone attending a conference or public function, whether inside the country or abroad, to stand and make a show of vigorously walking out if Taiwan is ever referred to as the Republic of China or if the Taiwan flag is displayed. More than policy, it was a law.

On the other hand, abandoning your own reception, which you are hosting, especially when feting an international delegation of this caliber, is not easily done. Virtually impossible, in fact. They just don't cover this one in protocol class. We were in uncharted territory and nobody knew what to do or say.

Instructions circulated telepathically among the Chinese: *Remain calm. Nobody make any sudden moves. We are an ancient people. This, too, shall pass. We hope.*

Our hosts stood as immobile as the terracotta warriors of Xian. No one spoke or moved, even to sip their drink. The void was total. All sound, air and light had been sucked from the room by the sheer power of the worst possible sin one can commit in that place and time. It was a singular occurrence as one judges such things, rather like an irreproducible work of art, in its own way. The perfect *faux pas*.

What was amazing was that the ambassador was able to maintain a posture of benign gentility, his glass held slightly higher than waist level with the other hand cupped lightly under it. Still smiling as pleasant as Mary Poppins having tea with the Queen, he spoke to me out the corner of his mouth, almost without moving his lips. "Goddammit," he said quietly, emphatically. Surveying the wreckage around us, I thought that pretty well summed it up.

It seemed the ambassador was down for the count, but the gentleman who had negotiated the postwar mutual defense treaty that still exists between the U.S. and Japan wasn't finished yet. The man who, when he was ambassador to Iran, had kept his cool as his car was ambushed and machine-gunned to smithereens around him, and had saved the lives of his chauffeur, his wife and himself by getting everyone to the floor—still held cards he hadn't played. The nephew of "I shall return" was about to kick into action.

He spoke in a voice infused with statesmanship, so sonorous and warm the ice sculpture on the buffet table began to melt. "Larry," he said in a grand voice that could have been followed by "someday all this will be yours." Instead it was followed by, "why don't you offer a toast?" Big ol' smile. The voice in my head screamed a deafening "*noooooooo*" that only I heard. The room was so quiet I could follow the sound of my own blood rushing in my ears. I thought, *That's it?! That's your plan?!*

But I knew it was. I even thought I could see it, although it wasn't a plan as much as it was an awareness of there being a shortage of options, a very small number of diverging paths of lesser evils to choose from. Like maybe one. The ball was in our court because there was nothing our Chinese hosts could say. Not if their lives depended on it. They had seized up like a brigade of collective farm tractors without oil. Also, the ambassador could not say another word because, at this point, just clearing his throat would set off a panic. I looked out over a roomful of bureaucrats and shoulder surfers, frozen in the headlights, with surreal grins bolted to their faces.

I would like to say that my toasting strategy, forged in the fires of adversity and honed to a keen edge in that moment, was to ramble incoherently. It wasn't my strategy, but that's what I did. Mainly I was thinking, *Just don't screw up. Keep it harmless and maybe this reception can get back on track.* Every man, woman and child in the room sure as hell wanted it back on track, that was clear.

Harmless? I can do harmless. Lightly amusing? No sweat. I proceeded to make agreeable noises, babbling about "hands across the sea" and international good vibes and such. I segued into the unrivaled beauty of China, the art, the culture, the Han Dynasty, the symbols in the carpet. I was starting to mellow a bit and I realized the great truth of proposing toasts: as long as you do no harm, *it doesn't matter jack what you say.*

I know I violated the Geneva Convention two-minute rule for toast-proposing but it seemed not to matter because, more than brevity, what everyone wanted was the healing of time and distance. The expressions on the faces of our hosts and the ambassador told me if I stayed clear of the minefields and well away from a certain disputed island, they were content to let me take my time and rhetorically wander the whole Middle Kingdom if it suited my fancy. After all, patience was a Chinese invention.

I didn't really get traction, though, until I got onto some historical references. History, being mostly lies written by the winners, offers enough vague refuge to comfort any well-educated group. I proposed we all recognize and appreciate past serendipities that have conspired to bring the worlds of the East and West into mutual awareness and ultimately, cooperation and friendship. "Cooperation" and "friendship" conjure up a most-favored-nation, duty-free coziness and are always good to include in a toast.

Important safety tip: When toasting in a communist country, if you choose to invoke history, go as far into the past as you can without bumping into the dinosaurs. But definitely avoid the recent century. For example, a quote from Confucius is safe anywhere, but not always Chairman Mao. There are still too many exposed nerve endings lying around.

Nobody would have mistaken my remarks for eloquence, but they weren't too shabby either. I concluded, "... and so, fellow citizens of the world, here's to Marco Polo." As clever as I like to think I am, I have to say that last part was inspired by some benevolent force outside myself. The gods of smoothness had been with me when it counted. We got a bemused chuckle from the multitude and the gaffe meter was reset to zero. And me, I got one of those not-bad nods, a smile and a wink from MacArthur. It felt like how getting a medal must feel.

I sauntered over to the buffet feeling pretty good about everything, having helped save mankind and all. As I piled dim sum onto my infinitesimally petite cocktail party saucer with "made in Hong Kong" stamped on the bottom, I recalled other historically memorable slips of the tongue, some quite high-profile. There was Jimmy Carter telling the people of Poland he understood their desires, a sentiment repackaged by his State Department interpreter and submitted to the gathered dignitaries as the American President telling them he understood their carnal lusts. And of course President Kennedy's, "*Ich bin ein Berliner*" ("I am a jelly donut.")

Life really is a game of inches. A word here or there helps grease the affairs of state or shoots them down in flames. An incorrectly chosen phrase at the end of a long day of business negotiations, and the deal is suddenly on thin ice. You shoot one little archduke and the whole damn world goes to war. Like other great statesmen before me, I find Latin expresses the dilemma best: *cogito ergo dim sum*—I think, therefore I am a pork bun.

RollyCoaster

we were young, supple as green twigs, bouncily
in full manic panic, absurdly
to a window where hearts
drawn in dust from contented times
are retraced in future hope.
then quickly to the shelves
where comforting memories are dried,
pressed into books for safekeeping
by paladin fairyfolk who come round
to remind us to breathe,
and even carry us a ways.

then zip zip away on lubricated thought.
engraved crusted-over bygones of
childhood betrayals and abandonment
lie glowering in wait
so we can find them now and then
accidentally and suddenly,
like an always forgotten missing step
on darkened basement stairs.

then back again, upward, skyward
dreaming, guffawing for no reason,
but expectantly.

remember?

EGO TE ABSOLVO...

Ego te absolvo a peccatis tuis in nomine Patris
et Filii et Spiritus Sancti. Amen.

I absolve you of your sins in the name of the Father and of the Son and of the Holy Ghost. Amen.

In Argentina, as in many Latin American countries, it is a custom among observant Catholics here to cross themselves whenever they pass a church of their faith. However they are traveling—walking, bus, train, car—they make the sign of the cross on themselves as they rumble past. Just the act of watching people do that makes me feel protected, as it must do even more so for those who make the sign.

It's a fleeting, discreet movement, which though it takes place in a public setting, is not at all a public moment. Up, down, left, right, kiss the back of the thumb.

... in nomine Patris et Filii et Spiritus Sancti ...

I'm not Catholic and don't need to be, I think, to feel that my fellow passengers make the sign of the cross for as many reasons as there are people doing it. Maybe deeply held conviction or a parochial school autonomic reflex, or a momentary reconnect with eternity in a life that is otherwise temporal, secular and self-absorbed—nobody knows. In the darkened back seats of the Avenida Maipú bus at 1:00 a.m., it's one of the rare human acts utterly without political motivation. A handshake with the unseen God.

I spend between two and three hours a day on mass transit to and from the office. It's a complicated trip from the backwaters of the suburbs, hitting the whole sampler of urban public conveyance: bus, train, subway and my own two feet. Occasionally, it's the commute from hell, but it gives me a lot of time to read and watch faces, so I mostly forgive it.

te absolve ...

Among the faces is a dark-haired woman on the subway, early 30ish, office worker by her clothes, but not management. A book has her full attention. Her head tilts forward to reveal an area of thinning hair on top near the back that is evolving into a strikingly noticeable bald spot on an otherwise attractive head, face and body. Men expect to lose their hair. How terrible it must be for a woman.

A man who shares my subway car almost daily (inbound, third car from the end so as to be right by the exit when it stops), has a red birthmark around his eye. It is his further misfortune that the blemish is not dark enough to be an obvious birthmark, which people would notice and then studiously ignore and not comment on. It's just red enough to resemble the result of a run-in with a door three days ago. I know it's permanent because I've seen it for months, but strangers who sit next to him say, "Ooo, I see the missus clobbered you a good one." He gets this a lot, and whatever he thinks, it's probably way beyond *What did I ever do to deserve this?*

When I round the corner of the stairs heading for the lower level of Retiro Station every morning at 7:21 there are one or two or three young boys asleep on the bare floor next to the wall in this unheated passageway. Sheltered from the wind, but not the cold, the boys have their sweatshirts and dirty jackets pulled as far over their heads as they can get them. What is most jarring is that these are young children, eight, maybe twelve years old, and they live at Retiro Station. They are still asleep at that hour, and commuters hurrying past set food down beside them. But it's mostly snack cakes and cookies—coffee break junk at the bottom of the nutrition spectrum.

No matter how many times you walk past them, it's not something to which a person can get accustomed. And this is nothing. I've seen a great many more doorway children (*"gamines"*) in Colombia and Mexico. There must be zillions in Brazil, where cast-off children live downtown, begging and stealing or selling their bodies. A mini-scandal erupted in Rio de Janeiro a couple years ago when it was revealed that a businessman's organization had hired thugs to go through the alleys at night and kill the street children to thin their numbers.

When blessing-counting time rolls around, as it does for all of us now and then, a millisecond on the street in the presence of real poverty is all most of us need to dredge up a sincere there-but-for-the-grace-of-God. It's so easy to find a reason to make the sign of the cross.

Misereatur tui omnipotens Deus, et dimissis peccatis tuis, perducat te ad vitam aeternam.

May Almighty God have mercy on you, forgive you your sins, and bring you to everlasting life.

My observation is that one or two people per bus or train car, and every fourth or fifth taxi driver, will do the sign of the cross upon passing a church. When I first came to Buenos Aires, I noticed it, but it took a few weeks for me to associate it with the presence of a church. There is one spot on my train commute, near the horse track, where I still haven't been able to locate the church. People swirl their hands across their foreheads and chests as we zip past what looks to me like a small string of establishments that includes a fitness center and a bar. Maybe one used to be there. Maybe it's on the other side of the block.

I'm sitting on a crowded late-night bus from the train station, the final leg of my homeward commute. I never met a third world country (or "emerging nation" as we Argentines like to call ourselves) where the buses aren't packed solid all the time. It's easy to see why. Most can't afford a car. It's related to why you see so many young people passionately kissing on the park benches, in the grass, leaning against lamp posts on the corner. You have no car, you live with your parents; the park is the most intimate setting you've got. It's here or cold turkey abstinence. We're talking extreme heavy passion under the statue of *El Liberator*, José de San Martín.

The bus is coming up on a small cathedral and I'm playing a game I invented where I try to predict who of those around me will make the sacred gesture. I'm nearly always wrong it seems. I think I've guessed right maybe once, and that was a nun, so it hardly counts. It isn't always the little old lady or the man put on the social margins by his physical deformity. Often it's the hunky young turk, fast-tracking at the firm, and the virile female secretary who pay homage to the custom. I have yet to see the cross made by a couple, a man and woman together, for whatever reason.

Standing in front of me on the last bus of the night is a red-haired man in his 20s. Lean and strong, he hasn't shaved in four, maybe five days.

On his arm is a tattoo of what looks like an oak tree with a big grinning skull embedded in the trunk. A snake crawls out one of the eye sockets. As we pass under a street lamp, light skims across the man's bare arm. It's not an oak tree; it's a naked woman. Boy, am I tired.

He scowls through eyes dark and twisted. He looks over at me in my hoity-toity suit and tie, registering angry confusion. He keeps looking at me and I stare back at him way too long. I'm fascinated and I realize I'm not breaking eye contact as the rules dictate. *What do I think I'm doing? Larry, are you nuts? You have five children to think of.* I look away, but he doesn't, not for a long time. *I'm dead meat.*

I would like to say that in the moment of our contact I could sense in his dark recesses, a tiny spark of original humanity, something in there a compassionate man could reach out to and connect with, given enough time. A beautiful thought, and it would be so very Bing Crosby, wouldn't it? Like in the classic "Going My Way"—jaunty Father O'Malley in black clericals and a straw boater turns a hardened street gang into St. Dominic's choir. Maybe God was speaking to my heart at that moment. I'm now looking for the humanity in my knuckle-dragging brother, and for the Bing Crosby in me, but it's a tough sell either way. What would Father O'Malley say to him? "Would you like to swing on a star and carry moonbeams home in a jar?"

The problem is, there doesn't seem to be anybody human at home behind those eyes. Not even remotely so. To the very core of his bottom corpuscle, he looks like Central Casting's alienated postal worker—Arlo Guthrie's "biggest, meanest, mother-raper of them all."

Then it hits me. I am so totally wrong about people that this guy will probably defy all odds and cross up a storm when we pass the next church. I bet myself five pesos he does. He's probably a future saint, on his way to donate a kidney. What he'll probably do is cross himself. And then, after that, he'll come over and kill me for looking at him too long because, well, because this is Argentina.

I'm nearly ready to bet the ranch on it. We pass the church. He doesn't do it.

But I do.

I have to say there is something foundationally powerful in the Catholic tradition. Something there for me. I admire their … I don't know exactly what. The faith they place in faith?

I remember in 1973 when I was 24, seeing an old woman in Oaxaca, Mexico, advancing the last hundred meters to the basilica doors on her bare knees. She inched forward a foot or two at a time along a dirt path with sharp stones that cut into her kneecaps and legs. She wrung her hands and cried and cried and cried, wailing loudly, fervently. Whatever had broken her heart, the stones had nothing to do with the essence of her real pain.

Two small daughters or granddaughters placed a scarf on the ground for her to crawl over as she slowly advanced. As she passed, they retrieved it and brought it around in front for her to pass over again. The scarf and the hem of her dress quickly became streaked with blood.

She made the sign of the cross.

Dominus noster Jesus Christus te absolvat …

Our Lord Jesus Christ absolve you …

I was a hitchhiker then, just out of communication grad school, a *mochilero* with a backpack and jeans. I felt self-conscious and a little embarrassed, but I stopped and watched her anyway. Other people were walking past like this happens every day. And maybe, in their lives, it does. I think I may have promised myself that as repayment for my intrusion, I would remember what I was seeing. Someday I would tell somebody about this and maybe it would help them.

As it turns out, I am the one helped. That moment liberated me to be as fully one with anyone's earnest attempt to touch God as my own maturity will allow. My intuition tells me that before it's over, every one of us will be that old woman at least one time in our lives. If I want it to be my course, and risk the risk, and set my heart ablaze daily, and toil in the vineyards of the Lord and be about my Father's business, then I can be her lighted candle. I am free to be all faiths, to make all Gods my God, all people my people. I am all of them.

I am unificationist. I make the sign of the cross. I crawl up the mountain to the Tree of Blessing.

Five guys laughing

LMoffit/2008

This photo of five vendors was taken in a marketplace in Paraguay. I told them a joke, which I can't remember now, and they thought it was hilarious. Turns out, after further conversation with them, they didn't understand the joke at all. What amused them was my Spanish, which sounded to them like something that had fallen off the back of a truck on the way to grammar school. They enjoyed my ineptness, I enjoyed their enjoyment, and they further enjoyed my enjoyment of their enjoyment. Such things make the world go round.

Shoeshine in HOTlanta

I went to Atlanta last Monday to fight for truth, justice and the American Way, and comfort the suffering soul of the South.

Okay, not exactly.

I went to Atlanta last Monday to stick some documents in a guy's hand and immediately fly right back to Washington, DC again. I like the first version better, but the second one is true.

I was finished with my business by 10:30 in the morning and then spent the entire rest of the day and evening trying to get out of the airport as US Air canceled one flight after another (equipment problems). Refugees from those flights scurried over to Delta which was already overbooked from its own earlier cancellations. In the South they say that even if you die and go to heaven you still have to change planes in Atlanta. I finally got a flight at 7:30 that evening, and with another hour to drive, got home about 11, dog-tired to the bone. I felt like I had been beaten with a stick.

However, I did get an unforgettable shoeshine in Atlanta from a beautiful blonde woman who shines the shoes of convention-goers at the Georgia World Congress Center. Shortly after handing off the docs, I'm looking around for an entrance that might lead to a main street and a taxi stand when I notice the woman shining shoes. I also notice she is inordinately well put together in terms of physical construction. Honestly, that last part was not a factor. But even so, the next thing I know, I'm sitting in the shoeshine chair and she asks me my name. I tell her.

"Ahm DEEE-na,"she hush-puppied, as generations of strong, feminine, southern women stood intertwined with her spirit.

She looked up at me and said, "Y'all have beautiful eyes." I could see her perception bordered on genius.

In all honesty, I would have gotten a shoeshine even if the shiner had been a 90-year-old bridge troll, because getting a store-bought shoeshine when I'm on the road is one of my long-standing travel rituals. It's just something I have always done. Still, I hate it when my own thoughts and actions remind me what idiots middle-aged men can be when a beautiful half-their-age woman pays any kind of attention to them.

We talked about all kinds of innocuous things (including, for the record, my wife and children). But all the while, I could feel the heat of her delicate hands and fingers massaging my foot through the leather of my high-gloss, corporate-image wingtip shoes. And the reason for this was her "beautiful eyes" opener, the initial flirt that primed the pump of our repartee.

People are absolutely spiritual beings, for better and worse. We really, really are, and it works as fast as electricity. It's interesting, and quite amazing how, for both good and bad, substantial spiritual elements zip from one person to another through a variety of channels. Take the eyes for example. If someone is standing 30 feet away, you can tell whether they are looking directly into your eyes or somewhere else close by, say, at your cheek or shoulder. That's because when two pairs of eyes meet head-on, an inaudible conversation takes place between them. Undeniable messages are exchanged. We all know it happens; most of us experience it several times a day. Science is clueless on how and why, but some have figured out it's a spiritual communication. Good for them.

That was how the game played out between me and DEEE-na. Little eye messages, which, when accompanied by smiles and nods, between men and women, are what flirting is made of. She played me like a Paganini playing a Strad. For my part, I was quite happy to be her instrument. I gave her a nice tip—and really, that was the whole point of the entire interaction.

Later that afternoon at the airport I replayed the whole thing in my mind and concluded if the Angel of Death had arrived for me during the shine and I had keeled over, tumbling off the shoeshine stand with a massive heart attack, my last words and deeds recorded on the big computer in the sky would have been me exchanging foolish giggles with a cutie pie young enough to be my daughter. Any of my various messiahs would have called it "judgment by shoeshine."

Definitely, I would much rather have my final entry into life's computer be me saying, "I will always love you," to my wife and children, gathered around my bedside at home. It would look a lot better on my spiritual résumé, that's for sure.

As I said, I arrived home quite late, and Taeko was waiting up for me. I had been in touch by cell phone all day so she already had a blow-by-blow of the flight delays and was appropriately sympathetic. Wonderfully so, in fact, but that's how she is. After a light snack, we sat at the kitchen table with tea and I told her all about my shoeshine.

I have always thought it unwise and needlessly cruel for married people to confess to one another the whole history of all they did before they met. But in everything that happens afterward, a couple should keep each other updated on what goes on, especially as it concerns any dealings with the opposite sex. This, by itself, has simplified my life incredibly and I recommend it for everyone. Just knowing I'm going to tell her everything sooner or later, keeps me out of serious trouble, especially in a marriage where there have been scores of overseas business trips and separations lasting months, including one that lasted more than a year.

I'm not one hundred percent consistent in applying this tell-all policy on a day-to-day basis, but nearly so. Regarding anything of significance, I stay current. It's not just about reporting one's missteps and temptations; it's really about connecting to one's life partner in all aspects. It's so easy for little pockets of shadow to form in the folds of complexity within a relationship. Continual talking and reporting pumps fresh air and sunshine into those shadows.

Taeko is a gifted listener. At some point she asked, "When she said your eyes are beautiful, did you tell her that hers are beautiful too?"

"Yes, I did." I had forgotten about the ground-penetrating power of the wifely radar.

"And what color were they?" she asked.

"Blue," I said immediately, casually.

Even as she concentrated her attention on squeezing the excess water out of the teabag before setting it on the side of the saucer, I could have sworn I saw an almost imperceptibly raised eyebrow. "Blue?"

"Uhhh … well …" I paused, "yeah, blue" My understanding is that all beautiful strangers have blue eyes, but what I was in the process of realizing is that I actually didn't recall anything about her eyes. Not even the color. Which was strange.

Taeko wanted more. "What kind of blue?"

I thought, *What kind? There are* kinds *of blue?*

Finally I had to say, "You know, it might be that I'm not really sure about the color."

Propped on her elbows, Taeko held her teacup at eye level, peering through the mist. She took in my whole face in one gulp, and regarded it for the length of time it took for her mind to develop the snapshot. Her words were soft and unhurried, carrying not even a shred of complaint or accusation. "Then how do you know her eyes were beautiful?"

Damn good question, so simple, and an excellent opportunity for me to step up to the plate. Which I did. "Well, the rest of her was beautiful."

"And so you actually noticed other parts more than her eyes?"

"The thing is, she was bent over my shoes, wearing a very loose-fitting blouse with the top wide open. I could see all the way to Disneyland." (pause) "Sorry."

I'm reminded how off-course is almost everything in the world in the man/woman arena. In an ideal world, flirting is nature's first blush of courtship on the road to eternal true love. The way it's generally done today, flirting is the shallow end of the relationship pool, with genuine concern for the other person being virtually nonexistent. Not noticing her eyes meant I was not seeing a human being. I was seeing a sexy *thing*.

Taeko rolled her eyes. "You *felt her fingers* through your shoe leather?"

Remorseful stupidass grin from me. Having your stuff replayed back to you by your spouse is absolutely the downside of "fessing up." Taeko finally nodded and commented, more as a note to herself on the overall state of Larry, "You're getting there. It's not over yet, but you're getting there."

We drank some more tea. We held hands, talked about the kids and work, as we toyed with each other's fingers across the table. We flirted. Married flirting is really interesting. You'd think married flirting isn't as edgy as the other kinds because the outcome is somewhat mutually understood from the beginning. But it can be a genuine adventure if neither takes the other for granted. What's more, it has the potential to be infinitely more in the deep end of the relationship pool. I think love really is meant to age much better than it usually does the way it's currently practiced.

The reason we don't do love all that well is because we are squeamish about discussing it and it doesn't usually get talked about in a constructive way. And because people think it's dirty, then by default it all too often gets left in the hands of pornographers to teach our children the sublime art of loving. Those people are scum because they manipulate desire to transform human beings into *things* devoid of all caring and commitment.

There is not enough of the teaching of how to mold and shape our love to fit the changing circumstances presented by each passing decade in our lives. Married flirting, for example, doesn't come as naturally to some couples as it does to others, and therefore it should be taught in community colleges. I would say as a for-credit course, since it's so vital for human happiness.

We also need to teach a course about being grateful for love. The premature demise of a partner puts the relationship on ice for a while. I am told by those who have been left behind by their life's partner that, while it helps to maintain an awareness of the eternal nature of the marriage bond and the melting together of two spirits forever, the passing of your mate is equal to the passing of one half of yourself. Taeko and I spoke of our gratitude for one another—of how fortunate we feel to be physically present together, here and now. It won't always be this way. Nothing that depends on earthly existence can remain the same forever. That's another good reason to develop married flirting while you're both still alive.

This has been a huge, unintended digression, but I think I'll let it stand.

I continued my report, telling her about eating extra spicy buffalo wings and drinking Starbuck's coffee at the airport, and about watching a guy and his wife get romantic in the waiting area. (They both had on wedding rings so I assume they were married to each other.)

Make that partly romantic and wholly ironic. He was trying to kiss on his wife's ear while she was trying to ignore him as she read a romance novel that was probably at that very moment describing a guy nibbling a woman's ear. It was clear that the woman was tolerating, but not interested in, the actual real-life *schlurping* that was happening cheekside. She was much more into the fictional account. Truly, the pen is mightier than the tongue; even the tongue in your ear.

I watched the couple. The man kept upping the ante, getting ever more aggressive on the ear lobes. I wondered if he was going to dive into her breastworks just as she got to the bodice-ripping part of her novel.

Or maybe his and her different realities would somehow mystically meld together and he would find his way into her heart by insinuating himself into the book's plot, the two of them harmonizing in spirit—becoming the book right there in the waiting area ... *pulling her down onto a mound of new-mown hay, still warm from the afternoon sun, infused with the scented grassy musk born of mid-summer's heat ... and ... and yes! Yes, I cried—YES!*

I concluded my description and waited.

"Hmm," Taeko said, gazing intently at me for a long time with no expression I was able to read. The mystery of us continues.

BEASTS OF BURDEN

I have a rather involved fantasy I dip into now and then when there's nothing else going on at the moment. I'm on a television quiz show where the top prize is a million dollars. I get past the half-million level and the big question comes. "For all the marbles," the celebrated and color-coordinated game show host asks, "which of the following four Native American tribes was not one of the so-called 'five civilized tribes' of the Oklahoma Indian Territory?"

I look down at the list of possible answers: (A) Cherokee, (B) Choctaw, (C) Seneca and (D) Seminole. The question is so obscure and hairy that half the nation's viewers have beads of sweat popping out on their foreheads on my behalf. The rest head for the fridge, unable to deal with their emotions.

The rules of this quiz show allow me to phone a friend for help, or poll the audience or even have two of the incorrect answers removed from consideration. I don't do any of these things. I look calmly at the host, his cobalt blue silk tie set against a powder blue dress shirt and light gray suit.

I think: *Man, this guy is one majorly attired Kemosabe. Then I think: Alright now, about these tribes …*

I lean back, staring into the depths of my own wisdom, and thoughtfully begin to enumerate aloud on my fingers. "Well, hmmmm. Let's see, Regis. In Oklahoma, we have the Cherokee, Choctaw, Chickasaw, Creek and Seminole. I guess that leaves (C) Seneca. That's my final answer."

Regis hesitates a long, long time. Frowning, almost a pained look. "Are you sure?" he pleads. "Final answer," I tell him again, calmly reaching for my water. He frowns, sucks in his breath and slowly exhales as he shakes his head. Taeko, sitting behind me in the support chair, has fainted. All over America, people are soiling themselves. Regis lets a pause big enough to drive a truck through hang in the air. Then: "YOU'VE JUST WON A MILLION DOLLARS!"

If you attend elementary school anywhere in Oklahoma, you study the state's history and you memorize those, quote, "five civilized tribes" end quote. At the time I was learning their names, along with the widely held truism that the Cherokee were the first Native Americans to have a written alphabet, I sometimes wondered how any of this stuff would ever come into play at any time during the rest of my life. I also thought the same thing about algebra. The answer is you will only encounter a need to know the five civilized tribes of Oklahoma at the million dollar level on a TV quiz show. You will never, ever need algebra.

I lived in Tulsa from the fifth through eighth grades but spent most of my childhood summers on my grandparents' farm 80 miles northeast, near Fairland, in the far upper right corner of the state. My mother, Margaret Blanche Brown, was born and raised on that farm, from whose front drive we could spit and almost hit Grand Lake of the Cherokees. Mom was a redhead but nonetheless a quarter Cherokee, which makes me a more diluted one of those.

At the Cherokee headwaters of my lineage stood great-granny, a small darkish woman (as her daughter-in-law, my grandmother described her) who was in the Oklahoma Land Run in 1889 with her big Irish husband, or so the family legend goes. She died long before I was born and all I've ever heard about her from the elders is that she was one mean-tempered woman. But then you can't please everyone. The Indian blood has been further watered down by the Irish to the point where there is nothing recognizably Indian about me at all.

The farm had a few ponds, some forested land and several big fields where oats and grass for hay and grazing were planted. It had a big garden, a long chicken house and a barn with a corral and a stock chute for loading animals into the back of the pickup when it was time to take them to the auction. The barn had a dozen or so cats at any one time, feral and vicious, who lived only on whatever they could catch.

Mom's parents, Grandad and Granma Brown, ran a family farm of less than a hundred acres. Farmer Brown and the missus were Grant Woods' *American Gothic* right down to the pitchfork. They were the genuine article. He drove a black '52 or '53 Ford pickup with tobacco juice stains streaked down the outside of the driver's door.

To start the truck, he had to push in the brake and the clutch, turn the key, press the starter button on the dash, and spit out the window, all at the same time. The truck's rubber mat floor was littered with burned up strike-anywhere kitchen matches. Grandad liked to work a cigar from both directions while he drove, lighting one end and chewing on the other until they met in the middle. When he wasn't doing that, he gnawed on a plug of Red Man Chewing Tobacco that lived in the breast pocket of his bib overalls. Sometimes he'd be explaining something to me and his words would trail off into incoherent gurgling as he jutted out his lower jaw and kept his lips almost closed while searching for a socially acceptable place to deposit the loathsome wad of dark brown spit growing in his cheeks.

Grandad gave me my first-ever drink of beer. It was Pabst Blue Ribbon, and it came out of a can cold as a witch's bosom. He fished it out of a tall, metal milk can filled with ice water that sat on my side of the stick shift. Be assured this wasn't the wholesale corruption of a minor, just an infrequent sip now and then from the one he was drinking as we cruised along at his customary eight miles an hour on gravel roads maintained by a county grader. And anyway, it wasn't like I was a baby. Hell, I was ten.

Farmer Brown was a local saint as far as I could tell. I was listening on the extension when he answered the phone out in the egg house one day. "Clyde, you busy?" the fellow up the road asked. His car wouldn't start and his wife needed a ride into Fairland to pick up some medication. "Never too busy to help someone," he replied. He stopped what he was doing, fetched her and took her into town. I was impressed to the degree that, 40 years later, it's the one utterance of his life that when I recall it, I think I can actually hear his voice.

Memories coated with the rust of age have a way of shaving off all but the very best and the very worst parts of experience, rendering Oklahoma to me as a Norman Rockwell rural idyll of bare feet and fishing holes, of rippling heat rising off the two-lane blacktop, and me and my brother flinging dried cow chips at each other down by the dog pond.

In the summer of 1960, I was fresh out of the fifth grade and still protected from life's brutality by a cultural cocoon that allowed innocence to endure to an age unheard of today. Only occasionally did the adult world seep in, usually through the nightly news. A guy named Kennedy wanted to be president—an occurrence that, if it were to happen, Brother Glenn at Fairland Methodist Church assured me after one Wednesday evening service, would make Pope John XXIII the *real* president. I didn't ask for the details. I was still three years away from eighth grade civics, but I thought it must be true if it came from Brother Glenn. Since I got most of my Jesus from him, I figured I could count on him to deliver up my politics too.

Two years later there would come the Cuban missile crisis and talk of atomic war. A friend's parents bought a fallout shelter and buried it in their back yard. They provisioned it with canned food and a handgun to shoot their friends and neighbors. We did "duck and cover" drills at school. We were told that squatting under our desks with our arms over our heads would protect us when Nikita Khrushchev nuked Eli Whitney Junior High. And, as an indicator of how resilient our innocence was, we bought it.

It was a more relaxed era then than it is now, maybe due to there being fewer lawyers. Folks in junky old pickup trucks drank cold beer as they drove the red dirt backroads, and nobody I knew had ever even seen a seat belt. I was ignorant of evil, of intrigues and regrets, of whole areas of complexity that would become my daily existence three or four decades down the road. All I knew for sure back then was that Jesus saves and that Pope John XXIII was president, and that his wife, Jackie, was about as pretty as it's possible for someone's mom to be.

The farm is forever July in my mind, because, with few exceptions, I mostly spent my summers there. Except for when I consciously force myself to think otherwise, Oklahoma has blackberries and wasps all year around.

It was right here on this very farm in the summer of my ninth year that one of life's pivotal realizations marched into my awareness. We were down by the barn one morning when we saw a heifer mount the back of another heifer and start humping away. (A heifer, by the way, is a girl cow, just to make sure we're all on the same page.) Grandad explained that when two heifers go at it like that, it means the cows are in heat and ready to be mated. In fact, that was the signal he relied on for knowing when it was time to make a phone call to the breeder and put Mr. Bull into the game.

The huge Black Angus bull glowered at me, smoldering behind the bars of the breeder's large trailer. I briefly considered reaching in and petting him, making friends. I walked up close to the trailer and he snorted, stamped his foot and made a sudden feint at the bars. I jumped.

"Careful, son. He'd kill you if he could," the man from the breeder's association said.

Reading my mind, Grandad cautioned, "Don't put your hand in there. He'll snap it off like new beans." He made a garden green beans snapping motion.

I could see he would, too. Then, just as suddenly, the bull was no longer thinking about me. The breeze had shifted and he caught the scent of the heifers. He turned his gaze toward the corral and any notion of crushing me under his hooves was now a million miles away. His pink slender penis snaked out from beneath him, longer and longer. This was getting really interesting.

The breeder maneuvered the trailer to make it flush with the corral gate. "You better go sit on the fence, son," the breeder said. "We're gonna let Duke out and that ain't the place you wanna be if he gets loose on us." I scampered up onto the illusionary safety of the wood rail fence, and the breeder pulled a rope that raised the rear gate on the trailer. As Duke backed into the corral, his manhood was all business. It looked like it hung down about a foot and waggled back and forth as he walked, twitching like a living all-beef Slim Jim.

The bull weighed at least a ton and the mating act looked like one giant eighteen-wheeler truck climbing atop another. They were only five feet away from me as I sat on the fence and the whole scene was *gigantic*, way out of proportion to any other experience. It was the first time I ever saw living beings making babies. These were giants, with giant parts and giant pushing and giant snorting and grunting. As Duke lurched forward on his hind legs to better his position, the ground shook. This was the first time in my life my mind had ever been filled fuller than full, because this was intimately personal in the way that only something that is the real thing can be personal.

Granddad must have noticed my wide eyes and mouth hanging open. He hocked a wad of tobacco juice at an anthill, wiped his chin with the back of his hand and commented, "You'll be doin' that too, 'fore very long." I was stunned. I knew my life had many unforeseen adventures ahead, but I never imagined I was going to be required to have sex with cows.

My knowledge of sex at that time was a scattered jigsaw puzzle whose pieces included approximately: it was a word you didn't say in front of your parents, and bad high school girls did it in the back seats of cars. What they did, I had only a glimmer of an idea. Oh, and also there was the bare-breasted princess of Bali in the pages of National Geographic. I suspected, and hoped in my heart of hearts, that she had a place in the big picture.

Maybe it was God's original plan that Adam and Eve learn about sex from observing the animals. That would be natural. But what would have been really helpful during this two or three year period of my own awakening would have been for a grownup just to calmly sit down, give me a few basics about the pneumatics of mating and what parts went where. Also something about the spiritual importance of saving my purity and modesty for my future wife—and then to conclude the conversation with, "You're going to have questions later on about some of this stuff, and when you do, I want you to come and ask me the second one pops into your head, because *I will be there for you.*" That would have been very alright.

In addition to baby-making, I guess there was one other adult thing of which I was becoming aware, a kind of undercurrent reality in a farmer's life. This was a no-nonsense working farm and Granddad forbade us to give a pet's name to any animal that would eventually be slaughtered for food. That way we wouldn't get too attached to them. We could name the dogs and the cats and even the possums and a coyote we called Lamb Chops, whose glowing eyes we briefly caught in a flashlight beam one night. He got his name, not because of Sheri Lewis' famous puppet of the same name, but because he literally chopped lambs.

However, we were specifically not allowed to name any of the chickens. This was all a nice theory but it fell apart pretty quickly because if you're around the same animals all day every day, you get attached to them anyway. Add to that the fact that Grandad regularly violated his own dictum. Every morning and every evening we put the baby steers on the cows to nurse, two per cow, one on each side. There was Little Britches, Spotty, Pooch, Maverick and so on—all Granddad's names.

Maverick belonged to me, an Angus-Holstein mix I bought at birth by taking out a $20 note from the bank (co-signed by Granddad), which I paid off to the tune of a dollar per week that I kept back from my allowance—my "earnings," he called it.

I helped castrate Maverick shortly after birth, thereby transforming him from a bull into a kinder, gentler steer. By then I had already figured out that balls come with an attitude, and that removing them makes sure certain issues never arise. I held him down while Grandad did the deed with his Purina feed store pocket knife, slitting the scrotum to expose the testicles inside. He cut them off cleanly and dropped them into a pail of water.

He dabbed some black disinfectant salve on the wound and Maverick hobbled off to lie down. He spent the whole rest of the day lying in the shade by the barn. He didn't get up for the evening feeding and didn't start moving around again until much later that night. On the whole, I thought he took it much better than I would have, and there didn't seem to be any hard feelings between us.

We cut about 20 calves that day and ended up with a small bucket of calf balls. I hadn't a clue why he would carry them around in a pail, assuming it was just part of the medical procedure. I just have to say, though, that I was more grateful than I have words to express that my grandmother waited until way, way *after* breakfast the next morning to explain what mountain oysters are.

Maverick was both my pet and my 4-H Club project in the fifth grade. I talked to him, read the Hardy Boys to him, played my clarinet for him. I played "Faith of our Fathers" and the hook from "Take the A Train," mimicking what my grandmother remembered of it, which my band teacher assured me bore only a homeopathic resemblance to the real tune. But Maverick thought it was in the ballpark, and he ran to me whenever he heard me practicing down by the creek. To have your calf seek you out and walk right up to you just from hearing you play the clarinet is an intimacy whose beauty cannot be adequately conveyed in words.

In the back of my mind I knew that one day we would twist their tails and push Maverick and Little Britches up the loading chute and into the back of the pickup truck for the ride to the stock auction in Welch or Joplin. I knew we would sit in the stands with the other farmers and meatpacker reps, awaiting our turn when our guys would be run out into the small arena and the auctioneer would crank up his stuttery jabber, the only part of which I could ever understand was the "whatcha gonna give for 'em?" that he would drop into his spiel now and then like a firebreak.

I knew the scene. The meatpacker reps nodded imperceptibly or tapped their canes or lightly brushed the bills of their caps as the auctioneer spoke in tongues on his high bench, pointing to acknowledge the bids. At some point, his "budda-budda-budda" voice would catch with a little "hut!" as he abruptly changed cadence, slowing to a more halting, jerking step that sounded just as unintelligible as before but meant he was winding up and calling in the final bids. Rhythmically the sudden downshift, with the syllables still spilling out all over the room, made me think of a train slamming on the brakes and all the cars behind banging into one another like an accordion collapsing.

Finally he would end it with a sentence clear and clean as a cucumber, "Soooold to Cudahay," or "Sooooold to Swift Premium" and that would be it. Maverick and Little Britches would be prodded out the gate, happily stupid, headed for Jimmy Dean's Country Smoked Heat-n-Serve Links.

I knew all that was going to happen. I had seen it many times before with other people's livestock. I didn't dwell on it with their steers and I would try not to dwell on it with mine. To do so would be in bad faith with the pact that has always existed between farmers and the earth, perhaps the second oldest covenant in human history, next to don't eat the apple. Farming is the original Plan B, mankind's first contingency plan after getting kicked out of Eden.

It's hard work too, and you're always poor. Working the land makes you old, destroys your body, and farmers don't do it out of some sense of romance. They live or die depending on what the land returns to them in exchange for their effort and luck. They form a partnership with the Creator, with their part of the bargain being to grow grain and vegetables and raise chickens, hogs, sheep and cattle as food and commerce. God's part, the heavy lifting in the contract, was inventing the Earth, the plants and animals. And also maybe to send a little rain now and then if He don't mind.

Farmers accept their inborn responsibility to the next generation. They feel called by God and the spirits of their forbearers to raise strong sons and sensible daughters, and to teach them the ways of their fathers and mothers. Exercising a loving dominion over the beasts of the field is what they do in order to make that happen. You plant and propagate the herd; you harvest and you butcher, and you eat. Then you sow the seeds of your own children and give them their role in the cycle.

I never heard one of them speak of any special reverence they felt for the animals. A conversation about it would probably embarrass most of them and they would likely hoot and dismiss it if you brought it up, because frankly, farmers just don't say all that much, period. But the respect is clearly evident in the way that nothing is ever taken for granted; nothing is wasted. The partnership is that sooner or later, a farmer returns everything to the earth, including himself. In return the beasts of the earth carry our burdens and die that we might live. Nothing more and nothing less.

Vegans would disagree, saying one can live even better and healthier without killing animals for food. I won't argue the point, but the reality is that a good portion of the world gets its protein from meat. And that goes double for Oklahoma.

My grandparents' primary income came from raising chickens, a thousand hens in cages. They began laying as "pullets" at 22 weeks and continued putting out almost an egg a day for the better part of a year. When their laying days were over, they were taken to the butcher shop, killed and dressed for sale to stores and restaurants in town.

They were all white leghorns except for about a dozen barred rock hens, beautiful black birds with white stripes that lay the brown eggs you pay extra for. I came back from Vacation Bible School one afternoon and was dismayed to see half of them peeking out from between the bars of a wire cage sitting on the tailgate of the pickup. Their egg production had been dropping for several weeks and they were on their way to the butcher shop to get dressed for dinner. So to speak.

The barred rocks were special favorites. I spotted Dagwood and Blondie and Snuffy Smith and Tonto and Cherokee and Choctaw on the tailgate. I cried under the covers that night, paying the price for clandestine chicken-naming.

At the end of that summer I had to go back to school in Tulsa. Granddad was kind enough to buy Maverick from me for $65, a far more than fair price at the time. He would finish raising him for market. The money burned a hole in my pocket and I irresponsibly squandered most of it driving go-karts and caught hell from my dad, but that's another story.

When Maverick was a yearling and ready for the auction, he and Little Britches and the gang were grazing in the south pasture. One of Tornado Alley's famous instant thunderstorms sprang up that afternoon and a bolt of lightning shot down and killed Maverick in a split second. And that was that.

You pour all your energy and resources into raising crops, a family, a calf—cutting all kinds of deals with the angels and the weatherman. And then God takes him out in one stroke. You look at it philosophically and you pick up the pieces. You make do, you deal with it as best you can, and you don't give up because there's no place else to go but the grave or the old folk's home. With any luck, when you've outlived your best-if-used-by date, you will get a bedroom off the kitchen and a rocker on the porch where you can sit and watch your naked grandbabies playing with the dog.

How to light a cigar at the Manila Hotel

At the colonial, old-moneyed Manila Hotel, pride of the Philippines, the cigar lady, petite and of unparalleled loveliness in a shapely floor-length dress with a slit up the side, floats through the lobby bar on the gentle wind of her own exquisiteness. She carries a mahogany box of hand-rolled Philippine Tabacalaras. Her smile says hello, welcome, I can't live without you, and a dozen other things to as many lonely gentleman travelers.

She stops at your chair, presents the compartmented tray of elegant smokes of many sizes and textures and, in a voice that is liquid summer, suggests, "Cigar?" She takes the one you select, and places it capped-end-down into a snifter of brandy for a few seconds while she unsheathes a small scalpel. She removes the cigar and deftly incises the wet cap, cutting a small, rabbinical, v-shaped notch in the tip. Then she strikes a match and ignites a cedar twig. She holds the cigar close to the burning cedar, but not actually into the body of the flame, and with nymphet grace, rotates it evenly, toasting the foot of the cigar. Tenderly placing the still-moist barrel between your lips, she continues to hold the flame near as you suck slowly, evenly, on the other end.

Rich, buxom smoke rises into the air. After it begins to burn, she asks, "May I?" And of course she may. Fingers of delicate femininity retrieve the cigar, which she examines to make sure it's evenly lit. If one area is burning faster than the rest, she wets her middle finger with her tongue and touches it to calm the fire on the part too intensely ablaze.

Even to Freud, sometimes a cigar was just a cigar. Not so at the Manila Hotel.

EPIPHANIES AND HARD CHOICES

The French peasant maid carrying the heavy containers laden with cream-topped milk, still warm from the udder, suddenly straightens her back and stands tall, letting the pails slip from her calloused hands. She is stopped motionless by the vision crackling in the air before her, just beyond her reach.

"Yes—yes" she responds to urgings only she can hear. "Yes, I will leave Domrémy. I will raise an army. We will march to Orléans to lift the siege and drive the English back across the water. I will put the Dauphin Charles VII on the throne of France.

"And yes! I shall cut my hair short, wear men's breeches, don bosom-flattening armor and deliver my libido into God's care.

"Of course I'll irritate and frighten everyone, even those who follow me, until I am finally betrayed by my own side, turned over to the British to be subjected to an inquisition. After suffering great personal humiliations, I will submit to be burned at the stake as a witch."

"Joan! Joan!" Her mother's voice from the farmhouse door calls her roughly back to the present. "Whatchu doin', girl? Standin' there lollygaggin' ... dang, who you talkin' to? Looky there whatchu done. Get into this house right now!"

"Oh...huh? What? I'm sorry ... coming, Mother."

Years later, Joan is a settled housewife on a farm of clay and pebbles. Her husband is a good man, but not a visionary. Her children are good children, but not predisposed to glorious, doomed campaigns. Her little church by the river is a nurturing community, but the preaching is as dry as the communion wafers, and the holy wine keeps disappearing.

Joan peels the potatoes, setting the skins aside for the pigs. She looks down at her veined hands and wrinkled flesh of her arms, tries to remember if she actually did hear and feel the angel of the Lord that sweltering August morning in her youth.

Did that ever really happen? Did I dream it? Did I really see an angel and hear his voice? I wish I could remember everything he said ... or anyway, that I imagined he said ... or daydreamed. I'm sure it must have been just ... well, maybe ... I don't know.

You can be chosen, but saying yes or no, and choosing to act on it or not, is your own free will. The profound epiphany, with a blinding vision and sonorous angelic voice might last a full minute and leave you shaken to the marrow. It might knock you off your donkey and make you blind for three days, like Paul, or mute for a year, like Zechariah.

But then what? You will either own it for the rest of your life, or you won't. Owning it means walking a lonely path. You consciously take the other branch in the road's fork, moving determinedly toward an entirely new destiny. You need to find a sword, raise an army, get some funding. In the back of your mind, you know you will likely die in an utterly unexpected time and circumstance, and none of it will be pretty or tidy. And all the decisions along the way, chosen one, are yours alone to make.

LEGENDARY COOT REMEMBERS

I used to be immortal, a turtle's age ago
when the humor fairy double-dipped me
in the River Styx and I have never
thought it should have been otherwise.

I could swagger and remember,
laugh with all my teeth showing,
the membranes slick,
the good parts juicy all the time.

In my head I haul my dead skin cells
to the top of the rocky hogback,
running 200 miles naked like Jim Bridger.
Breathless, gasping, I stand around the fort,
dehydrated as a beauty queen,
mistaken for blue Indian summer corn.

Stunt cowboys toss one another
through sugar candy saloon windows.
The old coots watch, knowing they
could have done it with real glass.
Or so they think,
lying in bed with a wife-shaped husk,
along with their regrets
and self-justified ragged sense of time,
waiting for the angel of sex.

THE RUSSIA CHRONICLES

The Russia Chronicles

The Ministry of Bugs

Except for all the loathing, I miss the Cold War. What I miss about it is its clarity. The lines between us and them were sharply drawn. For people who like their good and evil rendered in angel wings and devil horns, it was the kind of era we may never see again. There was a dependability about things for those of us who traveled throughout and lived in the USSR in those days. For example, you knew you were being followed; you knew the hotel rooms were bugged. After 1990, when communism fell apart, we were no longer as certain. We still assumed our phones were tapped, but we never knew for sure anymore. A lot of government budgets were being cut and veteran spooks at the top of their pay grades were being laid off.

The Brezhnev era in Moscow was a golden age of skulking and lurking. For 99.999% of Russians, life was—and still is—a tedious forced march of getting things done, putting food on the table, and with what time remains, finding love, beauty, meaning in one's existence and the like.

But for one layer of the Russian bureaucracy that I came to know quite well during a decade of travel around the Soviet Union, life had much in common with spy novels.

That was a time when cloak-and-dagger clichés had real meaning for foreigners who went to Russia a lot. The government put extraordinary effort into sneaking around and following people, making dead drops of stolen secrets in parks, and planting bugs. To the ruin of many male travelers, the KGB was quite successful in the art of compromise. The women of the "honey traps," were not the gorgeous stunners of the James Bond movies, but were ordinarily nice-looking secretary types.

It's a lesser priority today, and the mafia in Moscow is now much better armed and better run than the KGB.

Graft is everywhere in Russia these days, whereas it used to be that the government was one-stop-shopping for all your corruption needs. Only the government had guns, and if they didn't shoot you, nobody shot you. Today, the heavy hand of Big Brother is largely gone and everybody's packing heat. Chaos reigns. One hardly knows who to bribe anymore. Are a couple of twenties too much or not enough?

An American family I got to know, Kevin and Barbara and their kids, lived in Moscow during the early 1980s, when I first began going there to organize meetings between U.S. and Soviet business people, scholars, media and such. Kev and Barb worked in a company that had some cooperative arrangement with a Russian counterpart firm, and lived in housing provided by their Russian partners.

While discussing household expenses in their kitchen one night, talking about how stretched they were, Kevin commented that if they could only bring in another 300 rubles every month, they would easily be able to meet all their obligations. Two days later, Kevin was in a cafe and met by happy accident a Russian man who spoke good English and was in a line of work similar to his. They seemed to have many interests in common and Kevin was delighted when the Russian decided to accompany him on the ten-block walk to the metro station. It was the beginning of one of those rare and beautiful friendships between two guys in which everything about one resonates with the other.

The Russian had an interest and solid experience in Kevin's line of work and his educational background. Kevin grew up not far from the Catskills in upstate New York and, like Kevin, the Russian had a lifelong infatuation with that region and its cultural heritage. Like Kevin, he had read all of Washington Irving's work and had visited the place generally thought to have been Irving's location of the fictional Sleepy Hollow. Like many Russians, he had a fondness for allegory and Kevin was fascinated by his amazingly forthright commentary (for a Russian living in Moscow, anyway) on Rip Van Winkle as a metaphor for the communist state at the end of the twentieth century. Leninism's children, he told Kevin, are awakening like Rip at the dawn of the new millennium in the Age of Information to find their gun rusted and their dog dead, and that the world had gone on without them.

As they approached the subway, the Russian asked Kevin if he would be interested in doing a little work on the side for his company. It was an innocuous task, nothing illegal, nothing that would interfere or compete with Kevin's current work, and was exactly suited to Kevin's expertise.

"We'll pay you 300 rubles a month."

The pattern for this kind of encounter, and it's a well-established one, is that a connection is made and a friendship set in motion. The professional relationship would be above reproach in the beginning. But as we know, there are a thousand shades of gray in any normal business and friendship, and we all constantly make moral decisions on the fly. In Kevin's case, things would be moved incrementally toward some desired goal, whether it be the relatively benign gathering of information or confirmation of things already assumed—or some outright illegal activity that would end up with Kevin being owned by Soviet agents.

One could argue that their encounter and the job offer was nothing more than a coincidence, although 300 rubles was a handsome sum at that time and almost nobody was making that kind of money for part-time gigs. Almost assuredly it wasn't coincidence. Things were extremely weird between the U.S. and Russia at that time, and the American Embassy was a repository of countless cautionary tales about exactly this sort of thing.

What an interesting commentary on that era, and on U.S./Soviet relations, that out of all the perfectly rational reasons for a chance meeting of two men of similar nature and experience—plus an offer of 300 rubles a month for some harmless freelance work—the most plausible explanation is that your kitchen is bugged.

Organizing delegations, meetings and fact-finding trips took me all over the Soviet Union (and later the Russian Federation), to Moscow, Leningrad (later St. Petersburg), the Baltic states, Minsk, to the Central Asian republics of Kazakhstan and Uzbekistan, to the Ukraine, even all the way out to Sakhalin Island, 11 time zones to the east.

We stayed in myriad hotels run by Intourist, the state tourism agency. There was a sameness to them all: frayed carpets, small, boxy beds, latherless soap and toilet paper that was a non-absorbent cross between waxed paper and the Big Chief tablet you used in grade school. None of them had room service, and when you ran out of soap or toilet paper it would not be replenished until you complained about it.

A fellow in one of my delegations remarked in his room that he might feel a lot better about this country if they would serve borscht. After all, the beet and cabbage broth soup was a Russian classic. Chicken Kiev would be much appreciated too, since that was also Russian. Sort of.

And the bathroom towels reminded him of the sheets a coroner uses to cover corpses.

"Wouldn't it be special to have real terrycloth towels for a change?" he opined aloud.

Terrycloth was unheard of in Intourist hotels and I never encountered it once in all my travels through Russia and the republics. What you got were big, wide things that were slightly more than bed sheets but a little less than canvas. "Lenin's linens," one guy called them. There were other jokes about the same fabric being used for Russian lingerie. A little unfair, but these were hostile times. Our friend used all these put-downs and more in his little in-room monologue. Of all the people on all my trips to the Soviet bloc, only this one man ever had terrycloth put in his bathroom, which he announced rubbing his palms together with undisguised glee that evening as we sat down to a dinner of hot borscht followed by Chicken Kiev.

I had a friend, Vitaly, who was a deputy chief editor for the government newspaper *Izvestya*. At that time he was in his last few years before retirement. He passed away shortly after that. In 1966, as *Izvestya's* bureau chief in Rio de Janiero, he had been declared persona non grata and kicked out of Brazil on suspicion of being a spy. Which he was. Vitaly did some work on the side for me, not spying, just helping make introductions for me. Since everything in the Soviet Union slid more smoothly on the lubricant of relationships and exchanged favors, Vitaly was a big help. He would have been an even bigger help except that he drank a great deal and I could usually count on him to be bombed out of his skull when I most needed him to be hitting on all cylinders. That was true even if it was 8 a.m.

But whether drunk or sober, Vitaly was the consummate old pro. Whenever we sat indoors and began talking about anything more substantive than the weather, he would touch his lips and make a cautionary pointing gesture at the ceiling. This meant that whatever I had to say, however innocent, could wait until we were able to go outside away from walls and imbedded microphones. This was right near the end of the Soviet Union and the system was as tired as Vitaly was; but lifelong habits die hard and large staffs of bureaucrats in some Kremlin directorate were still tapping the restaurants and hotels frequented by foreigners. Our best conversations took place on walks through the park, preferably next to a fountain whose gurgling waters negated long-distance listening devices. We weren't swapping state secrets. He was all out of them and I never had any. We were just two friends who were no longer cold warriors. Say what you want about spies, but they are excellent listeners.

One evening in the Japanese restaurant of the foreigners-only Mezhdunarodnya Hotel in Moscow, he began to talk about the surveillance. It was quite uncharacteristic for him to open up in a place that was routinely bugged, but I chalked that up to the fact that he had already inflicted serious damage on a bottle of scotch in my presence, and God knows what before. He was at least eight and a half drinks to the one I would sip all night. He leaned in close, his breath burning my face like a desert wind.

"My good friend is the former chief of the division that monitors hotels." He leaned back for a moment and smiled a smile of fond remembering. At Vitaly's age, most things that make one smile are in the past. "Yes," he confided, "we used to drink at his dacha on weekends and listen to the tapes he brought home." The Ministry of Bugs' Greatest Hits.

After the Cold War ended, I made arrangements for a delegation of scholars, professors of public affairs and policy, to meet with counterparts in Moscow, St. Petersburg and Odessa in the Ukraine. In Moscow, our first city, one of the professors met a woman in the hotel bar between sessions. Joseph noticed her sitting there reading an English-language book (a Tom Clancy Cold War novel, of all things), and he commented that he also liked Clancy, early Clancy. She was Russian and was reading to keep up her English. She had read all of Clancy and also acknowledged the superiority of *Red October* and *Red Storm Rising*. That was a pleasant surprise, but what should have surprised him more was that a Russian woman was sitting in the bar of an Intourist hotel. Places where foreigners stay have a wall of doormen outside for the purpose of keeping Russian nationals out. At that time, Russian women who got into the foreigner's hotels were hookers or government agents or, often, two-fers.

To say they hit it off well would be an epic understatement. They found hours of common interests to talk about and Joseph missed that afternoon's round of meetings. Well into the early evening over drinks at the bar, and later, espresso at a small side table and then dinner, they generated much light and even more heat.

We didn't see him the rest of the evening and by the next night Joseph was no longer staying at our hotel. As our conference arrangements called for us to bunk two conferees to a room, he began sleeping with her at another place, "over by the river," he said, which meant exactly nothing. Still, he showed up alone each morning for the meetings and tours.

His lady friend joined us one evening for dinner and a show at a club or the ballet. Our Intourist guide, Natalia, openly detested her and we understood that the jezebel's presence placed our government chaperone in some jeopardy because guides are responsible for knowing where their charges are and who they're talking to while they're in the country. A few of our number also considered her an unwelcome intrusion and looked at her the way Paul, George and Ringo must have viewed Yoko Ono.

The rest of us found her quite pleasant and interesting to talk to. Her name was Irina, and though not an official member of the tour, she wasn't intrusive and didn't disrupt anything in any real sense. Still, I knew the dangers for Joseph and tried to point them out on more than one occasion. "I paddle my own canoe," he said each time. After that he wouldn't talk any further on the subject.

When the Intourist guide was out of earshot, Irina was quite forthcoming about working conditions and daily life in the Soviet Union, even politics, about which she held strong opinions. That made her a valuable educational resource for many of us. We left Moscow to fly to Odessa a few days later and I commented to our guide that we seemed to have weathered the problem okay. The guide looked at me the way a patient teacher looks at a first grader extolling the joys of Santa Claus.

"We haven't seen the last of Irina," she said.

And whaddya know? Guess who "showed up" in Odessa? She appeared in St. Petersburg as well. Like a camel who slowly moves into your tent, she became part of the group, joining us for meals and tours, and never missing an evening event. "Little Red," as we called her, gradually overcame the resistance of most everyone except our guide, who told me she had been reporting on Irina to her superiors from the first day. But nothing ever happened to Irina that we could tell. She was never whisked away in the dead of night by Ivan's skulkers and she waved goodbye with a big smile for us, and blown kisses for Joseph, at the airport in St. Petersburg as we boarded the flight for home.

You never can tell whether a woman like Irina is a KGB "honey trap" or just another single gal looking for a ticket out. Russia has an abundance of both.

An associate who was also a frequent visitor to Moscow told me about a U.S. businessman friend of his who met a girlfriend under circumstances similar to Joseph's. The man was visited by State Security one afternoon as he sat in a coffee shop near Red Square. They were making an unsubtle point of letting him know they knew where he was all the time. The plainclothes security officer was charming and unhurried, impeccably dressed and conversant in American English. He smiled, introduced himself politely, sat down and said quietly, and without the slightest trace of judgment in his voice, "We know everything you've been doing."

The officer pulled out a cassette tape and slid it across the table to the now very nervous man. "Don't worry, you haven't broken any laws here," the officer assured him. Then he paused for one very pregnant eternity and added a nonchalantly posited question: "So tell me, who opens the mail at your house, you or your wife?"

I visualized Sergei and the former Chief of the Ministry of Bugs, listening to a tape of Joseph and Irina in their hotel room or her apartment. I visualized Joseph's wife in Memphis getting an audio cassette in the mail.

A few years later, I led an international delegation of media professionals, men and women who were editors, publishers and reporters of various news-gathering organizations. In St. Petersburg, three of us went out to dinner one beautiful summer evening. For two or three days in late June the "white nights" mean round-the-clock sunshine that far north. The sun drops into the treetops and scoots along the horizon, creating an all-night sunset before rising again on the new day.

After dinner we decided to walk back to the hotel. It was nearly 11 p.m. and the sun hung low in the sky at our backs, bathing the city in warm ochre tones. It looked as if everything had been dipped in a bath of melted gold. The world shimmered. The green and white Baroque-style Winter Palace (now the Hermitage Art Museum) and the Neva River behind it looked like an orange sepia print. The streets were packed. Surely not one person in the whole city was home in bed, and few would be during the non-stop party that is St. Petersburg's White Nights Festival.

The giant plaza in front of the Winter Palace was a big, churning fiesta. Street musicians occupied their separate spaces and a man maneuvered on very tall stilts across the slippery, uneven cobblestones near a 155-foot red granite obelisk. The Alexander Column was built in honor of Emperor Alexander the First, to commemorate Russia's victory over Napoleon, and it dominates the Palace Plaza. It weighs 600 tons (Intourist guides always tell you how much monuments weigh) and just sits there on top of the pavement without any underground foundation or support of any kind. The man on stilts stood in the column's shadow and juggled butcher knives and bantered with the crowd. They loved him and filled his pickle can with kopek coins and folding money.

We were caught up in the circus, marveling to one another when we heard a feminine voice. "Ah, you speak English." The three of us turned to see three very beautiful women. Golden women, so stunning they *shimmered* in the sunset, like a poem waiting to be written. One asked with only a slight accent, "Are you from America?"

"Yes," my friend, the editor of a large plains state newspaper, replied.

Like us, they were nicely dressed, also just returning from dinner. Like us, they were all from out of town—Moscow. Like us, they were pleasantly surprised to hear English being spoken in this unforeseen happenstance on the streets of St. Pete.

Like us. Like us. Like us.

"Your English is excellent," I said. "Did you study abroad?"

"Why, thank you. It's a great compliment coming from native speakers. No, we have good schools here and we practice every day. We work for Radio Moscow in the news division." They were bright and perky and all three were really in the moment, responsive. We chatted and the conversational atmosphere evolved so pleasantly that it soon had only a barely recognizable colleague-to-colleague tinge, and had acquired a palpable ambiance of man and woman. Anyone over the age of 14 knows the difference.

We all thought simultaneously: *Well, shut my mouth! If this isn't simply an astounding coincidence. We're in the news business too. There's three of you, three of us. You're alone in this big bad city and we are too. We're quite a bit older than you, more than a bit, but it's clear you're impressed with our manly attributes. Must be our pot bellies.*

We talked amicably at the end of the bridge. The wake from a barge on the Neva slapped gently against the stones below us. They said they were in town on business and were staying at the posh Astoria Hotel (where we had wanted to stay with our group, but it had been packed). They mentioned the hotel's beautiful and historic bar, which had to be seen to be appreciated. The high beams in their eyes were blazing and they were perched on their tippy-toes waiting for us to suggest we all pop over to that ol' historic bar for a look-see and a drinkerooty.

They were articulate and personable but they were not, in our opinion, news people. A collegial vibe exists among those who gather news for a living. It's an attitude more than anything, straightforward but with a tastefully veiled skepticism. One might describe a wine that way. Whatever it is, it's global in our profession and we found it in our dealings with colleagues in the USSR's state-controlled media. But not with these gals.

Whatever they gathered for a living, it wasn't breaking news. And at some level, that bothered all three of us. We were standing there on square one, knowing that square two would have been nothing more than a pleasant evening of conversation, and I'm sure we all could have arranged to maintain the Radio Moscow charade. Still, it didn't seem right on a bunch of other levels and in the end, we opted not to go there. We talked about our work for a few minutes, pumped their hands goodbye and moseyed across the Nevsky Bridge. Our unanimous conclusion was that women that beautiful are wasted on a blind medium like radio.

The RUSSIA CHRONICLES

GET MOOSE & SQUIRREL

Hunting-gathering in Moscow, the KGB
and Tanya the heat-seeking missile

omiko Duggan, my associate, and I found the flat in the hard winter of 1990-91. Like many Moscow apartments ("flats" in the British vernacular taught in Russian schools), ours was terribly overheated during the cold months with radiators through which hot water was shoved from some central hot water plant miles away. The radiator didn't have a knob for turning off the heat, which meant the only way to regulate the temperature in the flat was to open the windows. In my youth, if I did that, my father would shout, "Hey, are you trying to heat the whole neighborhood?" Here, the answer would be yes.

For two weeks before that we had been staying in a rented college dormitory room that was only partly heated from 9 a.m. until 6 p.m. each day. We would have been grateful for a little overheating and wondered why the Ministry of Hot Water and Warm Beer (as we called them) in the most wasteful government on earth had chosen our little college to bone up on their economizing skills.

It was bitter cold, bottoming out one day at minus 40 Fahrenheit. Even Muscovites, who take pride in their hard winters, knuckled under and closed the schools that day. They don't do "snow removal" in Moscow, as much as they just shove it over to the curb where it piles up until God removes it in the spring. Foot traffic on the sidewalks packs it into hard "*skreet skreet*," so called by Russians because of the sound your boots make as you walk over it.

Our purpose for being in the USSR was to visit legislators, deputies of the Soviet parliament who worked in the "White House," the tall pale concrete building that houses Russia's legislature, trying to convince them to attend a series of seminars in New York that dealt with the philosophical basics of setting up a government to allow for democratic processes and a return to religious freedom.

Tomiko and I had been asked by a non-profit organization to help recruit parliamentarians for their educational seminars because we had spent a lot of time on the ground there, dealing with Soviet government officials and media. She and I had worked together well for 16 years, organizing numerous fact-finding trips for U.S. opinion leaders and media on all sorts of issues.

As a team we divided our conferencing duties roughly into politics and logistics. I secured the speakers and meetings with officials, while Tomiko organized hotels, airlines, meals, meeting venues and managed the budget. If a hotel or conference center staff was poorly trained, Tomiko whipped them into shape in no uncertain terms, marching into the bowels of the kitchen to knock heads with the catering chief if that's what it took. Hotel conference and banquet managers were impressed with her exacting attention to detail, even if she had to harass them until they gave her what she wanted. On the final day of a conference, hotels often tried to hire her away from us with the offer of an executive position.

Our merry band in Moscow was completed by the arrival of Jesus Gonzales, from Spain, one of the CAUSA organizers who joined us after we had been there a month. He brought his good humor, optimism and generous faith to the mix. This particular mission didn't have a conference-organizing aspect in Moscow, so the three of us haunted the halls of parliament together, introducing ourselves to the legislators.

Tom Ward, the CAUSA director back in New York, sent encouragement and care packages, one containing an enormous warm coat for me since I had gone to Russia unprepared for the winter. Like Napoleon, Tom pointed out.

It was a tremendously interesting time to be in the USSR, and rough days for the socialist utopia. Communism was sucking wind, staggering into the ropes at the end of the 15th round. *Glasnost* and *perestroika* were on queer street, with knees of jelly (only boxing metaphors will work here).

Gorbachev couldn't deliver the goods, and the sclerotic system mocked his efforts to try. Everyone could see it, feel it, smell it, taste it. If the Soviet Union took over the Sahara Desert, it was said, after five years they would have to import sand. Communism's warts had never been very well hidden, but now nobody could ignore that the power structure had always been a twisted caricature of government. It was a very insecure time for everyone in the country.

The leaders we spoke with had all kinds of confused notions about how money is made in the real world. For them, wealth was created by cooking the books and fabricating goals out of the blue sky to make the revenue column balance with the expenses. Amazingly, this can actually work, but only for a few people at the top of the food chain, and only as long as the system remains a closed loop, but even then only for a limited time. In the case of the Soviet Union, that was 70 years.

So there we were, taking a taxi to the Parliament Building every morning to see who we could get in to meet on a cold call, or by using the name of someone we had met the day before. It's not an easy way to get appointments, even with people who aren't very busy. And we were trying to see Peoples' Deputies, who were running around like the crew of the post-iceberg Titanic trying to hold the USSR together.

A successful encounter in working the Parliament Building was defined by the Deputy offering us coffee. We knew we were received when he opened the steel safe in his office and pulled out the jar of Folger's Instant Coffee Crystals, bought from a hard currency shop with dollars or Deutschmarks. The powdered creamer, sugar, cups, saucers and guest spoons were kept in there, as well.

Our days were divided between the Parliament Building and our rented flat, the living room of which we converted into an office. The flat was in a *Khruschova*, an apartment house built during the Khrushchev years. It was at the qualitative low end of Russian housing, made of prefab concrete slabs bolted and caulked together.

The most sought-after flats were in the ochre-colored concrete block buildings erected by German POWs during Stalin's time. Most of those were close to the center of the city. We lived farther out in the Moscow Hills, not far from Moscow University on Ulitsa Schvernika just off Ho Chi Minh Square and the Akademicheskaya Station on the Orange Line Metro.

By the way, the shortest restaurant review I ever read in my life was for Hanoi, the Vietnamese restaurant on Ho Chi Minh Square. The entire review was three words: "Don't do it." The reviewer had gotten food poisoning from her visit.

In our Khruschova we lived among the common people, but being foreigners, we were automatically a few steps higher on the food chain. Our living allowance wasn't much but it was paid in dollars. This fact alone made us wealthy in the sense that it increased our options. For example, we could shop in convertible currency shops where they had all the goods and only took dollars, Deutschmarks, pounds sterling and the like. However, these shops were expensive and we couldn't use them all the time. But once a week or so, we bought eggs, imported canned foods, fresh fruit and vegetables as easily as we did in the states. Just knowing we could go to these special shops in a pinch was a tremendous psychological comfort not available to Ivan Sixpackovitch.

Valya, one of our two assistants, came to the flat one morning beaming like a sunrise. Had she fallen in love on the metro? Even better, she said. "Last night, I found a line for eggs that was only 45 minutes long. It still makes me smile thinking about it." A popular saying at that time went, "There is nothing in the shops, but there is everything on the table." It meant that despite the empty shelves and empty stores, the resourcefulness of Russian women still somehow managed to feed the family at night.

Tomiko had to return to Washington after the first month, leaving Jesus and me to soldier on alone. We missed her organization and can-do spirit.

At some point, Jesus and I decided to shun the "hard currency" stores and go native, foraging for food in the local shops, even though it meant changing more of our precious dollars into rubles, a form of reverse alchemy. Saving money was the main reason, but we also figured that if we wanted a better understanding of the culture, we couldn't do it by hopping into a cab and running down to the German supermarket or McDonalds whenever the urge hit. But mostly, I think we were compelled by the challenge of living on the edge, going toe-to-toe with the most user-*unfriendly* consumer economy to ever walk the earth.

Until then, our food shopping experience in Moscow had been limited. The few stores that were marked had signs that said *produkti* (products). And those were always empty. One day, we saw an old lady walking down the street clutching the string bag shoppers typically carry, whose Russian name translates as "just in case." She looked like a fellow hunter-gatherer, so we decided to follow her in the hope she would lead us to vegetables or butter or meat.

We trailed her at a discreet distance. She went into a darkened, deserted *produkti* and down a dark hallway, into a back room. The unmarked room was set up as a butcher shop and fruit stand. We bought some mystery meat. The vegetables looked like they had been delivered to the market by being shot out of a cannon. We bought a few of each anyway, and on the way home tried to figure out the best way to cook it all.

From the old ladies we learned tricks like sniffing the outside of instant soup packets for mold.

Many stores sold just one thing, butter for example, so we would buy a kilo, sometimes two (nearly five pounds), because we never knew when we would run into it again.

There was a bakery nearby that usually had a short, 30-minute line, and we bought a loaf of bread there every other day. The bread was round and dome-shaped, like a yurt. We tucked it unwrapped under our arm and continued foraging. Milk, for our coffee, was always a problem. No matter where we bought it, it was always at the very end of its life. No matter what expiration date was written on the carton, it would be stinking and rotten in our fridge, deader than Elvis, by breakfast the next morning.

That's when we had a shopping epiphany. On one of our daily scavenges we went into a store we hadn't seen before. There were the usual bored employees standing around, smoking. The store was completely bare, with the exception of a large wire bin in the center of the floor that was filled with Similac, powdered baby formula, in cans the size normally used to sell house paint. With great glee, we saw that this would solve our coffee creamer problem. The price in rubles was equivalent to twenty-five cents each so we bought four huge paint cans of Similac and carted them home, one under each arm, thrilled as we could be, laughing and congratulating ourselves.

The reality of Similac (powdered breast milk essentially) is that it takes some getting used to in coffee. In fact, the combination is downright strange. The first time I put some in my coffee and drank it, I made a grotesque face. The mixture was awful. "Yucck! This," I said, holding my cup out to Jesus, "is why nursing mothers shouldn't drink coffee."

Ultimately, we did get used to it, and even grew to like it. The Soviet Union was the land of shoving square pegs into round holes and then documenting the damage with a self-congratulatory report. Since all the laws go against prosperity's self-interests, the advent of privately-owned business in Moscow was accomplished on the shoulders of one under-the-table workaround after another. In the late 1980s, all businesses operating openly were owned by the state, and there was no advertising, so you either found out about a shop, or you didn't.

The first private enterprise restaurant in Moscow was named "36 Kropotkinskaya," which was also its address. When someone mentioned the restaurant, you automatically knew where it was. Clever.

And it worked. Time Magazine wrote in its July 27, 1987 issue:

> It is 11 a.m., an hour before opening time. Already the queue at 36 Kropotkinskaya Street extends around the corner of the elegant green-and-cream 19th century building. People are waiting patiently for a chance to experience one of the first visible signs of economic reform, a free-enterprise restaurant. "We've got a big problem here," Manager Andrei Fyodorov says. 'Too many customers."

As the Cold War began to wind down, so did the routine surveillance of foreigners. While we always conducted ourselves as if our phones were tapped, it was likely our apartment and phone were bug-free. The days of serious skulking in the alleys seemed to be behind us, and besides, the KGB now had bigger problems. The mafia was the rising power in Russia. They were running drugs and prostitutes, and laundering money from extortion, and the government couldn't stop them. The KGB, outspent and outgunned by the mafia, had become a toothless tiger.

In effect, the spy game had become something of a comic exercise. You could still get your camera confiscated for taking a picture inside the terminal at Moscow's big public Sheremetyeva Airport long after we had satellites that could photograph all the runways of all the secret military bases in the world. It was tempting to think of the KGB as a version of the old Rocky and Bullwinkle cartoons. Boris and Natasha, the two inept spies always decoded the same message from Fearless Leader: "Get moose and squirrel." And of course they bungled it every time.

But the KGB brand name and reputation still counted for a lot in Russia and we knew that even a weak tiger is still a tiger. While making some calls for us one day, Valya apparently misdialed. She said hello and then went silent for a long time. When we finally noticed her, Valya was sitting in her chair immobilized with terror, unable to speak or move. She held the phone to her ear and her mouth hung open. Finally she mouthed silently to us, "KGB!"

She had been calling one of the many agencies that share the KGB's three-number prefix and had dialed one wrong digit, which had put her through to the cloak-and-dagger division, where some authoritarian harvey wallbanger picked up the phone. He was giving Valya a heavy-handed third degree: "What's your name? How did you get this number? Speak up. We can trace where you're calling from. We know who you are." All the color had drained out of Valya's face and tears began to spill out the corners of her eyes.

Jesus was the one who acted. He crossed the room to Valya, calmly removed the receiver from her petrified hand, listened for a few seconds, and hung up the phone. We told her not to worry about it and tried to go on about our business, but Valya's composure was wrecked for the rest of the day.

Whoever this goon was, we never heard back from him or the KGB, nor did we get their traditional 3 a.m. knock at the door. We figured he was just some impotent bureaucrat in the basement of Lubianka Prison longing for the good old days. He was blessed with an intimidating gravel voice from a lifetime cigarette habit.

This was the closest Jesus or I ever came to witnessing the genuine fear felt by citizens of the USSR toward their own government. It was a sobering wake-up call for us as visitors, and another reminder that, notwithstanding the relative total freedom we enjoyed in the USSR, the bear was far from dead. Boris and Natasha still had real teeth, and Russia could still be a very nasty place for any average citizen who could not leave.

Our other assistant and translator was Kirill, who normally worked for the North American Division of Novosti Press Agency. Natalya Yakovleva, director of that division, allowed us to hire Kirill on a freelance basis at Tomiko's request a few days after our arrival in Moscow.

Kirill was in his early 20s and spoke good colloquial American English. (He said "truck" instead of "lorry," and when we said, "thank you," he replied, "you're welcome," instead of the British "not at all.") He looked like a young Leonardo DiCaprio, with moppish hair and a sweet face.

We jumped right to the point, telling him we wanted to hire him to go around with us as a translator, and that we would pay him in U.S. dollars. He blanched and looked at Natalya for cues. Dealing in dollars was still officially a crime, although everyone did it all the time.

Naytalya waved her hand dismissively and told him, "I'm not here." That was all he needed. Kirill leaned forward on the table with a lopsided grin that was part baby and part Huck Finn. "How can I help?"

On a shopping expedition shortly before Tomiko returned to the States, we made the mistake of taking Kirill into a hard currency food store. The windows were covered with movie posters so Russians wouldn't be able to see all the food they couldn't find in their own shops. You had to show a foreign passport to get in. Kirill came in with us and was deathly quiet the entire time. We bought some eggs, milk, bread, fresh veggies and some microwave popcorn. We paid, grabbed a taxi and left—all without Kirill having uttered a single word. This was very unlike him, and he looked depressed as he could be.

"Kirill, what do you think when you see this kind of store?" I asked.

"I wonder what I have done that was so bad as to not deserve anything like that." Going into that store with us, Kirill visited the true front line of socialism vs. free enterprise and had peeked over the edge into the other side. There was nothing we could say that would be of any comfort to him.

Someone Jesus and I still mention when we reminisce about those days is Tanya the Heat-Seeking Missile. We encountered Tanya one day in mid-summer while foraging. She would have been a major head-turner anywhere in the world—blond, shapely, magnificent. We saw her coming up the cut-through path toward us as we made our way to the corner to see if the veggie vendors were open. She smiled and we all said "hello" at the same instant. Her English was good, so we fell into conversation about which food shops had anything decent.

"What are you doing here?" she asked. "Are you sovietologists?" Academicians were about the only Americans living in cheap housing this close to Moscow University. We gave her the stump speech version of why we were there and found out she lived in the building next to ours and was a single mom with two kids.

As Jesus and I walked to the veggie stands, I asked, more to myself than Jesus, "I wonder why her marriage broke up."

"Oh, the usual," Jesus said. The usual. That was Jesus' shorthand for the full array of issues that have separated men from women since the dawn of time. Jesus had studied the male-female dysfunction from every angle, and had even written books about it, a true Fall of Man specialist. One tennager in Uruguay, where Jesus had been the senior pastor, told me he and his friends always like to go to church when Rev. Gonzales gives the sermon, because they know he's going to talk about sex.

A lot of guys look at a beautiful woman superficially, swearing if they could ever be so fortunate as to have the love of such a goddess of a physical specimen, they would never think of looking at another. But that's not how it works of course. When we met Tanya, two things were clear to us: She was the prettiest woman in that neighborhood and she was also about the loneliest and most unhappy.

We almost got some butter in the shop on the corner (the lady ahead of us bought the last kilo), but amazingly, we did find some watermelons that didn't look like they had been scrounged from the dustbin of history. We bought a couple, including one for Tanya. We went to her apartment and gave it to her. At that time, we met her kids as well, and invited her to stop by for a cup of tea when she had time. We were happy to have met a local friend who came with decent English and pleasant femininity.

A day or two later, Tanya popped over for that cup of tea and we talked further. I was typing a letter on the computer in our living room office while Tanya sat on the couch with Jesus. He was showing her a book of photos of his wife and kids back home.

I looked over my shoulder once or twice and noticed she was leaning in rather close to him. I turned full around in my chair and made eye-contact with Jesus. She had leaned in farther, her head close enough for him to smell her hair, and Jesus was definitely not having fun. He was now talking about his wife with greater emphasis and urgency, but it wasn't making Tanya cool her jets. In fact, it seemed to be having the opposite effect. She was almost in his lap now. Even when Jesus held the book of photos out toward her, she still managed to find ways to wiggle in closer to him.

He was saved by the tea kettle whistle. Tanya went into our kitchen to pour tea for us all. Jesus fell back against the couch cushions. He looked like he had been hit by a truck.

"Oh my God," he laughed, miming wiping away sweat.

"Be standing up when she comes back," I advised. "It'll be less intimate."

El wrong-o.

When she came back with the tea, Jesus had put the photo album on the shelf and was standing by the couch with one foot up on the rail that held the seat cushions. It was a goofy, unnatural nonchalance he was affecting, but an admirable attempt. Tanya served the tea, set the tray down and walked up to Jesus to resume the conversation, standing way too close. She planted herself "inside" his propped-up leg, not very far from fig leaf country. Jesus, always the perfect gentleman, tried to use his hot teacup to force her back a bit.

At some point, I invited Tanya into the kitchen, figuring that putting a table between us would change the vibe. The problem was the table wasn't much bigger than a postage stamp, and Tanya was somehow able to be all over it and all around it at the same time, pressing forward, an unstoppable Greek phalanx of boobs, lips and eyes.

Jesus came and stood in the kitchen doorway to her right, which helped because we divided her attention. Together we began to speak about our families and our marriages, but more specifically, of examples we had observed of how purposefully inviting God's presence into our families had transformed our lives in beneficial ways.

As a team, as brothers, Jesus and I just quietly kept to the high road, sharing our hearts and as we did, the effect on Tanya was visible. She turned off her infrared, heat-seeking tractor beam. She sat back in her chair, calm now, no longer radiating the lonely *do-me* vibes.

With the sexual tension erased, Jesus and I were able to appreciate and enjoy her sisterly qualities and the feminine beauty with which she graced our apartment. Every human being suffers from a deficiency of unconditional, non-sexual love and in the setting we were able to create, the original flowers of Tanya's character blossomed. This was a valuable lesson for us in the importance of changing the atmosphere of an encounter, from where it is at the beginning to where it needs to be.

We saw Tanya a couple more times after that when we stopped at her apartment to say hello. By the time of our last visit, she had found a boyfriend and it was obvious he had moved in with her.

The three of us, Tomiko, Jesus and I, went back and forth to our Moscow flat at various times throughout 1991 and were living there during the August coup that toppled communism. But that's another story.

The longest our team was there at any one time was three months. We met many fine people and developed lasting friendships with some of them. We had meetings with high officials and were routinely invited into parts of the Kremlin no tourist ever sees.

The Russia Chronicles

Gorby Gets the Flu

The Russia Chronicles

On Sunday afternoon, August 18, 1991 at 4:50 p.m., Mikhail Gorbachev was working at his *dacha* on the Crimean Sea, far from Moscow. His aides knocked on the door to inform him that Yuri Plekhanov, a top official of the KGB, had arrived with a delegation of military and party officials and that they wanted to speak to him. The visit was totally unexpected. Perhaps sensing something, Gorbachev tried to make a call. All five separate phone lines were dead.

At that moment, Gorbachev's chief of staff, Valery Boldin, entered the room to inform him that the delegation had been sent by the State Committee of Emergency.

"The what?!" Gorbachev had never authorized such a committee. Boldin, speaking for the group, said that Gorbachev must sign a statement declaring a state of emergency in the USSR, and authorize other unspecified "special measures." He was told that if he didn't sign, Vice President Gennady Yanayev, head of the Emergency Committee, would take over as president of the country.

Gorbachev told Boldin to tell the leaders, who became known as the Gang of Eight, to go to hell. Soldiers came in to occupy the dacha and put the Gorbachevs under house arrest. First Lady Raisa Gorbachev suffered heart palpitations from the stress, and had to lie down most of the time, under medication.

Meanwhile, the conspirators, who included the military leaders, ordered thousands of troops to head for Moscow and Leningrad as well as Latvia and Lithuania. They also took possession of the "black box," the executive briefcase containing the launch codes for the Soviet Union's mighty nuclear arsenal.

At the center of the crisis was a new treaty being prepared by Gorbachev for signing by all the countries within the USSR. The new agreement called for the decentralization of much of the power that had once been strongly in the hands of the Soviet Government. The satellite republics would now have a great deal more autonomy. Conservative members of the Supreme Soviet who read a preliminary draft of the text were horrified. They saw this as the unraveling of the Soviet Union. Yeltsin, a liberal, supported the treaty. Things were already very tense in the Baltics. Lithuania had declared its independence the previous March, and had taken over the main TV station in Vilnius. Soviet troops re-took the station, killing 15. In Riga, Latvia, anti-Soviet riots were put down with five deaths.

The one hitch in the conspirators' well-orchestrated plan was their failure to arrest Boris Yeltsin. Yeltsin had unexpectedly left for his office in the Parliament Building 45 minutes earlier than was his custom. Even though Yeltsin was Gorbachev's most outspoken critic, he refused to go along with a military coup that would put the most hardline commies in control of the country. Yeltsin locked the doors of the building (known by Muscovites as the "White House") and said he would not leave until Gorbachev was released.

That was Sunday night. No news had been made public, and Jesus and I had probably been out shopping for food or visiting friends while all this was going on. The next morning was Monday. Jesus was in the kitchen when I turned on the morning news on TV. But there was no news. There was a symphony orchestra playing classical music.

Hmmm. Wrong channel? I glanced at the dial. *Nope.*

It took a good 30-seconds for my early morning brain to process why classical music was on television where the news usually is. And then the gears finally caught.

Ooooh shit.

"Jesus!" I hollered, "Come here—something's going on!" He came running into the living room and understood immediately. We both knew the drill. Everyone in the USSR knew the drill. Whenever a Soviet leader died, the commies replaced any live news programming with a classical music videotape while they huddled up to decide what to do next. Communist governments, being generally fond of taxidermy, don't have much time to commit to a plan before the body starts to become less than presentable (as was the case when Chairman Mao died in China; but that's another story).

Gorby's dead? we wondered. An hour later, at 8:30 a.m., when I knew he would be in his office, I called my friend, Vladimir, a somewhat senior official at the Central Committee Building. Vladimir's portfolio was based on his experience in the Central Asian republics, but he would know what was going on. The Central Committee of the Communist Party is only a block away from the KGB headquarters on Dzherzhinski Square. (One of the most enduring images of the collapse of communism was the crane removing the huge statue of Felix Dzherzhinski from the middle of the square. Dzherzhinski was the founder of the Cheka, Lenin's secret police, the forerunner of the KGB.)

"Vlad, it's me. Can I come to your office?" I asked.

"Yes," he replied and immediately hung up. Vladimir was quite gracious and effusive in person, and I had learned to accept that our phone conversations needed to be terse. Stalin had had Vladimir's parents killed when he was a boy and he was never on the phone without thinking some third party was listening to his every word.

Soldiers were everywhere as I walked from the Metro to the Wedgwood-blue Central Committee Building. A guard looked at my passport and called Vladimir's secretary, who came out to escort me to his office.

"Well, you know, Gorbachev has the flu and some back problems," Vlad said, sounding sympathetic. He leaned back in his shirtsleeves and suspenders, sounding like a country doctor comforting a concerned relative. "He will have a chance to get some rest. This is for the best."

He quoted to me from memory that morning's official blurb: "Because of Mikhail Sergeyevich Gorbachev's inability to perform his duties as the president of the USSR, due to health reasons, in accordance with Article 127 of the Constitution of the USSR, the vice president of the USSR has temporarily assumed the office of acting president." I tried to get Vladimir to elaborate but he looked a little distracted and that was all he would tell me.

Okay, fine. I went back home to brief Jesus. By now, the news was all over the place and everyone had an opinion, which mostly seemed to be in support of Yeltsin. Even though glasnost and perestroika weren't delivering the goods, and Gorbachev's popularity had fallen into the basement in recent months, nobody wanted a commie takeover.

Curiously, the coup didn't seem to be very well organized. For one thing, the phones still worked. We had no problem calling the States. Yeltsin and the other opposition leaders weren't arrested, even during the early hours before people had surrounded the "White House" and started erecting makeshift barricades. Yeltsin was on the phone with leaders of other nations, drumming up support. At one point, a delivery car from the new Moscow Pizza Hut pulled up and a guy carried several large Supremes inside. Yeltsin and his staff had ordered siege food.

Yeltsin phoned the coup organizers, the so-called Emergency Committee, and told them to shove it. Later that day, he went outside and climbed atop a tank to address the crowd around the building, which had now grown to 20,000. He seized the moral high ground, declaring the coup unconstitutional, called himself "the guardian of democracy" and called for a general strike. The mayor's office supported Yeltsin. Other officials decided not to say anything one way or the other, waiting to see which way the wind would blow.

Jesus and I, strolling past the armored personnel carriers parked bumper-to-bumper across Tverskaya, watched the whole thing in person.

Interestingly, the news photos of Yeltsin on the tank also showed an aide next to him who bore such a strong resemblance to me that it fooled my brother, Mike, who worked for Mobil Oil in Houston. Mike called the head of the international division, who at that time was trying to get a foothold in Russia for joint venture oil projects. He showed the division chief the newspaper photo and said, "If you want to get into Russia, talk to my brother. That's him on the tank with Yeltsin." This case of mistaken identity led to me being hired by Mobil for a lucrative consulting gig that opened doors for them to Russia's oil and gas power brokers. (More on that in the next chapter.)

By early evening, the crowd had grown to well over 100,000. A large number of Afghanistan war vets showed up to organize the erection of serious barricades and the making of Molotov cocktails.

The building was surrounded by high school and college students, pensioners, priests, street sweepers and, increasingly, soldiers who were defecting from the army. Many carried automatic rifles. They climbed on the tanks placed all around the building by the Emergency Committee and shared cigarettes with the young recruits who made up the tank crews.

The tanks were there on orders from the Army, which was supporting the coup, but they were manned by kids only a year or two out of high school and their hearts weren't in it. Nobody felt the slightest danger from the tanks, in spite of street talk of an impending military crackdown by the coup organizers.

A curfew had been imposed by the Committee but nobody paid any attention to it. Jesus and I hung around until about midnight before heading back to the flat. It was a warm summer evening and the streets were filled with people strolling, talking to the soldiers. This would be history and everyone wanted to be a part of it.

The next morning, Tuesday, August 20, the defense of the White House continued in earnest. Rumors of the imminent arrival of troops continually pulsed through the crowd like electric surges.

Popular revolution had been a required subject in high school and college, so the young people knew how to man the barricades. They also had been schooled on the moral virtues of the Sandinista National Liberation Front (FSLN) during the 1980s in Nicaragua, so they knew how to work a crowd. They chanted the Sandinista slogan in Spanish, "*Un pueblo unido jamás será vencido!*" A people united will never be defeated.

Barricades rose skyward as mountains of construction debris, scrap metal, sawed lengths of telephone poles, air-conditioner shipping crates, furniture and concertina wire were all intertwined. Anything they could find that could be made to stay in one place was added to the pile, fastened to an empty cable spool or some old tires to hold it in place. Someone drove their car alongside the barricade, got out and called for people to come flip it on its side to be added to the barrier.

A reporter for CNN described the scene with the barricade in the background. "The action around the parliament building is reminiscent of an anthill. People continue to build barricades, although the entrance to the building is already blocked with layers of material, and all the nearest points are firmly secured. Granite blocks are surrounding the building, cars have been turned on their side. In the past several hours, security headquarters has moved to the center of the parliament building, where people are working out the plan for the defense of the building and coordinating the action of the defenders. The defenders have at their disposal automatic weapons and bottles of homemade incendiary liquid, boxes of which are standing right here."

A revolution needs a flag, and this one moved under the banner of the old Republic of Russia. Sprouting from apartment windows and hung like capes around people's necks, the white, blue and red was fastened to spikes jutting out of the rubble defense works.

Moscow has a handful of unique 1950s-era buildings scattered around the city. The "Seven Sisters" are of a style called "Stalin Gothic," with an evil genius quality of spires and eerie wedding cake ornamentation. They look like they were designed by an architect trying way too hard to get mentioned in history books. Today, two of them house government ministries, two are hotels, one is Moscow University, and two are apartment buildings.

One of the Stalin Gothics is near the White House, just on the other side of the American Embassy. The students went in and denuded the lobby, carrying out couches, big stuffed wingback chairs, tables, potted plants, doors—moving it all like lines of ants from the building to the barricades where they would pass it up, hand-over-hand, to some folks on the top who had just the place to put a sofa from yesteryear.

Several young demonstrators emerged from the apartment building carrying a piece of Stalinist flotsam. It was a huge section of antique staircase banister. One of them told us, "We are using Stalin's architecture to build the barricades of our new revolution." Soviets love allegory. It sustains their literature and their films in a signatory way, like masa flour in Mexican food. They weren't just looting a building; they were looting *this* building, *Stalin's* building, and everyone coming out of there carrying the headboard of a bed or a sink understood this. For several days I tried to put a name to the expression I saw on the faces of the students stripping the staircase. Not smugness, not victory. And then I understood. I was looking at closure.

The famous Russian cellist, Mstislav Rostropovich, flew in from Paris and played his music near a window in the upper stories of the White House. Someone put a microphone near him and piped the sound by loudspeaker, out to the revolutionaries.

That night, the streets filled with people. Rumors of troops coming in by helicopter and fresh tank divisions were on everyone's lips. The crowds began to place themselves across streets and bridges. At midnight, tanks and armored personnel carriers finally did arrive, and the crowd met them, determined to block them with their bodies. Two people were shot and one was crushed under the treads. But that was it as far as violence went. Even when the crowd swarmed over the vehicles, the army didn't open fire, not even after people set fire to one of the armored personnel carriers. The tanks and carriers pulled back and left. They couldn't wrap their hearts and minds around the idea of killing civilians, and so decided to take Yeltsin up on his offer of amnesty for all military personnel and police who refused to support the coup.

By the next day, Wednesday the 21st, the coup was coming unraveled. Coup leaders were stopped trying to get out of the country. Yeltsin sent a plane to the Crimea to pick up Gorbachev, who looked drained when he arrived in Moscow the following morning.

The State Emergency Committee had eight members: Gennady Yanayev, vice president of the USSR; Valentin Pavlov, prime minister; Vladimir Kryuchkov, director of the KGB; Dimitri Yazov, defense minister; Oleg Baklanov, of the Soviet Defense Council; Vasily Starodubtsev, member of the Soviet Parliament; and Alexander Tizyakov, president of state communications. The Committee members were all arrested, except for Interior Minister Boris Pugo, who shot himself in the head.

People were happy to see Gorbachev returned because it meant the end of the coup; but the real hero in everyone's mind was Boris Yeltsin. Ten days later, Yeltsin ended communism with a decree suspending all activities of the Communist Party. Gorbachev issued his own decree to end communism. The party newspaper, *Pravda*, was closed, as were the Central Committee and the KGB. Party offices, limos and spacious country retreats were seized and suddenly everyone was falling over themselves to declare they had only been lip-service communists and had never truly bought into any of it.

Four months later, on December 21, 1991, the Soviet Union went out of existence. Where the USSR had stood for 74 years, there were now 15 independent republics. Four days later, Gorbachev resigned and Yeltsin became President of Russia. The transformation was immediate and everyone slipped into their capitalist skins without effort because, in truth, they had been practicing for this moment for years.

The day the coup failed, I phoned Vladimir at the Central Committee, just a few hours before his building was emptied and padlocked. He was at his desk. I was at least savvy enough to know not to say anything stupid over the phone, like, "Sorry your coup failed." But Vladimir didn't know that. He knew Americans could be oblivious at times. That's why, when he picked up the phone and heard me say "hello," he jumped in immediately, all hyper and excited. "Larry, great news! We got the sons of bitches!"

"Way to go, Vlad!"

The end of communism spawned a migration of sorts, of unificationists who went there and lived for years and years to help build whatever was to follow the era of Marx and Lenin. Jack and Renee Corley were among the first of those. (In 2006, the Russian Orthodox Church helped orchestrate the Corley's eviction from Russia and return to the States, but not before they had established a solid foundation of core members who are still active today.)

All of us who observed and participated in the relatively bloodless revolution that changed the Soviet Union, from a multinational empire into a country in search of its soul, were forever changed in ways large and small. Countless personal revolutions were set in motion within individuals and families throughout the entirety of peoples and cultures in the now shattered USSR. The transformation was every bit as elemental as Russia's seasonal passage from winter to spring, and on into summer.

The RUSSIA CHRONICLES

TAKING ONE FOR THE TEAM

On a summerish September day in 1991, my brother Mike called to congratulate me for being enough of an insider to have been standing atop the tank with Boris Yeltsin in Moscow when he made his grandstand defiance of the coup organizers a month earlier.

Mike was a landman for Mobil Oil Corporation and thought this was really cool because he knew people at his company who lusted after partnerships with Russia's oil powers, and would kill to be able to have the kind of access I had.

I reminded Mike that my picture was all over the front page, four columns wide in every newspaper in the world. It was taken by Associated Press and had become the signature image of Yeltsin's courage. What would have been even better would have been if that had actually been me in the photo with Yeltsin. But it wasn't. I remember thinking, when I first saw it on the front page of various newspapers: *That aide standing next to Yeltsin sure looks a lot like me.*

I told Mike as much and he went silent on the other end. He informed me that he had bragged about me to his friends who were on the team assigned to open up oil and gas rights in Russia and Central Asia. He had told them his brother was Yeltsin's buddy, and that they should hire me as their door-kicker-inner in Russia. He had showed them the photo as proof.

I assured Mike that, while I was not on the tank, I was standing a few feet away and I did have demonstrably good access to top leaders, and might make a valuable contribution to Mobil. Ask the team in Houston to send me a ticket to go down to speak with them, I suggested. Mike did, and they did.

Mobil already had a couple of get-into-Russia consultants, an American and a Russian who had formed a company whose only client was Mobil. The Houston team leader said that if I were hired, it would also be partly as a way of sending a motivating message to their current consulting group who had been slacking. *Terrific,* I thought, *I'm a wake-up call, a mine-shaft canary.* And what better way to make sure this first group of hired guns (hereafter called "the evil consultants") hate my guts before having even met me?

In my initial meeting with Mobil's Russia team, they unrolled a map of Sakhalin Island, just north of Japan, where the USSR shot down Korean civilian airliner Flight 007 in 1983. One man pointed out that the capital was Yuzhno-Sakhalinisk in the south and that all the oil refineries and apparatus were located in Okha on the north tip of the island.

"You should immediately open up a charm offensive in both places," I said. This apparently meant something to them because the team leader jumped on the phone and asked someone else to join our meeting.

A Poobah and an assistant came in, and they asked me to repeat what I had said. I did that.

"Why is that?" His Drillsmanship asked.

"This is just based on my overall experience, because I've never been to Sakhalin Island," I said. "But in Moscow, would-be foreign investors discover that the sole ownership of every building or piece of land is claimed by a half-dozen entities: the federal government, Moscow Oblast (state level government), the office of the Mayor of Moscow, the district or precinct within Moscow, the office of that particular economic region or *ekonomichesky rayon* (wowing them with my use of Russian), followed by whichever ministry normally oversees the activity that will be conducted on that land. Therefore, there is almost certain to be a longstanding rivalry between Yuzhno, where the political leaders are, and Okha, where the revenue is."

"You sure?"

"I wouldn't bet the ranch on it, but I *would* bet the main house."

"So what do you recommend we do?"

"We'll need to see when we get there. What's certain is that you're going to need a full buy-in from both factions to make an oil deal work. That much I *would* bet the ranch on."

I found out later that this was exactly what they had been discovering as well. Furthermore, this was a minefield they hadn't been warned about by the evil consultants. And so I was added to the road trip, as a second-string quarterback consultant.

They phoned me in DC a week later and offered me a mind-blowing per diem. The rate would equal what they were paying the evil consultants. I was giddy after hanging up the phone. I started my billable time that very minute, working the phones and faxes (email was not yet available to the public).

While eating a sandwich at my desk, I computed that I was earning $125 just for eating lunch. I had never been paid even remotely this much, and am certain never to be again. Mobil flies their people first class if the flight is longer than six hours. The upshot was that I was even earning money during the time it took me to fly to Moscow, while sleeping under a soft blanket in the movie-star section of the plane. Thank you, Jesus, for Big Bourgeois Oil.

The evil consultants quickly began living up to my name for them. They told the Mobil Vice President, and leader of the group, "Larry doesn't know anyone in Russia." They assured him, "All Larry is doing is getting people's names from a directory."

One afternoon, the evil consultants took me to see their new offices, still under construction. They were gutting and building out a large suite of offices in central Moscow. The place was wall-to-wall in drop-cloth, miter saws, painters and carpenters. Everything in there was going to be either hardwood, or marble shipped from those mountains down near Kazakhstan.

As we exited the chaos of construction and stood on the street admiring the building, I asked them if it wasn't a bit premature to be doing all this permanent remodeling, being that they were a consulting firm with only one client. I speculated aloud that after we opened the doors for the company and made the introductions, they would sign contracts, make toasts to each other's grandness, and would no longer need consultant door-openers.

The evil consultants chortled kindly, head-pattingly, at my naiveté. This is a very, very, very complex country, they informed me. Ninety percent of anything anyone tells you is going to be bullshit.

Yes, I thought, *these people would make good Texans.*

A million things can go wrong in a business deal, things you have no idea about, they condescended. Mobil will always need a guide in Russia, they educated.

No they won't, I thought, *Russians and Texans were made for each other.*

Over dinner at the Metropol Hotel, just off Red Square where we were staying, the vice prez said he had been questioned by the bean-counters back at Mobil's accounting office as to how he could have spent $5,000 for meals on an earlier ten-day trip to Russia. The VP's answer, "by skipping lunch," had failed to amuse.

There was a lot of information laid between the lines of that anecdote, the active ingredient being that even with hiring expensive consultants, flying us first class and putting us up at the swanky Metropol—there were still grown-ups back home who were watching expenses, and who never slept. I saw this as further confirmation that the tenure of us consultants in Russia would be a beautiful, but finite, blaze of glory.

But for now, Mobil needed all of us and we worked Moscow as a group—our fearless leader executive, a handful of personable geologists and geophysicists, the evil consultants, and me.

Communist countries don't have directories and phone books. Everyone phoned by me or the evil consultants, were people we either knew personally or had acquired coordinates for by dropping names, promising unspecified future favors, or simply using an important-sounding voice— the way stuff gets done in a lot of places. But in truth, knowing someone personally was not as big a factor as being able to say, "I'm calling on behalf of Mobil Oil Corporation." Best little door-kicker-inner I ever used. The evil consultants made some appointments and I made some, and we seemed to be operating more or less equally at that point.

The vice president decided to move the group to Alma-Ata, as the capital of Kazakhstan was called then. Mobil was competing with Chevron and British Petroleum for Caspian Sea drilling rights. Kazakhstan loved the thought of oil money, but not the thought that oil spillage in the Caspian could kill the sturgeon and, with them, the caviar business. So we needed to knock on some doors.

I already knew Dr. Chan Young Bang, an economic advisor to President Nazarbaev, who founded the Kazakhstan Institute of Management,

Economics and Strategic Research. I had met him earlier that year on a visit to Alma-Ata to recruit participants for an American Leadership Conference in the States. It was refreshing to meet one as learned and competent as Dr. Bang in Kazakhstan who, as an advisor to the government, was sorely needed there. "Most of what I do comes down to teaching Economics 101, basic reality, to people who have never operated by supply and demand," Bang told me.

Bang had a young grad student assistant fresh from the U.S. I phoned him before going there for my second trip. I told him I was coming with a delegation from Mobil and asked him, "Do you want me to bring you anything from the US?"

"Anything?" he asked.

"Of course. Whatever you're homesick for, I'll bring it." I almost could have predicted his request.

"Why are you taking two jars of peanut butter into Kazakhstan?" one of the evil consultants asked me when I opened my bag for the customs inspector at the Alma-Ata airport.

Through the helpful, and freshly peanut-buttered assistant, I got us in to see Dr. Bang without a hitch. He spoke with our delegation at great length about the ins and outs, the do-and-don'ts of doing business in Kazakhstan. He offered to make calls to the leaders of various governing factions for us. His assistance shortened our work and reduced considerably the possibility of us stumbling onto some internal political turf war and becoming identified with one faction or the other. That is always a potential problem in Russia and the republics.

One of the more personal calls I made was to Gennady Vasilyevich Kolbin. He had once been First Secretary of the Kazakh Communist Party and was now serving in the Supreme Soviet as the Deputy Chairman or Deputy Prime Minister (memory fails me). Secretary Kolbin had been to one of our American Leadership Conferences in Maryland in April of that year. During his visit to the States, we did some shopping together one afternoon. I had helped him find a few souvenirs and we had a pleasant dinner together later that evening.

I secured an appointment with Kolbin for that afternoon and took everybody with me. The evil consultants were still pouting about the

Dr. Bang appointment. They had no idea he even existed. On the way to Kolbin's office, they talked the vice president's ear off, assuring him that, like Dr. Bang, this was another cold-call name I had pulled from my wondrous directory.

We were ushered into Kolbin's enormous office. He wasn't there yet, so we stood around admiring the artwork. After several minutes, a side door near his desk opened, and out walked Kolbin. His face brightened when he saw me and he headed straight toward me. He was short, stocky, with a tough guy's mug and a quasi-oriental look. He opened his arms to embrace.

"Laaaary," he smiled and growled. He put one hand on each shoulder, pulled me toward him and kissed me square on the mouth. No prissy Hollywood air kisses for Kolbin. This one was big and wet and smack on the lips.

"Gooooood," he snarled playfully. "Gooooood to see you." He pulled me in again for a bear hug. His hair smelled like Lilac Vegetol.

The vice-president turned to the evil consultants and said, "I think they know each other."

Later, when I reported all this to the family, Taeko asked me, with a mischievous smile, if the Deputy Chairman was a good kisser. I said he was okay, but that her job was in no danger.

To Russians, a kiss on the mouth between men is an intimate greeting for people who feel the kinship of brotherhood. It's a beautiful tradition, but not something Texas is ready for. My Mobil friends saw me as taking one for the team, and told me they were impressed.

We all flew to Sakhalin Island after that, where I was able to get a Mobil infomercial on local television just by walking into the station and introducing the vice-president to the station manager. In Russia, where the first measure of a man was taken by noticing what kind of shoes he could afford, the manager took one look at our leader's Bruno Magli calfskin oxfords and thought, *I think I'm going to try to be a good friend to this gentleman.*

Earlier I had asked Mobil's marketers to give us a Russian-language version of the 20-minute video, and to add a few words in support of the future prosperity of the people of Sakhalin Island. There was always a shortage of decent, locally-relevant content on Sakhalin television and the station manager liked the piece (and the VP's shoes) so much, he ran it every night for two weeks.

The president the international division, the ultimate boss, had flown in by company jet to hobnob with the Sakhalin authorities. He was plain-spoken, with a down-to-earth personality that went over very well there, although I can't recall his name. We worked hard every day and brought good results; we met the right people and shook the right hands in Yuzhno and also Okha. The VP was kind of a cowboy who shot from the hip, but he was a good judge of people and a skillful negotiator. Much of whatever success Mobil had on the ground in those days when Russia and the Central Asian republics were the wild frontier can be credited to his leadership.

After a fortnight, His Vice Presidentsmanship told me they would be sending me home in a day or two, and would also send the evil consultants back to Moscow. Mobil had accomplished their initial objectives, thanks to our help, and therefore they would not need our services any more.

"Makes sense," I told him. "It's been fun. I did two months of work and will invoice you."

"Fine," he said.

I flew back from Sakhalin Island via Anchorage, to Dulles Airport on the private jet with Mobil's international president. Mobil has more company planes than some countries have in their entire air force. The steward on board served chili dogs (my favorite cuisine), and the president took a nap on the couch while I watched the late-afternoon winterscape of the Kamchatka Peninsula and the Koryak Range of Eastern Siberia unfold below me in the cloudless, crystal air. In its pristine remoteness, it was desolate and embracing at the same time.

As I looked out the window, I thought about Korean Airlines Flight 007 and the fact that we were flying in reverse—and with permission this time from Soviet air controllers—almost exactly the path that had gotten the airliner shot down just eight years earlier. How quickly everything was changing. And it was just the beginning.

GARDENING

Windowlight sunshine speaks to me in birdy
from the bluejay on the weathered fence,
beckons to let the sensorial me unfurl.
Time is now to till the soil, put seedlings deep
and in one leap, stand astride the world

Hillocks and rolling rivulets reveal
the garden too long untended beneath
my touch lays bare and fallow, my gaze
a trace of warming breath excites
bountiful land, and I lay stunned
in the presence of your grace. I yawn,
entwine your legs in mine, you touch my face.

How like a tongue the earthworm moves
through undulating mounds of fecund loam,
taken, carved, curved made spade-available
earthworks, breastworks, all this my home,
cradled, caressed and furrowed
by God-crafted tumescent garden flesh.

Downy velvet moss sodden with dew
in tranquil restlessness upheaval and sighs,
visit my soil mister good to be true,
mister bright eyes, mister warm-to-the-touch.
Smooth my clumped, lumpen, rich, leafy clods
under your nails, under more than I can stand.
Hold me, roll me, envision my pungency
then rush into my garden zucchini man.

Dog Canyon

Coyotes howl at it. We fall in love in its presence, and maybe even partly because of it. The first thing most of us were told about it is that it's made of green cheese. It can be tragically inconvenient when it rises full, changing us into werewolves just as we're sitting down to Monday Night Football with nachos and friends. On the other hand, it comes to the aid of poets by rhyming with June.

Some nights you can even read by it. On the two-lane strip near Dog Canyon in Big Bend National Park, tucked away in the far southwestern corner of Texas, the full moon on a clear desert night is all the light you need. The roadside marker informed us that Dog Canyon, a little black hump barely visible in the distance, was so named because a traveler in the 1800s hiked in and found a dog guarding an ox-drawn wagon. Whoever was driving the wagon was never found and nobody knows what happened to him or them.

The three amigos—Smitty, Tom and myself—stopped in the middle of the deserted two-lane and looked out in silence over the two-and-a-half miles of unmarked wilderness between us and the canyon. "Whadya think?" Smitty asked.

More silence. Tom leaned an elbow out the driver's window, looking to the side for a long time as he thoughtfully stroked the end of his moustache, his "bush," between forefinger and thumb. Finally, "Nice moon." It was. Big and juicy as a garden slug, and perched right on his shoulder. He pulled off the pavement, killed the engine and walked back to the trunk.

That was as much conversation as we needed to reach agreement to hike in and spend the night. We left a note on the dashboard telling where we would be. We did this for two reasons, one being that we didn't want the rangers to think the car was abandoned and tow it, and two—taking a lesson from the ox wagon driver—only an idiot hikes into a wilderness without telling anyone where he's going.

The three of us had gone to high school in Midland, Texas, and later hung out together at college in Austin. Midland is West Texas desert country, but a whole different kind of desert than what you have in Big Bend. For one thing, Midland's desert is not postcard picturesque. Midland doesn't have giant tree-like saguaro cactus with spiked arms upraised and an owl nesting in a hole near the top. What sticks in your mind about Midland is that the town is surrounded by sand and cursed with endless tracts of mesquite trees.

Mesquite roots go twenty feet down and suck up every drop of water around. Upper East Side Manhattan residents will pay ten bucks for a little bag of mesquite chips to use in their patio hibachis. Ranchers around Midland will pay you decent money to come in with your chain saw and chop 'til you drop, hoping you'll clear enough mesquite so they can build a road from the house to the main gate.

Therefore it shouldn't be surprising to hear that people who know and appreciate the arid patches would be willing to leave Midland's desert and drive eight hours to vacation in a much better one. And we had done well by it over the course of a week—hiking at Persimmon Gap, climbing rocks in Boquillas Canyon, having a spear fight with wild bamboo growing on a pebbled beach along the Rio Grande, making an "unofficial" border crossing into the Mexican village of Boquillas del Carmen to eat mystery soup in an outdoor market. We were in the home stretch of what had been a pretty full week.

We loaded our packs with water, dried fruit, and beef jerky, and set off toward Dog Canyon, following a dry creek bed under moonlight. Our spirits were still buoyant from the sunset a few hours earlier. Sunsets last longer in the desert than anywhere else except the ocean. Although not really flat at all, Big Bend has wide expanses of unobstructed view all the way to the mountains in the west.

Usually the pollution from the factories on the Mexico side of the Rio Grande creates an awful brown pall over everything, but a stiff northwesterly wind in the morning had blown the haze away and escorted in the rarest of all phenomena—potential rain clouds.

It had rained briefly, and hard, earlier in the afternoon—a thirty minute *aguacero*, before moving on. There is something about sunsets after a rain, when the sky is breaking up, that make them particularly spectacular. The light on the horizon paints the bottoms of the clouds a shocking pinkish orange, the color of a clown's buttons. And they're really in your face because, having been born as rain clouds, they're as low in the sky as clouds ever get. The leeward edges away from the sun were a shade Tom called "harlot's eye shadow purple." For an hour that afternoon we had stared up at shameless exhibitionist clouds slapped over a sky that blue velvet was named after.

"You know," Tom had observed as we watched all this going on, "if nobody had ever seen a sunset before, and you came along and painted a picture of one like this, with all that purple and orange, people would say you dreamed this up on your own. But nature does it, and everyone just says, 'Wow, neat!' " Tom is a sky man. He is also a computer programmer and a jazz drummer. Smitty, on the other hand, is a blues guitarist and a geophysicist, an earth man. Jazz and air, blues and dirt. I'm sure we can all see the fit.

But now, it was night. The last of the clown buttons had broken up and the sky above us was clear while far off to the West, we heard thunder and saw flashes of light behind the clouds of a second storm system following a day or two behind the first. April is a good month to be here. These parts only get about 10 inches of rain a year, but sometimes it comes in just a couple of doses. When that happens, the waterless creeks and arroyos are prone to sudden, dangerous flash floods, sometimes on a clear day when there isn't a rain cloud in sight. Signs are posted in low areas and all the park literature warns of flash floods. We were mindful of that as we made our way along the dusted wash called Bone Draw, which leads into the canyon.

The clouds and rain were headed toward us ... maybe. Or maybe not. No way to tell, really. The earlier rain had hit us, only lightly, four miles from here but had not touched this place. Another peculiarity of the desert is that it can rain on one side of the road and not on the other. Literally. But for now, the thunder gnomes were playing nine-pins far away in somebody else's sky.

It was the most interesting night sky any of us had ever seen, even Tom, who was a connoisseur. Unimpeded by city lights or pollution, the Milky Way was as rich and chunky as its namesake candy bar. We could even see the dim "seven sisters" of the Pleiades cluster in the Taurus constellation. Add to that the lightning show hugging the distant hills. The continuous rumbling just over the horizon was probably farther away than it seemed. We experienced the distant clatter the way the citizens of Harrisburg, Pennsylvania, experienced the fighting over in Gettysburg.

The terrain is classic Chihuahuan Desert—sandy rock and scrub. It covers parts of southern Texas, New Mexico and Arizona, and a large portion of northern Mexico. It seems every plant comes with thorns. The spines on the barrel cactus can go right through the tops of your boots, and one doesn't hike, even in daylight, without spending a lot of time watching the ground.

Smitty and I fell about fifty feet behind Tom. We were discussing the foliage, and he pointed out several lechuguilla plants, unique to this kind of desert. They have a swirl of thick leaves with nasty thorns on the ends. Just as we were talking about it, we heard a loud scream up ahead, followed by a string of Nixonian expletives. Tom had found a lechuguilla too.

Smitty was expounding on a now-familiar theme about how water drives everything. "Quench," he called it. Nothing is born here or makes a move without taking quench into account, and every living thing has a strategy. Many plants have small, waxy leaves to limit water loss through evaporation. The most extreme case is the cactus whose leaves are so small and slender we call them thorns. Some plants, like the ocotillo, exist in a state of dormancy year after year, a stand of tall dried sticks. At some point, the ground moisture accumulates until the plant feels secure and its inner alarm goes off. It goes into a hurry-up offense over the next few days, erupting in leaves and flowers, making seeds and dropping them, hoping for the best. Its job finished, it folds in on itself, drying up and hunkering down to wait for the next wet year. No quench, no life. Water rules.

No doubt about it, the desert is hostile to everyone who doesn't belong there, especially humans. There are few benign creatures except for possibly horned toads. They're cute (to other horned toads), and at least they don't bite you. But everything else that moves in the desert— whether on four legs, six, eight or more—bites, stings, pinches or sucks. Other species, such as the two-legged kind that wear hiking boots and pitch tents, at various times do all four.

Night is when the critters all come out. Their water strategy is to do their surviving-of-the-fittest after dark, when it's cooler. Every other bush had a jackrabbit under it. There were plenty of coyotes, but they stayed away from us. We could hear them baying a mile off to our left. And by the way, they aren't howling at the moon like everyone says. Coyotes howl at each other. Tom said it's just that the notes are written on the moon. Sky man.

We saw large tarantulas, nearly stepping on them before noticing them. You don't normally think of a tarantula as being something that can hop two feet. They're essentially harmless; but try telling that to your mind. These are big, hairy spiders with big, hairy mandibles and hairy bug-eyes. The scorpions are out in battalion strength. I make a decision: I am not sleeping in this place.

The son of an oilman, I grew up hearing geologic terms with the same familiarity one acquires for the names of home-team ballplayers. Go ahead, ask me what a geosyncline is. During the Devonian Period, 370 million years ago, this area was an ocean. Amphibians were invented and test-driven here before becoming all the rage worldwide. By the Late Cretaceous, the shallow seas had come and gone several times before returning to swampland again. This was T-Rex country 65 million years ago when the giant dinosaur-snuffing meteorite is thought to have hit only a few hundred miles south of here, in the Yucatan. The big guys had a front row seat for the show, and died instantly. Smitty said the impact made the ground take on the characteristics of water, with earthen tidal waves throwing the giant reptiles around like Godzilla action figures being tossed in the air by a kid and batted over the backyard fence.

We threaded our way carefully along the creek bed, one eye watching where we stepped and the other enjoying the stars and the thunder over the hills. Dog Canyon is not much more than a hump on the desert, a small ridge with a slot eroded through it. As we approached, still almost a mile away, it began to take shape in the darkness. Smitty remarked how out of place it looked poking up out of relatively flat terrain.

In geologic terms Dog Canyon is a recumbent fold of a fully exposed Laramide thrust fault. But with the moon in a position to cast a sidelight, and from far away, it could have been the Dog Canyon dog, sleeping, curled up against the solitude of abandonment.

When we walked into the weathered groove a little after midnight, it was imposing—looking taller than it really is, dark, gothic with stark shadows. The canyon isn't very long and we could see out the other end of it. The moon shone right down the narrow gully; otherwise we wouldn't have been able to see zip. A short way in, we looked up on our right at a shallow cave about thirty feet above us. It had a ledge with a natural amphitheater eroded out behind it. The recess was about 20 feet across, 15 feet high and made a dimple with a floor 10 feet deep or so into the cliff. A pile of boulders below formed an easy stairway.

We climbed up and put down our packs. We called it the penthouse, with a great view up and down the creek bed. Tom decided he would walk to the other end of the canyon and check it out. Smitty pulled some dried mesquite kindling out of his pack and then took off after Tom, to see if he could find anything else to add to the campfire he intended to build.

I took our roll of toilet paper and climbed down to find a place to answer nature's call. I walked back out the way we had come in and then went another couple hundred feet until I found a small clearing. I checked the area very carefully for a long time. If I was going to drop trousers on Planet Tarantula, I wanted to make sure I had a secure perimeter. Finally, I leaned on a rock, sat on my haunches and waited for nature to finish calling and hang up.

That was when I heard a sound off to my right. Something big and rangy was rustling around in the brush. I didn't move or breathe. A wild peccary barged into the clearing and stopped when he saw me. Hard to say which of us was more surprised. I'm squatted down less than 15 feet away from the razor-sharp tusks of a belligerent-looking javalina, staring at me like I had just taken the last of the overhead carry-on space. He didn't run away, and gave no sign of having any intention of doing anything other than charging over to rip open my gleaming white, city-slicker belly. I could swear this was the exact same razorback pig that gave rabies to Old Yeller.

I slowly stood up and we regarded each other in silence. After what seemed like time without end, but must have been a good five minutes, he suddenly snorted and lunged toward me two steps and then stopped abruptly again. I froze and put out my hands, as if somehow that mattered.

If I hadn't already finished the business I had come here for, I certainly would have done it at that moment. Then he grimaced, or was it a smirk? He trotted off unhurried. We both knew he could have had me if he had wanted to and, in retrospect, I think his bogus charge was simply to make that point. I realized my pants and underwear had been down around my ankles the whole time, which could explain the smirk. I was shaking as I pulled them up.

I hauled buns back down the creek bed, certain the pig and his friends would be waiting in ambush. In a panic fueled by imagination, I sprinted up the rocks to the ledge. Smitty and Tom were on their hands and knees in front of a pile of sticks, focused on fire-building. Smitty was blowing on a piece of glowing ember that was moments away from becoming our fire. He looked up and grinned, waiting for me to compliment him on his woodsmanship.

I was still shaking. "I just met one of those killer pigs—up close."

"Javalina?" Smitty said.

"No thanks, just had one," Tom smartassed. Had he been waiting the entire week to say that?

The campfire was appreciated. The temperature stayed in the 70s all night, so warmth wasn't an issue. It was by its light that an earlier people would have illustrated their stories on the rock walls around us. But for us it was comfort and conviviality and, I hoped, a show of force for the killer pig community I knew was lurking just beyond its circle of light. The flames proclaimed, "We are fire-bringers, tool-users—two opposable thumbs. Top of the food chain, buddy, so don't mess with us."

We ate the last of our provisions, some Vienna sausages and jerky with crackers, and shared a big can of fruit cocktail for dessert. We were famished from the hike, and we judged the meal to be perfect in every way, except volume. We talked and laughed a lot, and dispersed now and then to forage for debris for the fire. At some point we nodded out, using our packs for pillows. Thunder rumbled beyond the horizon.

It was a bit before 5 a.m., "the dawn's early light," the song calls it, when we heard Tom shouting from down below. His voice cut through the daybreak's tranquility like a chainsaw in church. He was shouting something and it had the urgency of Little Timmy having fallen into the well. My body ached everywhere as I pulled myself together enough to get up and peek over the ledge. Tom stood in the middle of the creek bed forty yards farther into the canyon, gesticulating wildly. He was pointing, his mouth hanging open. Then we heard it. "Flash flood! Flash flood! Flash flood!" he hollered over and over again.

He had gone for a walk and had been taken by surprise, looking up just in time to see entering the far end of the canyon, a rampaging solid wall of water bearing down on him. It was six, maybe seven … inches high.

We looked beyond him but still couldn't see it. And then we could. It registered as a hand moving down Bone Draw, changing the color of the sand from beige to dark gray as the water soaked the soil for what could have been the first time in a year. Then we could see the rippling motion of the water itself and the leading edge of the tidal wave. It pushed a growing mass of debris ahead of it, hurtling toward Tom at the speed of an old woman strolling.

Smitty and I scrambled down the rocks. We arrived where Tom was at about the same time that the water rolled gently past. The flash flood was defined more by what it wasn't than by what it was. It wasn't Cecil B. DeMille's Red Sea taking out the Egyptian Army. It was no roaring cascade. It was silent, barely even a gurgle. All kinds of flotsam and dormant seeds from twenty or fifty miles away were coming into the neighborhood. This was Mother Nature rearranging the furniture. With luck, it could get real green around here for a short time. "Hey look," Tom said, "scorpions float!"

We gathered up our things and headed back to the car, splashing through the water. What was left of it anyway. Our big flood was only two inches deep now, and fading fast. It had crested at about six inches and immediately began to recede. The sand was thirsty and claimed its due. It was owed a lot of back moisture.

This would be our last adventure for this trip. We were out of food and running low on cash. We were aware of being way overdue for a bath, and fresh underwear. We had had it up to here with the whole gorp and guy-food thing. But we would never relinquish our sense of victory at having seen the great wilderness, having braved terrible dangers, exotic foods, wild plants and animals, and now a real, by God, desert flash flood. It was time to go home and sit around the cooking fires of our women, to inspire and spellbind them and the children until their eyes glowed like embers.

We resolved to remain different than we were when we had left the ordered, regulated world of shaving and doing the same things over and over again every day. The world of hypertension and twice-daily NASCAR commutes.

Smitty recalled the morning a few days ago, south of the Chisos Mountains, when we awoke not to a rooster's crowing, but to the unmistakable call of the white winged dove. It makes a sound exactly like someone calling out in a trill, "Who cooks for who?" That brought us to a grand consensus. Yeah, we concurred, let's drive over to that little place in Marathon where the chicken-fried steak and white gravy from last week still haunted our memories, where Betty the waitress called us "Hon" and brought us endless coffee refills.

"Let's go get ourselves cooked-for," the sky man riffed.

Lebanon—Tyre and Baalbeck

Walk on eggshells around Baal, the bad god

My flight home Saturday morning got scrubbed. British Airways had overbooked it by 80-plus people. Eighty-something people! I think it must take a very special gift to be able to oversell a flight by this much in the computer era. Outbound flights were crammed, so I wouldn't be back in DC until the following Monday night.

I was stuck in Beirut over the weekend with my business concluded. Pleasantly so this time; a few years earlier "stuck" would have implied being pinned down by sniper fire targeting civilians. But now it was 2004 and I was vice-president of international operations for United Press International (UPI). Having a couple of days not spoken for, my associate, Hangus, and I hired a car service to take us down through Sidon to Tyre in southern Lebanon. We wanted to take the opportunity to see the country and one of its beaches. Tyre is quite close to the Israeli border, and is in the traditional invasion corridor, so there is a certain military tension everywhere.

It was a subdued threat in those days, but definitely a hair-trigger ambiance of hostility. In southern Lebanon it's pretty much all Muslims, as opposed to Beirut's Christian, Muslim and Druze mix.

We drove past cornfields and orchards with fruit trees and date palms. There were small family farms interspersed with small commercial areas with farm supply stores, tea shops and gas stations—the support structure for rural folk. On the news broadcasts far away in America this is a geopolitical hotspot. But locally it is nothing at all like that. The land, the people and the way of life is rural. The concerns are local and seasonal.

I wondered if Jesus walked into what is now southern Lebanon, up to Tyre or Sidon. I thought I recalled the Bible saying as much, and wondered if the hills looked then the way they look now, or if that particular old and gnarled tree on the hillside could somehow be 2,000 years old. If he did, he probably would have come right past where we were because as soon as you get away from the shore, Lebanon becomes very hilly, so the road had to have gone along the coast.

We went to the beach, which is an unusual experience for me, having fair hair and skin. The sun is fierce here but after about 4:30 or 5 in the afternoon, I can handle it. We stood in the rolling waves of the surf, looking up at the hills behind us, imagining that Jesus slept along this shore. He spoke to people right here about God's Kingdom. He must have caught fish right where we were. We body surfed where Jesus body surfed.

The hills slope up broadly, but not steeply, away from the shore. The terrain looks like a massive hand on the earth, the eroded rivulets looking like fingertips reaching for, and barely touching, the sea. Up along the fingers and the back of the hand, there are cypress trees, banana orchards and vineyards.

Punctuating this Eden are dug-in army tanks and sand-bagged observation posts. The armed presence and checkpoints, though sobering, are not enough to leach away the powerful sense of being in the presence of sacred history. But still, tanks parked in the nooks and crannies along the highway, guns pointed at the traffic, get one's attention. They serve to remind the realist that this place never was a paradisiacal setting for a pastoral romp by Protestantism's chiseled and brown-eyed Jesus.

Lebanon has always been scary. Every now and then the Muslim sects and the Israelis still use this area to stage their endless rounds of payback. Before them, the French were here with their tanks, and before them there were the Ottomans (Turks) with horse-drawn caissons, each civilization parking their military hardware atop the rubble of the one just conquered.

Standing in the surf I thought, poor God. Nobody would live for the sake of the world, and how would they even know they were supposed to? Jesus knew what was needed, and maybe a scattered handful of holy people throughout history, but it certainly never made the six o'clock news.

Me and Hangus got to talking about America's role here—in terms of either living or not living for the sake of the world. Big powers perceive themselves to have a global mission. Some Americans think so, and England certainly saw itself that way during its 19th-century zenith.

Kings and emperors. Prophets and presidents. Their choices make it or break it for entire civilizations. We got into heavy discussion for a while about the rise and fall of empires and what the half-life of our current civilization is.

The Bible was pretty much invented where we were, and standing smack in the middle of all that can get a person thinking about things they don't normally ponder. We wondered what the world would be like if sometime a great civilization could actually manage to learn from the mistakes of those who went before? We definitely should have chosen a less historic place if our goal was solely to unwind.

The Mediterranean seems to be at least twice as salty as the Atlantic. When it goes up the nose or in the mouth, it's brutal. As I've mentioned in other writings, I have always liked the idea of the ocean much better than the actual ocean itself.

Soon the sun turned into a huge crimson wafer and dived toward the water, creating the expectation it would send up clouds of hissing steam. I think it's a good thing God was the one who chose the outrageous reds, oranges, pinks and purples for sunsets that He did. If you or I had picked out those colors, we would be accused of a lack of seriousness.

On our way back to Beirut, we decided to hire the car for a trip to the ruins at Baalbeck the next morning. "It's named after Baal, a bad god," Hangus said, looking up from the guidebook.

"Is it a good idea to go up there, tramp around on someone's sacred turf, invoke the requisite curse and irritate a bad god?" I asked.

But the driver seemed okay with it, so we arranged for a 7 a.m. pickup.

You can drive completely across Lebanon in about three hours and be in Damascus, in Syria in another 40 minutes. Baalbeck (alternately spelled Baalbek) is on the road to Damascus, only with a slight divergence to the north. By 2015 you wouldn't want to get that close to Syria with an American-looking face. But in another ten years, who knows?

The temple ruin sits in a long valley that runs most of the length of the interior of Lebanon. The valley, wide enough to be called a plain, was the central corridor for caravans in that part of the world for thousands of years.

Lebanon in general is a series of civilizations built atop the wreckage of preceding ones, and you have the same thing at Baalbeck, but with the added difference that this ruin rising high out of the plain still bears much physical evidence of each one of its predecessor civilizations.

Several buildings and courtyards occupy probably five or ten acres, creating a campus that was, in different ages, a sacred temple, a fortress, an open-air marketplace and a burial ground for VIPs. A shrine set into a wall by the Romans became a kitchen for the Ottomans, its ornately carved ceiling blackened by Turkish cooking fires. Everyone who came along— Greeks, Romans, Byzantines, Arabs, Crusaders, Mamluks, Ottomans, French and now, Lebanese—added their own rooms, temples, ramparts.

You can literally see the layers of time sitting atop of, and next to, one another. Holding up the same section of roof in the Temple of Bacchus are a fluted Greek pillar, a smooth Roman pillar and a square Egyptian pillar, each standing fifty feet tall and weighing a gazillion tons.

Here's how it began. You start 1,800 years before Christ with the Phoenicians. Good King Whatshisface marches from wherever his main city was to this relatively highest point on the plain. He rounds up 20,000 volunteer slaves and says, "Okay, we're going to build some really awesome ruins right here, better than anything Egypt's got." And of course, a huge cheer goes up.

At this point, ruins had barely been invented so the king has to further explain, "You start with a new building, a temple in our case. You build it and then you wait a really, really long time. You can do that, can't you?"

You kidding? Damn right they could and so, with lots of team spirit and testimonies around the campfire at night, everyone jumps to the task.

Baalbeck gets its name from the Bekaa Valley in which it sits, and from Baal. Baal was the Phoenician sun god. Hangus thought Baal might have been an orgy god as well. We're not sure and certainly wouldn't be surprised. Baal does get a bad rap in the Bible so we think he must have been up to something.

Anyway, if you're a sun god I assume that means your nights are pretty much free after sundown. And being that orgying is generally an after-dark activity, Baal could easily have worked nights as an orgy god. He also could have been just a generic nighttime god, or even had nights and weekends off. Then again, Baal could have been the tooth fairy, whose work is also done at night. Or he could have been the closet monster.

We mulled it over. Baal: mighty sun god by day, closet monster by night. The guidebooks were strangely silent on this point. Hangus and I both wished we could sit down for a long and leisurely lunch with a for-real Ph.D. historian, someone who could connect the dots between the various empires. We wished someone could create a thread running through them all, from Adam and Eve to the present, so we could talk about all the what's and the whys.

We would have been able to talk with our personal Professor Emeritus about why one civilization lost its lease and had to go down and be replaced by another, and why the dominant civilizations seem to rotate from continent to island to peninsula, and back. He or she would look for the fingerprints of Providence in the rise and fall of powerful nations and kings. Not every answer would be available, but a lot of them would, and we would all have raised some interesting questions and would have been in history nerd heaven experiencing this place where so much history has tramped by.

Lacking Professor Emeritus, we did what a scholar would have done. We pieced it all together ourselves. Except without the benefit of actual knowledge.

Thirty minutes into the tour, our guide was pointing out the Temple of Venus built by the Romans. It is the only circular structure among all the buildings. It is round and feminine, like the swollen belly of a goddess of fertility, love and beauty, the symbol of lakes and rivers.

When the Christians came along, they consecrated this temple to Saint Barbe (called Saint Barbara by our guide), and carved crosses into the walls. But even with that, and even as a nearly decomposed ruin, the roundness of the walls still impart femininity. Spiritual echoes of prayers and anguished supplications one might offer to a goddess of fertility still linger on the pitted steps leading up to its inner chamber.

The Phoenicians had a large hexagonal court inside near the entrance, with the sides corresponding to each of the six elements: earth, sky, water, fire, air and thunder. How uncomplicated and personal are such elements, ever-present in the lives of people who lived on the most intimate terms with the land and weather, sleeping at dusk and rising with the sun.

Thunder, more than any of the other ancient elements, carries in it the implied voice of God. It is the most "abrupt" of all the ancient elements; it doesn't even exist until it suddenly rocks your universe. I thought, *yes, thunder would have to be elemental.* To many of us it still is. Of course those elements of yesteryear are also ruins today, replaced by helium, chlorine, potassium, neon—elements surely, but not ones we relate to viscerally.

The hexagonal court featured animal sacrifices and dancing maidens. I am somewhat presuming about the dancing maidens because I think our guide mentioned sacrifices and dancing. I saw the pens below the court where they kept a big pool of water for washing the sacrificial animals, but didn't see a pen for prepping the dancing maidens.

So we're wondering, animals and maidens? Or just animals? Either answer would indicate obvious great differences in the nature of the religion, the cultural priorities, the morals, etc., but I don't know.

What would Professor Emeritus say?

There is an underground room near the Temple of Bacchus (definitely the go-to god for all your orgy needs). We saw several heavy stone coffins had been built but never used. On the outside of each sarcophagus are carved figures of lions or a man killing a wild boar, or planting. These carvings are thought to reflect the personality of the future occupant.

However, the sides of one sarcophagus on display were blank and we were told that people were often buried in sarcophagi that were rough and unfinished on the outside. Interestingly, historians think this practice was intentional, and not because the family was too poor to have the carvings made. It is thought, according the plaque next to one, they were left unfinished out of consideration for the futility of man's existence.

What?! really? I had to read the inscription on the plaque twice. Try to imagine people leaving their coffins uncarved as a silent protest of the pointlessness of life. To snub your nose at The Almighty like that is a very strong vote for nihilism. Takes guts for sure, and I think most people are much too uncertain about death and eternity not to hope with all their hearts that it all ends in paradise. So why, then? It boggles the mind.

What would Professor Emeritus say?

The biggest part of the ruin is the Temple of Jupiter. Only six of the original 54 giant pillars still remain upright, but they crush into insignificance everyone who stands in their shadow. When born-again Christian Emperor Constantine came along, he dismantled much of the Temple of Jupiter and used the stones to build a church to his new improved God.

That's the way of it at Baalbeck, each god upgrade consigns a previously sacred site to being a suite of storage rooms again. Temples under new management, become kitchens, and altars become dining tables. Deconsecrated stained glass and Eucharistic incense is sold to the curio shops that have surrounded the temple grounds since the first barefoot army pitched their tents there. Statues of all-powerful deities become doorstops and cutsey hat racks in the offices of the new priests. The virgins of the old gods are let go and married off to peasants, and replaced by a new crop.

There are sobering lessons at Baalbeck, as there always are when you come across a civilization that was once thriving but is now dust, so dead that everything you touch crumbles in your hand. Of course the most sobering realization of all is that the modern world that lies all about us—our giant cities—might be the vine-choked ruins accidentally discovered by a farmer's wife two thousand years from now when she stubs her toe on a Chrysler Building gargoyle while planting radishes in what used to be Manhattan.

It would be different than someone discovering Baalbeck or Machu Picchu. The world today is so interconnected that in order for someone to unearth a long-forgotten Chicago or Paris would mean that humankind would have to first be driven to near extinction, existing only in tiny and isolated pockets of rural subsistence for hundreds and hundreds of years. It would take that long for a towering metropolis to be reclaimed by Mother Nature so fully as to make it invisible to a wanderer walking through what used to be skyscrapers and palaces.

But it could happen, and that's the sobering part. What can happen to Baalbeck can happen to London and New York. The principles are the same for all vanishing civilizations. Only the scale is different.

Baalbeck gives you the benefit of peeling back the layers of several vanished worlds without having to travel. History is like a set of concentric walled courtyards that, when you breach each one, working your way back to the original center, you find people and their gods behaving not altogether differently from the way you do things.

Unfortunately for each newly arrived civilization, their collective ego usually prevents them from considering the possibility that the changes they have brought about are not always improvements.

STICK A JADE MONEY FROG IN YOUR WINDOW

You gotta love Hong Kong. When daughter, Theresa, was three, she called it "Honk Honk." And it remains so to me today.

Feng Shui translates as "wind-water" in English. This is how the Chinese harmonize their existence with mountains and bodies of water. And come to terms with the hostile feng shui of the Bank of China.

The Bank of China's building in Honk Honk is triangular, so it has three edges or blades (a.k.a. "poison arrows") that point outward. They also have huge stone lions sitting on either side of the front entrance. One does not mess with the Bank of China.

A friend sat in an office for five years facing one of the Bank of China edges dead-on. His was an energy-sucking existence.

Finally, he called Great Teacher, who pointed out the problem with the bank's placement and said, "Also, you sit facing away from a pillar directly behind your chair. This is a knife in your back. Do you find that your ideas are chased into the street and their clothing ripped off and fed to howling dogs?"

"Yes, Great Teacher. My career is a sodden, drowned possum."
"You must reposition your desk to directly face the door. Cut a hole in that wall to give you a view of the harbor and sea. Put a jade frog in your window. A powerful money frog can defeat the poison arrow."

"I can move my desk, Great Teacher, and the frog is fine, but this is a skyscraper. Bashing a hole in the wall is surely another idea my bosses will pour deep-fried corndog temperature oil upon from atop the fortified gate. It may turn out to be my final idea. Ever."

"Then hang paintings of the sea there to make the wall disappear."

"Thank you, Great Teacher, oh supreme geomancer." He wore no ring so I just kissed his gnarled knuckle.

My home office in Bowie, Maryland violates all the rules. First, it's located in my bedroom, the portal to dreamtime.

The natural light is only so-so. There are no oxygen-producing plants (I have a brown thumb, and if you think no plants is bad Feng Shui, try dead plants). I do not sit in a commanding position to attract strong, successful energies. The dual sins of this are that my back faces the door and my face looks straight at a wall. Which may affect the quality of my prose, and could explain a lot.

"Grasshopper, you are a neutered duck."

"Yes, Great Teacher."

A WINTER'S DAY

The title is misleading. It's late July, early, early in the morning. Slightly post-pre-dawn. The sky only appears to be transitioning from dark purple to the lighter blue range. At this point, whether the horizon will ever actually brighten, whether the sun will finally rise, is anybody's guess. I stand in front of the window sipping coffee. If I hold the cup right under my eye and peer over the rim toward where the sky meets the horizon, I catch the purple in the steam.

Honey Nim comes out. "What are you doing?"

One eye closed, keeping the cup absolutely still, I focus like a Shaolin monk. "I'm steaming the purple."

"Go put on some clothes."

"I made you some coffee. Sugar?"

"Not today, and just a little arf-n-arf. Thanks. What are you doing?"

"Look, steam. And dark purple sky, over there near the ground."

She sips her coffee, looking thoughtfully where I'm pointing. "Yeah."

I switch gears, sing softly, "A winter's day, in a deep and dark December. I am alone, gazing from my window to the streets below, on a freshly fallen silent shroud of snow. I am a rock; I am an island."

"What's that?"

"Song ... Paul and Artie ... You know, '... and here's to you Mrs. Robinson, heaven holds a place ...' Those guys."

"Oh, yeah. Tall, curly hair, sings the high part."

"The song is about isolation and emotional detachment. I am an island. Look there. Did you know the bright thing closest to the moon is usually Venus? Venus reminds people of love."

She has this really nice quality of not rushing it when she thinks I'm headed somewhere with a thought. Conversations can sometimes drift rudderless for long minutes without either of us requiring a "point." Until one of us gets it, assuming there's something to "get," we're happy to wait it out in the conversational middle distance. It's a survival trick for when you find yourself in an international or interracial marriage. Not everything needs to make immediate sense in a linear A-B-C-D fashion. Silence can also be a form of conversation and so we exist together in silence.

She moves past me, closer to the window and gazes out, willing the deep purple to dissolve into sunrise. I stand behind her, talking into the back of her neck. "Which do you think is better, to give yourself freely to loving another even though you could end up broken-hearted, or to carefully protect your heart and settle for what's available, but in doing so, never feel the roller-coaster thrill of love?"

She turns, puzzled. "What?"

It's not a terribly complicated idea; it's even somewhat a cliché. Our gap is mostly technical, "languagey," in our local parlance, so I explain it again in more or less similar words.

She understands. "It makes him crazy," she says.

"Love makes you crazy?"

"Yes it does," she says. "Know what I mean, jellybean?"

"I know what you mean, crocodile."

I put my arms around her from behind, drawing her in to stay warm. Our arms mutually encircle one another entwined, cups clinking. I sing her another snippet. "I have my books and my poetry to protect me ..."

"Go put on some clothes."

Spare change basket atop the dresser...

Where the pennies, nickels and dimes go at the end of the day ... atop the dresser. What follows is my equivalent of that, bits and pieces I don't want to throw away. Some, I'm sure, would make excellent, illuminating essays, contributing wonderfully to the sum of human knowledge. Other bits are just bugs on the windshield that float around the cosmos until I smack into them as we circle the sun at 67,000 miles per hour.

A young friend told me, referring to himself, "I'm not really a poet." And yet he thinks and speaks in images, and writes all the time, filling notebook after notebook and will never let me or anyone read it. I told him that if you're a person who writes poetry, even if you never share a single word of it with another soul, even if you die and are buried in an unmarked grave along with your moldy poetry pages, never to be published posthumously, you are still a poet.

The poems and stories a writer creates are the writer's children. Through editing and rephrasing they become the writer's friends and companions. Through sharing they become the writer.

Great Tuna Road Trip

Just now sent Honey Nim out on her first-ever solo road trip to call on seafood managers at big supermarkets in Richmond and Virginia Beach. If I weren't pinned down at home in deadline hell, I would be in the passenger seat beside her, navigating. We just discovered that the print on the road map, which I so carefully marked up for her, is too small for her to read.

"I'll stop at a bookstore and get stronger glasses," she said.

"They don't make bookstores anymore. Stop at Amazon."

She does a fashion model tease of her summery blouse and light linen pants. "Does this look okay for, 'Hello, I'm your seafood representative'?" She shakes my hand in a businesslike manner.

"You look fine. They'll be happy that their tuna and salmon and yellowtail has a human face."

"Would you buy tuna from me?"

"In a New York minute."

Then, as she's getting in the car: "Is Richmond north or south?"

"Um… it's south. You're making me nervous, Honey."

"I don't panic." Big smile.

And off she drives. Her philosophy about driving and maps and getting from point-A-to-point-B is "all directions go someplace."

For the most part they do. Even a bridge to nowhere still goes somewhere.

⋅🐟⋅

It was a hot and dusty August day when the Texas Cannonball pulled into the station, blowing steam and trail grime onto the platform. Down from that train stepped a giant of a man …

… a Bible in one hand … a six-gun in the other. If he had a name, nobody knew what it was.

Turns out he was in town for a literary archetypes convention. He was seen getting into a cab with a boy and his dog, a nun with a guitar and a dancehall madam with a heart of gold.

⋅🐟⋅

When Theresa was about four (I think that was her age because we were living on Jodie Street), at the breakfast table one morning, she picked up two pieces of toast. In her little pixie voice she called out, "Clear!" and slapped them onto my chest. Butter and all. Looking for clues to her future in the makeshift defibrillator pads, I thought *medical profession*. But the key point was the toast itself. I should have been thinking *chef*.

We generally take it as a given that if a tree falls in an empty woods, it makes no sound. But nobody said there had to be a human being present. If there is even an earthworm in the vicinity, or bacteria in the soil, or a brain-dead, wife-beating redneck ("You hadn't oughta said that.") and his attorney, it makes noise.

This iconic story about the pioneering film director Cecil B. DeMille, reminds me of projects I have seen and/or been a participant to.

DeMille was famous for directing giant epics of biblical proportions. He once directed a film that required an enormously complex and expensive battle scene with the traditional "cast of thousands." Filming on location on the Sinai Peninsula, the director set up multiple cameras to capture the action from every angle. It was a sequence that could only be done once.

DeMille yelled, "Action!" Thousands of soldier extras stormed across the field, guns blazing. Riders on horseback galloped over the hills. Cannons fired, pre-set explosives shot debris and fireballs into the air, and battle towers loaded with soldiers came toppling down. The whole sequence went off perfectly. He had outdone himself as a director. It was beyond spectacular.

When the charge ended, and the bombs, fires and crashes were done, DeMille yelled, "Cut!" He was then informed, to his horror, that three of the four cameras recording the battle scene had failed. In Camera #1 the film had broken. Camera #2 had missed shooting the sequence when a dirt clod was kicked into the lens by a horse's hoof. Camera #3 had been destroyed when a battle tower had fallen on it.

DeMille was at his wit's end when he suddenly remembered he still had Camera #4, which he had placed along with a cameraman on a nearby hill to get a long shot of the battle sequence. DeMille grabbed his megaphone and called up to the cameraman, "Did you get all that?"

The cameraman on the hill waved and shouted back, "Ready when you are, CB!"

When you get to be age 65, your employment prospects narrow. If you have a "cottage skill" such as editing or consulting, you can do that as long as you keep the customer satisfied. Otherwise you settle for niche jobs such as piece work, after-hours shelf-stocking at Trader Joe's, anything that needs someone with a strong work ethic to show up reliably every day, on schedule, rain or shine, to do some task. Something like pressing a button on a machine that, if the button isn't pushed every day at 10 a.m. sharp, the Yellowstone Park caldera will erupt with the obliterating force of 10,000 atom bombs. An old guy, with a deeply ingrained sense of responsibility, would push that button every day without fail, rain or shine.

<hr/>

"A racist is someone who thinks there's more than one race." That was told me personally by James Bevel when we met in Washington, DC in the early 90s. A leading strategist and architect of the 1960s Civil Rights Movement, he helped organize the Montgomery bus boycott after Rosa Parks was arrested in 1955. He organized numerous lunch-counter sit-ins and is sometimes called the "father of voter rights." He and Martin Luther King, Jr. walked, arms linked, along Main Street(s) throughout the deep south, past the nightsticks, the German shepherds and crew cuts owned by people who were certain there is more than one race. It turned out they were wrong.

<hr/>

A rule of music to teach your children: There's no protection against stupid lyrics other than turning off the song.

<hr/>

Religion is a guy sitting in church thinking about fishing. Relationship is a guy fishing, thinking about God.

<hr/>

Honey Nim handles the bill-paying. I do other stuff. Important manly stuff. You try to match the tasks with the natural abilities, like rabbits do the running and monkeys do the tree-climbing. Problem is, Honey Nim also does the forgetting to do stuff, a task I thought I was in charge of. As a result, we never get utility bills anymore—just pink-edged impending turn-off notices.

"Always take the time to offer sincere devotions, prayers and other conditions. Offer them when you get up at dawn, when you are on the borderline between the spiritual world and the physical world and your optic nerves are just starting to function after a restful night. The spirit world will show you something spiritual. Through such experiences, you will be given knowledge. Then you will be able to predict, *Today this or that will happen, or today such and such a person will come by.*

"A capable doctor can tell what kind of illness their patients have just by looking at their complexion, or by seeing how their patients walk. Likewise, your spiritual antenna must be long and have the sensitivity to appraise things. For this to happen you need to offer conditions of devotion."

Sun Myung Moon speaking informally on November 11, 1990, said the above. I have tried versions of this for brief periods and found it to produce results I could verify. I say brief periods because maintaining any spiritual discipline with unwavering consistency, through revolutions, famine, birthings and hurricanes is iffy. Friends who observe various different faith traditions, confirm the value of this. Therefore I park this one in the arena of universal principles. For everyone to chew on.

Jen Kiaba, a friend who is a widely respected art photographer, posted this question on her website: "If you could create anything, regardless of struggle or money, what would it be?"

I responded: A high-ceiling space with large windows and skylights on eight compass points. The windows would be infinitely adjustable with translucent scrims that can cover any window to simulate every degree and color temperature of light. It would have a wrap-around porch for contrasty sun and natural, open shade.

In that space I would seek my holy grail: creating great art and breath-taking composite photos with believable light and shadows, digital drawings. I would use them to illustrate things I and others write. There would be some elves hanging around of course, and I would let them help out, but they have to show up sober.

I and Honey Nim would live in a nearby tree house with a woodstove and a view of a river and a mountain (within easy access of our children and grandchildren). Every day I would write essays and short stories and my danged poems to go with the photos. I would never get out of my blue jeans except to put on a tux to go to White House dinners.

※

What would Jesus shoot? A gun is just a tool, the same as a hammer and nail, or the bolt locking your front door. It helps you get your work done and keeps you safe. There are certain things only a gun can help you do. Like shoot stuff. So what would Jesus shoot? He would shoot food to feed his followers. He would shoot wolves to protect his flock (literally if not metaphorically). Would he shoot money-lenders, beauty-hating Philistines, dirty rotten liars, Goliath? From what we've read, perhaps not. But he would be tempted.

※

My dog, Nikki, pulled a slice of chocolate cake off the table in the dead of night, and had her way with it. Choco is poison for dogs so we are watching her to see if there are ill effects. None so far. We tried to shame her with our scolding voice and wagging finger, but she would have none of it.

She looked me right in the eye and spoke to me aloud, in English: "Puny Earthling, this is just the beginning." Whoa! Two important things to know here: chocolate cake makes dogs bilingual, and dogs are interstellar aliens. Warn everyone.

※

At eight in the morning Honey Nim sends me to the store for some danged arugula. Arugula! Seriously, I'm not kidding. Turns out it's a vegetable. Again, warn everyone.

※

If you are on the receiving end of seriously bad luck, which some may tell you is evidence of God's neglect, or even cruelty, you can interpret every bit of it only as God's love for you and it will be your greatest weapon against every hardship imaginable. It will make you impossible to defeat.

Blue and green are colors naturally calming to the human spirit. Hence sky and trees. There was never a moment in building this Earth when God was not thinking of us.

In the process of give and take, a process that is honored by every person of conscience, we often pay little attention to the "take" part of it. Sometimes we must open our hands and happily receive so that the other person, the giver, can also have an opportunity to grow in giving.

The boy stood on the burning deck … (Felicia Hemens)

Sitting on the back deck barely post-sunrise this morning with Honey Nim, coffee and a pear. I informed her that my stellar prose, laced with humor, had gotten yet another rejection email from The New Yorker magazine. I read aloud: "Dear Larry, We're sorry to say that your piece wasn't right for us. Thank you for allowing us to consider your work." An email?! What happened to the nice 3-by-4-inch pink or yellow paper of traditional rejection slips?

"From now," Honey Nim said, "they will decline." To underscore her point, the prophetess flipped her middle finger in the direction of New York City. I think I may be morally obligated to call and warn them.

She cut a slice of pear and slipped it into my mouth, uttering twenty-first century words of romance: "Less fat, more fiber."

It's official. My yard is 100% clover. The rest is sort of weeds. Clover, by the way, is also classified as a weed, and not a flower, simply because it is able to grow by itself, without the help of Corporate America. How wrong is that? I don't put pesticides or harsh chemical weed killer on my yard. I claim my reward while sitting at sunset watching the bunnies and the bumbles working the clover blossoms. The little bunnies are hopping and nuzzling and wrinkling up their tiny noses, and I'm thinking: *God is great*. My faithful dog beside me is watching the bunnies too, and thinking: *One bite. Gushing arterial neck wound.*

"Blueberries have anti-oxygen," Honey Nim said as she spooned some into my bowl. "They take out poison and bad stuff."

Antioxidants of course, and the Japanese and American language-warp continues at Chez Moffitt. Talking with Honey Nim is its own universe, and navigating it can be like transposing music from E-flat minor into G, while you're playing it.

We work through it with gentle coaching, repetition and some laughter, until the word eventually becomes "anti-accident." Close enough.

Amid the spinach, kale, almonds and carrots, Honey Nim substituted cucumbers for berries in the green smoothie she made for me in the blender. She took a sip first. "You may not like this; it tastes kind of pukey," and handed me the glass of green, foamy glop.

"You sure know how to sell it," I said. I guess she never saw The Exorcist.

Turned out it was delicious. Just slightly salty in addition to the natural sweetness of the other veggies. So cukes turns out to be the secret sauce. You heard it here first. Encountering cuke juice in your green smoothie is like falling in love across a crowded room.

Not really. In fact, not at all. But it was early in the day when I wrote this, and the comparison happened to be lying atop the analogy pile.

Honey Nim made me a big ol' salad of shredded cabbage, tomatoes, celery and cukes with a bit of olive oil, salt and pepper on it, and placed the air-tight rubber container into my hand. "This will make your intestines happy," she said, and tucked me into my car.

"The first gulp from the glass of natural sciences will make you an atheist, but at the bottom of the glass God is waiting for you."
—Werner Heisenberg (father of quantum physics)

Son John, the nursing student ("Dad, go ahead, ask me anything about vaginas."), refused to eat a donut peach, a white peach that looks like it was flattened in a panini press.

"It's deformed," he said.

"John, let the scales fall away from your eyes. Eat the damn peach."

He took a bite. Then: "Wow, Dad, this is mad GOOD!"

Bada-bing! Every time John learns something, an angel gets his wings.

><del>᠊᠊᠊</del>

Reminder for Kathy, David, Theresa, John and The Hwa

One day, when you are older, and I am living and working my ass off somewhere on the other side of the rainbow bridge, you may be sitting at a sidewalk café, trying to write a song or a poem. You will be on the doorstep of realizing that NOTHING in English fully rhymes with "orange" or "dangerous." (However "gangrenous" comes close to dangerous as a near rhyme, and what poem of love I ask you, is not made better by the appropriate insertion of gangrenous?)

Taking a break from that creative exercise, you may begin idly watching people walk past, noticing everything you can about them. You might draw a few circles on your paper and label them "wearing tie" or "tie with red" or "women without earrings" or "men with earrings" or "pants unzipped" or "looks unusual enough to have been drawn by a cartoonist." You may start making a mark in each circle for each passerby relevant to which category.

At some point, between doing that and inventing words that rhyme with "hostage," you will recall whose child you are. The thought will make you smile as you hoist your cappuccino frappiato pizzicato grande heavenward in greeting.

><del>᠊᠊᠊</del>

Speaking of rhyming, I don't recall whether it was Ogden Nash or e.e. cummings who added letters to words to make them rhyme. Nash certainly enjoyed mutating the language at will, and with great whimsy. Today we take it for granted that you can do that with poetry and still be accepted in polite society.

In the days of Dickinson, Yeats, Whitman, etc., poetry was also a discipline. You had rhyme schemes that you didn't wander far from. You had capitalized first letters of each line, and so on. Punctuation even. The classic Shakespearean sonnet is a straitjacket to write, and yet when executed perfectly, rolls off the tongue and through the ears effortlessly, as though flowing down a frictionless slope.

Today, poetic "free verse" can be so utterly lacking in structure that you're actually reading ungainly prose broken up into lines of short length (like the way Chinese cooks hack up a chicken with a meat cleaver). That's the other extreme. My preferences fall somewhere in between the super-structured and the loose-as-a-goose. A bit of each. Ultimately, in poetic expression, I side with Louie Armstrong, who said of music, "If it sounds good, it is good."

~~~

Spelling Rule: i before e

Except when you run a feisty heist on a weird beige foreign neighbor.

~~~

You're walking down the street when a dog steps out of the alley.

He looks at you for a couple seconds, then, "Hey, I gotta tell you something."

"What?! Who's speak—"

"Down here."

"Omigod, you're a DOG!"

"I know, I get that a lot. Okay, here's the deal. You should love God and take care of people. Can you do that?"

"Um, yeah. I guess so ... Sure, I can do that."

"Cool. Before you go, could you do me a favor and rub my stomach?" He lays down and rolls onto his back. Later you're thinking about it. "You should love God and take care of people."

Question: Is it any less true because a dog said it?

~~~

An elderly couple has just finished dinner at the home of some friends. The two wives are in the other room momentarily and the husband begins telling the host about this fabulous restaurant he and his wife had dinner at a few nights ago.

"Sounds great" the host says. "What's the name of the place?"

"Uhhhhh … well" the elderly man says, "Ummm … well, let's see." He scratches his head and finally asks his friend, "What's the name of that flower? It's red and has thorns …"

"A rose?" the host offers.

"Oh yeah," the elderly man says. Then he turns his head in the direction of the other room and calls out, "Rose! What was the name of that restaurant?"

In the kitchen with Honey Nim this morning. I'm pouring cups of coffee for her and me. Behind me she says in the most sweet and loving voice, "You're so beautiful, you're sooo beautiful. What am I going to do with you?"

I turn around to say something endearing in return.

She is not looking at me. She is speaking to two flowers she had just put into a small vase and was carrying to the table. Instantly I saw all three daughters and both sons contained in her spirit, her face, her voice, hands, everything. The universe contained in one second.

When our family was living in Buenos Aires, it was sometime during 1997 or '98, I asked my son, David, what he would wish for if he could have only one wish. He was probably in the sixth grade at that time. He said, "I wish dogs could talk." The older I get, the more that answer makes me smile, even though it would create huge problems. Dogs see a lot of stuff that goes on. And you can bribe them with a tennis ball.

Betsy Robinson's birthday wish
February 7, 2015

Have a meaningful, if not happy, birthday, Betsy Robinson. No, wait, have a birthday where you're, like, polishing an antique oil lamp, and out pops a genie who talks like Robin Williams. No, like Charlton Heston's Moses, only more liberal. And you get three wishes and as usual you totally waste the first two. You idly wish Starbucks still had pumpkin spice lattes, and then when one appears with that "poof" noise that wishes make, and you realize you blew it, you say, "gimmie a freakin' break," which technically counts as your second wish if the genie decides to be a hardass, which this tired, letter-of-the-law autocrat apparently does.

You duct-tape your mouth shut for a couple hours while you try to get your thoughts together. And then finally, you settle on wish number three and you rip off the duct tape, taking part of your lip and your incipient lady moustache with it. You gasp out, "I wish for the ability to bring happiness to people." The poof sound happens and within the next hour, you rescue little Timmy who had fallen into a well, and Tiny Tim gets his lifesaving operation (what is it about Tims and their bad luck?).

So anyway, you get your danged wish and spend the rest of your days going around helping people find the richness of love and completion they long for in life, including yourself, because you're a person too, party of the first part, and are therefore included in the language of said wish, to wit: "... happiness, one each, shall be applied."

><del></del>

Most of your life will be a wrestling match with selfishness.

><del></del>

We have telescopes that can count the freckles on the face of another galaxy, and that can see a star going nova in an event that actually happened long before the earth cooled, but the light from that event is only just now reaching us. When I ponder such bigness, my conclusion is that people who worship nature, and those who worship God for creating the natural universe—are cousins who play different positions on the same team. I keep two extra places at my table for each of you.

><del></del>

In the big, mixed fruit salad of the cosmos, I see, and even hear and smell, the fingerprints of God.

><del></del>

The young people in my life don't always make wise choices (in fact pretty much never), but their energy and inventiveness keeps me vital, strong, fresh. My eyes are bright. And though I am too old to die young, still I am amazed at everything. "I see the stars. I hear the rolling thunder."

I wish the day had forty hours, and human life a hundred and twenty years, not because I fear the end of physical life, but because I need every second of that time to get existence right. The God I know is an actual entity with a consciousness and an unquiet heart. God is fully male and female, otherwise there could be no men and women. Moses' burning bush and the laws of planetary motion have the same author.

>*The God of religion does science at times.*
>*Science, religion are of the same vision.*
>*And life is unfair, but it rhymes.*

Q: Why was war invented?

A: To teach geography to Americans

(joke I heard in Australia)

Caroline Hampton, a sweet and brilliant daughterish waif who used to live with us while attending school, was proposing a toast one morning (toasting a piece of bread in Moffitt jargon). She buttered the toast and laid the knife across the edge of the dish.

I was in crabby mode, for some reason, and barked at her. "Hey, don't just leave the knife there!"

"Oh, I thought this was the official butter knife of the day." She took it to the sink and washed it off.

I think about that now, every time I butter a piece of toast, set the knife on the edge of the butter dish and walk away. I had done it a thousand times before that morning, and have done it thousands since. That one morning was like some kind of glitch, a vortex in the space-time continuum. But anyway, a foolish consistency is the hobgoblin of little minds, right?

This morning while proposing a toast and buttering it, I raised my cup of coffee to Caroline in the usual kind of toast. On this, Ludwig van's 245th birthday, here's to you with my apologies, Caroline, and to the Official freakin' Butter Knife of the Day.

From William Selig, a hospital chaplin in Washington, DC, "Lessons of Illness and Death," December 21, 2015, from Applied Unificationism, a blog of the Unification Theological Seminary:

> *Father Moon spoke often about the spiritual world and taught that there is purpose behind everything in creation, including death. When he said, "Do you know why I am talking about death? I talk about death in order to teach the meaning of life." I understand this to mean we need to prioritize our life values. Most people get caught up in the materialistic side of life and often it is only at the time of illness and death that we become serious about getting our priorities straight.*

Here's something important. Be madly in love with God, so much so that you are connected in the details. Take pleasure in flattening the cardboard boxes before you stick them into the recycle bin because you think it pleases the earth when you invest your effort, even if it's only just the exertion of you pulling the boxes apart. That way you are very small, and enormous, at the same time.

Jury duty yesterday. I was in two pools of candidates but did not get selected. In one case, a felony, the defendant was accused of taking 18 items through the 12-or-less checkout line. The second trial was an eight-year-old girl apprehended while running with scissors. Pretty much an open and shut case from what I could see. The memory of the day for me was when I left the courthouse at 4:30 and was standing at the shuttle bus stop waiting to be taken to the parking area. In the bus shelter, a young woman stood up and asked if I would like to sit down. I said, "Oh, no thanks, we should prolly save this for the elderly." She laughed. I thought to myself, that's how you know when you are actually getting old. Someone accidentally informs you.

"Find what you love. Then let it kill you and eat you."

Something similar to the above, altered slightly by me, was adapted from something allegedly said/written by poet Charles Burkowski. It appeals to me as being life-affirming in a kind of counter-intuitive way that I can't explain. I include it in this book in case it strikes you in some similar way.

><del></del>

When we lived on Jodie Street in New Carrollton, at the time John and Hwa were born, the kids had guinea pigs, hamsters and rabbits at various times. Pets in cages live as long as they live, and it's not a great existence, even though the kids took them out to play in the back yard now and then. As Allison Boothby observed, "It's hard to love something in a cage." One day the rabbit died from something. Theresa and John, ages 6 and 3, took it the hardest. We buried the little furball in the back yard with solemn words said about (I forget his name), and what a good and righteous rabbit he had been.

What moved me the most about the funeral was when Theresa handed John a carrot to place reverently atop his grave. Sustenance to help little whatshisname on his journey to the afterbunny. I told them their love gives meaning to his life. They didn't understand that completely at the time, but they liked that idea and the notion offered some comfort. As the song says, "You're nobunny 'til somebunny loves you."

><del></del>

Mid-morning in the 17th floor Lounge Club of the *el swanko* Sheraton Walkerhill Hotel in Seoul, Korea. One of the hosts just came over, bowed deeply. Big apologetic smile. "I am sorry," he said, "It's our cleaning time. There will be some noise" (meaning a vacuum cleaner). I smiled back, said, "I have five children." No further words were needed.

><del></del>

Young people are confident they know so much. But I'm told it is only when you are old, and really and truly only in your final moments as the final angel is beckoning you to step into the light, that you suddenly comprehend so much you never understood at all, but thought you had, all those years. When that time comes for you, may a merciful God grant you a couple of extra seconds of life and lucidness so you can utter, "Oh, wow! Thanks."

Honey Nim is making California roll sushi and she asked me to go buy three avocados. The avocados are for RIGHT NOW, so they must be in exactly perfect condition. If too hard, there is no taste; if too soft, discolored overripe, very unsexy. There's a huge bin of them and they are all over the map in terms of readiness—from granite to gooshy. Jesus strike me dead!

I am in avocado purgatory, a twilight state that knows neither victory nor defeat. I HATE shopping for avocados. I bring to bear all my training. Bear says, "Don't bring training to me, Kemosabe. Bring to avocado." Good idea.

I use my Zen powers, slowing my breathing and heart rate. They say it is the avocado that selects the person. I focus on healing blue light. Or is it green? Amber? Dang. I try the whole spectrum and finally, I am chosen by three sisters of semi-soft perfection. Joy is manifested.

A few autumns ago, as someone's guest, I found myself alone in a camouflaged tree stand, dressed warmly, deer rifle in hand. Thermos of hot coffee. There were scattered clouds and a light on-and-off mist that made the orange leaves glisten in the fog. V-formations of birds silhouetted against the peek-a-boo sun told me which way was south.

There were deer everywhere but I kept forgetting to shoot them. I composed love letters to them in my mind that all started with, "Dear deer..."

When you're shopping for lip balm or a pocket comb and you wander past the greeting cards, and spot the perfect card for your perfect person... whether it's a birthday card, anniversary card or just a generic "glad you're not dead" card—buy it! Grab it and buy it right then and there. Take it home and stick it in your hidey hole until needed. Do that because when the special occasion finally comes round, someone else will have purchased that card and it will not be there. And that one pitch-perfect expression of your heart for your perfect person, saying exactly what you would say to them, only so much better, if you had been gifted with the tongue and pen of that poet or author—will be gone. And you will have to settle for giving them a copy of this book. This is information you can actually use. This is wisdom.

><

Prayer is an unnatural act, but talking with God is as natural as breath.

><

Eat dessert first because there is no tomorrow. Do you hear what I'm saying? You can gaze out over acres of yesterdays filled to their brims, some unfortunately with regrets like tiny painful paper cuts. But there is just one now, and there are zero tomorrows. I recommend going for the now, and giving it all your attention.

You grab the *now* by not saving the gourmet chocolates for a special occasion. Make an otherwise nothing moment special with someone you care for. Don't save the best wine for later; don't put off wearing the posh frock. You don't have to have a reason to reach out and touch his hand. When he looks at you puzzled, tell him "This moment is the anniversary of now."

Pay rapt attention when she speaks, look into her eyes. (This is harder to do if you've been married for umpteen gazillion years, because a couple gets accustomed to what the other is about to say, and they tend to not listen closely to one another. But you can do it.)

If you love someone, tell her now. Later may never come. Yes, it's a risk. She might get all scared and say, "Oh it's too soon. You've frightened me, and now I must run away," and off she goes down the road, around the corner and out of sight, and you're thinking, *whiskey tango foxtrot*?!

But you were true to you. You grabbed life by the you-know-whats. You *carpe diemed*. It don't mean you won't end up with the coppery taste of your own blood in your mouth now and then. I assume you weren't planning on living forever anyway, were you?

This sort of thing is what makes you a golden human being. Know this: Someone out there who understands the value of gold, who wants to live and die in the arms of true love will step out of the crowd to grab you up and never let you go. When that happens, be worthy of it.

⟡

Some days I wake up grateful. Other days I just wake up. Today was the whole enchilada. I wish I could suspend in amber, such a feeling as today, like brontosaurus DNA locked in tree sap for 65 million years. Scientists would find it, cut it open and say, "Hey look, 65 million year old gratitude. I wonder if it's still good?" *November 13, 2017*

⟡

World peace begins in the bedroom.

⟡

Dear whatever doesn't kill me,

I'm strong enough now.

Thanks.

Photo by Nadya Neal Hinson 2008. Text by Kathy Wakile who is forever credited with uttering this little gem, picked up by Someee Cards (© 2014). Used with Someee's permish.

ACKNOWLEDGMENTS

Truly supportive friends are glorious freaks of nature. Many have been of immeasurable value in the development of this book.

In addition to their native proofreading and grammarian abilities, they engage mind and heart to look at the big picture and details at the same time, examining word choices, context, nuance, and taste. They are cosmic beings of wisdom both celestial and mundane. Think of white-robed Jacob's ladder angels going up and down between earth and heaven, pausing occasionally to offer, "you might want to rein it in a bit, Bubba."

Over several years of creating these essays, some of you have assumed the role of Muse for me by reading, commenting and encouraging. You are, in no particular order, Deborah Russell, Thomas and Kathy Hwang, Randall Remmel, Kate Tsubata, Nadya Neal Hinson, Katie Heck, John Patrick King, Yoana Koleva, Betsy Robinson, Claire Bartolic Bowles, Judy Briley Osborn, Mary Ellen Legay, D.J. Brewer, Peter and Kimmy Brown, Maureen Spagnolo, Chiara Kelly, Anita Revel, Peggy Senger Morrison and Will Rogers. If you ever sat down and talked politics as a group, half of you would hate the other half (except for Will, who never met a man he didn't like). But I love and cherish you all. My apologies to anyone omitted.

Thank you Pamela Stein, my writing buddy for more than a decade. We have felt secure to share our half-baked, embryonic work with one another, marking it up and having our way with it. I love our soul-bending discussions. When we pop the hood and get greasy taking apart our motivations and the purpose of our creativity, God always enters.

Thank you Frank Kaufmann, for our many adventures, for never letting me get too comfortable and for never shying away from telling it like it is. You are a rare soul, a true brother and a damn fine friend.

Thank you Phyllis Edgerly Ring, for the technical expertise, wisdom and compassion you have brought to the final edit of the text and your advice in producing it. Making that first phone call to you was the best decision I made in getting this book out of concept and on the road to reality.

The next best phone call was to your friend and recommended designer, Marina Kirsch. Thank you Marina, for your design of the cover and your wonderful illustrations throughout, including the art for Tikal, the Russia Chronicles, Evolution of God and the Grim Reaper Commemorative Stamp. Your expertise in laying out the text and navigating the labyrinth of self-publishing were a great blessing. I happily recommend you and Phyllis to anyone working on a book.

In addition to Marina's illustrations, this book is made infinitely more interesting and readable by the addition of artwork, photos and quoted verse throughout. I am grateful beyond measure for permissions received to use the work of Andrew Marston, Stratton Wayne St. Clair, Bundesregierung/Engelbert Reineke and Someee Cards. Others are credited in the text.

Thank you Hannah Hunter, for your beautiful cover illustration. This book may never amount to anything, but the world will come to know and admire your art and beautiful nurturing nature.

To our children, Kathy, David, Theresa, John and Sunhwa. Your mother and I brought into this world, the friends we have always wanted. You and your spouses and children have done your best to keep me young for as long as possible.

Most of all, thank you, Taeko Sonoda Moffitt (aka Honey Nim), you are the soul of patience, my best friend, the rock I lean on, and my partner in this life and the next. Being blessed with you used up all my karmic credits, and now the universe never pays even the slightest attention to any complaints I have about the rest of life.

And finally, thank you to the Age of Information, and of course oxygen, for being there when I needed to breathe.

All errors of fact or judgment are mine alone.

This book is set in 11 point Optima Regular and Italic for text and 17 point Marcellus for titles.

I self-published this at CreateSpace.

About Larry

Larry Moffitt was born in 1949 between two other brothers, to a geologist father and a nurse mother. An "oil brat," he moved around the mountain and central states roughly every two years. There were two ways for a kid to fit into a new school—by fighting his way into a niche or through humor. Larry was a runt, and bully fodder, so he chose the latter. When it rained during recess, the other kids would beg the teacher to let Larry tell stories.

He acquired a bachelor's degree in Radio-Television-Film, with a minor in Photojournalism, and a master's in Communication, all from the University of Texas at Austin. He has been a spiritual seeker since childhood. In 1974 he joined Reverend and Mrs. Sun Myung Moon's Unified Family (now Family Federation) and that became the base for his continuing search for universal principles of truth and love adhered to by all the great faith traditions.

He has been a shoeshine boy, farmer, writer, beekeeper, radio disc jockey, standup comic, newspaper and newswire executive, and an evocative poet. His affiliations with mass communication and non-profit organizations, have enabled him to travel to more than sixty countries, including North Korea twice. He was working in Moscow when communism fell in August 1991, and walked among the students and their barricades.

In 1979, Rev. Moon suggested the former Taeko Sonoda of Yatsushiro in Kumomoto Japan would be a good wife for Larry. They both agreed and were blessed in holy marriage on July 1, 1982. They have five amazing children, all grown and doing interesting things.

"Honey Nim" on the book's dedication page, is one of Larry's terms of endearment for Taeko. "Nim" is an honorific suffix to the name of highly esteemed people in Korea. Taeko has been an American for several years.

Larry Moffitt
LMoffitt@sanviejo.com
www.sanviejo.com

Made in the USA
Middletown, DE
10 January 2018